AF717370

Lindah Mhlanga, Kefasi Nyikahadzoi, Tobias Haller (Eds.)

Fragmentation of Natural Resources Management

Defragmenting African Resource Management

edited by

Associate Professor Dr. Mafaniso Hara
(University of the Western Cape)

and

Prof. Dr. Tobias Haller
(Universität Bern)

PLAAS
Institute for Poverty, Land and Agrarian Studies

A publication of the
Institute for Poverty, Land and Agrarian Studies (PLAAS)
University of the Western Cape
South Africa

Volume 2

ACP S&T PROGRAMME

LIT

Fragmentation of Natural Resources Management

Experiences from Lake Kariba

edited by

Lindah Mhlanga, Kefasi Nyikahadzoi,
Tobias Haller

PLAAS

LIT

Cover images: Mohamed Hashim, Wilson Mhlanga, Cardo Kleberg, Mohamed Hashim.

The editors would like to thank the European Union (project AFS/2009/219017) through the African Caribbean and Pacific (ACP) Science and Technology Programme (Europe Aid/127860/D/ACT/ACP) for the funding that made this book possible. The contents of this book though are our sole responsibility and do not reflect the views or position of the European Union.

Bibliographic information published by the Deutsche Nationalbibliothek
The Deutsche Nationalbibliothek lists this publication in the Deutsche Nationalbibliografie; detailed bibliographic data are available in the Internet at http://dnb.d-nb.de.

ISBN 978-3-643-90400-3

A catalogue record for this book is available from the British Library

Klosbachstr. 107
CH-8032 Zürich
Tel. +41 (0) 44-251 75 05
Fax +41 (0) 44-251 75 06
E-Mail: zuerich@lit-verlag.ch
http://www.lit-verlag.ch

LIT VERLAG Dr. W. Hopf
Berlin 2014
Fresnostr. 2
D-48159 Münster
Tel. +49 (0) 2 51-62 03 20
Fax +49 (0) 2 51-23 19 72
E-Mail: lit@lit-verlag.de
http://www.lit-verlag.de

Distribution:
In Germany: LIT Verlag Fresnostr. 2, D-48159 Münster
Tel. +49 (0) 2 51-620 32 22, Fax +49 (0) 2 51-922 60 99, E-mail: vertrieb@lit-verlag.de

In Austria: Medienlogistik Pichler-ÖBZ, e-mail: mlo@medien-logistik.at
In the UK: Global Book Marketing, e-mail: mo@centralbooks.com
In North America: International Specialized Book Services, e-mail: orders@isbs.com
e-books are available at www.litwebshop.de

Inhalt

List of Tables

List of Figures

DARMA BOOK SERIES PREFACE

In Southern Africa the 'commons' have great livelihoods and biodiversity value, and they function as 'common pool resources' that are owned, accessed and used by multiple stakeholders in the region. However, as in many other parts of the world, management of the Southern African commons is fragmented. This fragmentation occurs in many ways and at different levels. For instance, authority is located in different government line agencies and technical expertise is divided among government agencies, non-governmental organisations (NGOs), universities and donors. In addition, actions take place at different geographic scales, and management networks are usually intra-sectoral (for example those in fisheries only know and network with others in fisheries). Funding for research and management also comes from multiple sources including foreign and international donors; and in some cases, commons transcend international borders, requiring international integration. Fragmentation in policy, legislation, knowledge base, authority and responsibility clearly makes a holistic approach to commons management difficult.

User stakeholders, especially the poor, usually draw upon the various resources (land, forests, fish, grass, water, wildlife) for composite benefits and livelihoods. If managed holistically, these commons can remain highly productive and sustainable. However, commons are in most instances under pressure due to their economic value and unco-ordinated management. Overexploitation and degradation occur particularly where ecosystem-based and ecosystem-wide institutional arrangements do not exist to overcome problems of subtractability that arise from open access.

In recent years, there have been increasing attempts to manage commons holistically as a result of the realisation and appreciation of the interrelatedness of both the ecological and socio-economic dynamics of natural resources – the so-called 'ecosystems approach'. This approach calls for partnerships between state agencies, research institutions, non-governmental organisations (NGOs), donors, traditional leaders, local communities and all other stakeholders. Effective links and collaborative partnerships among all stakeholders are critical for ensuring that the available scientific knowledge, indigenous knowledge, user knowledge and institutions are optimised. This book is an effort at demonstrating such a multi-disciplinary and inter-disciplinary approach in management of the Lake Kariba environs. It is based on contributions from various experts and users with long-term experience and knowledge of the area. The book reviews and evaluates policies and management approaches for the Lake Kariba environs, describes how these are fragmented and proposes a framework for defragmenting management.

The Lake Kariba case study is one of seven cases under the Defragmenting African Resource Management project (DARMA) in Southern Africa, which aimed to build networks and research frameworks that could integrate resource management. The specific objective of DARMA was to increase national capacity in five African partner countries (Botswana, Malawi, South Africa, Zambia, Zimbabwe) for integrated management of commons with the overall broader objective being enhancement of biodiversity of exploited commons while alleviating poverty at the same time. The main strategy for achieving these objectives was the development of scientific networks and integrated knowledge bases that can combine different relevant natural and social science disciplines in a way that will be of practical use for both biodiversity conservation and sustainable development. The final outputs of the DARMA project are a series of books and journal articles that will serve as a valuable collection for environmental policy makers and will, hopefully, serve as catalysts in future debates on defragmentation of natural resources management in Southern Africa.

The preparation of this series of books has been made possible with European Union funding (Project AFS/2009/219017) through the African Caribbean and Pacific (ACP) Science and Technology Programme (Europe Aid/127860/D/ACT/ACP). The contents of these books are the sole responsibility of the authors. They do not reflect the views and position of the European Union. We thank all the stakeholders and participants who generously donated their time and energy to making the DARMA project possible.

Development of the research frameworks for analysing fragmentation and defragmentation for the various DARMA case studies were developed jointly by the partners and associate partners. The DARMA partners and associate partners would particularly like to thank Professor Douglas Clyde Kongshøj Wilson (Innovative Fisheries Management, Aalborg University, Department of Development and Planning), an associate partner on the project, for all his contributions to the project.

Associate Professor Mafaniso Hara

DARMA Project Coordinator

Institute for Poverty, Land and Agrarian Studies

Faculty of Economic and Management Sciences

University of the Western Cape

South Africa

PREFACE

The chapters presented in this book are products of the Defragmenting African Resource Management (DARMA) Project. All the chapters are synthesis reviews of the information currently available on cross-commons interactions on land, water, fish, other aquatic resources, woodland and grassland and wildlife within the Lake Kariba environs. The reviews include both social and natural science aspects and reflect the experiences and views gained by researchers who have worked on Lake Kariba for more than 10 years.

The central theme of the book is that in order to ensure resource sustainability, research and management within the Lake Kariba environs should adopt an ecosystem approach. This approach to natural resource management emphasises the interrelatedness of the ecological and socio-economic dynamics of natural resources. At present, research and management on Lake Kariba is sector based and the ecosystem is now stressed and resource use conflicts are apparent. The typical characteristic of Lake Kariba, one of the case studies in the DARMA project, is that the area has complex resource uses and pressures. The demand for the various resources from users has markedly increased and this is presenting challenges to sustainable resource management. The book, which is based on the concept of ecosystem interactions, puts the Lake Kariba case in this context with regard to sectoral management of the resources and the consequent challenges. It highlights specific areas of sectoral interconnections between six main resources – land, water, fisheries, woodlands and grasslands, wildlife, and other aquatic resources – and analyses the impact that fragmented management is having on these six resources.

This book reflects the efforts of researchers who care about issues surrounding the management of Lake Kariba. The major conclusion by the authors is that resource management and research within this broad landscape has to shift towards cross-sectoral analysis and interdisciplinary approaches by opening up communication channels for knowledge sharing among disciplines at local and bilateral levels. We extend our thanks to the authors and various other stakeholders who contributed the chapters that made this volume under the DARMA series possible. Through their effort and willingness to document their experiences, they have provided an invaluable resource for new and upcoming researchers, resource managers and stakeholders, who can use the information contained in this volume as a basis to advocate for defragmenting natural resource management within the Lake Kariba environs. Beyond this, the book provides a synthesis deposit of all research that has been carried on Lake Kariba and as such can be used by researchers as background in establishing future research programmes. Special thanks go to everyone who assisted in making this book a reality.

Lindah Mhlanga & Kefasi Nyikahadzoi

Contributors

Portia Chiyedza Chifamba is a biologist with a Bachelor of Science general degree with a major in Biological Sciences and minor in Geography from the University of Zimbabwe, and a Masters degree in Fisheries Biology and Management from the University of Bangor, United Kingdom.

Vupenyu Dzingirai is a social anthropologist based at the Centre for Applied Social Sciences at the University of Zimbabwe. He has done extensive research within the Zambezi Valley.

Tobias Haller is a social anthropologist and Associate Professor for Social Anthropology at the University of Berne, Switzerland. He has specialised in ecological and economic anthropology and conducts research on institutions for the management of the commons in Africa.

Mafaniso Michael Hara is an Associate Professor at the Institute for Poverty, Land and Agrarian Studies (PLAAS), the University of the Western Cape, South Africa. He is a social scientist with more than 30 years' experience in social research and development work focusing on rural communities especially fisheries (both freshwater and marine) and, in recent years, integrated resource management in Southern Africa. He has published widely in these areas of his expertise. He holds a Doctorate from the University of the Western Cape (2001). He is co-ordinator for the Defragmenting African Resource Management (DARMA) project.

Gift Musinake is a doctoral candidate at Centre for Applied Social Sciences at the University of Zimbabwe. He is researching on decentralised resource management in western Zimbabwe focusing on water.

Lindah Mhlanga is a biologist who holds a Bachelor of Science (Honours) degree in Biological Sciences from the University of Zimbabwe, a Masters degree in Conservation and Utilisation of Plant Genetic Resources from the University of Birmingham, United Kingdom, and a Doctorate in Freshwater Ecology (Limnology) from the University of Cape Town, South Africa. She is currently a senior lecturer in the Department of Biological Sciences at the University of Zimbabwe.

Wilson Mhlanga is an ecologist who holds a Bachelor of Science (Honours) degree in Agriculture with a major in Animal Science from the University of Zimbabwe and a Master of Science degree in Applied Hydrobiology from Cardiff University, United Kingdom. He is currently a lecturer in the Department of Environmental Science at Bindura University of Science Education (BUSE) in Zimbabwe.

Kefasi Nyikahadzoi is a social scientist who holds a Doctorate of Philosophy in Applied Social Sciences from the University of Zimbabwe. He is a senior lecturer within the Centre for Applied Social Sciences at the University of Zimbabwe. He has done extensive research on natural resources management in general and fisheries in particular.

Jimmiel Mandima is a conservation practitioner with a Bachelor of Science (Honours) degree in Biological Sciences from the University of Zimbabwe, and a Masters degree in

Applied Zoology (Aquaculture & Fisheries Management) from the University of Kuopio (now Eastern Finland) in Finland. He is currently the Programme Design Director of Policy with the African Wildlife Foundation based in Washington DC, United States.

Crispen Phiri is a research fellow at the University of Zimbabwe's Lake Kariba Research Station (ULKRS). He received his Bachelor of Science (Honours) degree in Biological Sciences and Master of Science degree in Tropical Resource Ecology from the University of Zimbabwe, and his Doctorate in Zoology from the University of Cape Town, South Africa.

Acknowledgements

Funding to undertake the project Defragmenting African Resource Management (DARMA) was received from the African Carribean and Pacific Group of States (ACP Secretariat) through the Institute for Poverty, Land and Agrarian Studies (PLAAS), University of the Western Cape (UWC), South Africa. We wish to extend our thanks to Associate Professor Mafaniso Michael Hara (Senior Researcher at PLAAS), who co-ordinated the DARMA project. He also suggested the idea for this book and co-ordinated the necessary finances and together with Professor Tobias Haller for introducing us to a publisher in Germany (LIT VERLAG). Special thanks go to all the contributors who enthusiastically and positively supported the initiative. Finally we would like to thank the editors at LIT VERLAG (Germany) for their contribution.

Kefasi Nyikahadzoi & Lindah Mhlanga

January 2013

1. Fragmented management of natural resources in the Lake Kariba environs

Kefasi NYIKAHADZOI, Lindah MHLANGA and Tobias HALLER

1.1. Introduction

During the second half of the 20th century, the energy demands of growing economies after World War II caused a worldwide push for constructing new dams to generate hydro-electric power. This push led to the creation of Africa's first major dam in 1958, Lake Kariba, situated on the Middle Zambezi River between Zambia and Zimbabwe (see Figure 1). At the time, Kariba was the largest artificial lake in the world. The new development provided access to new wilderness areas and new resources for exploitation (Magadza 1986). Following the primary development for hydroelectric power generation, secondary activities emerged, which today include fisheries, tourism, livestock production, irrigated agriculture and water transport.

Although Lake Kariba is important economically and socially to both Zambia and Zimbabwe, there are major ecosystem challenges linked to the multiple resources that are being extracted and managed independently. The ecosystem interactions threaten the resource base and point to an urgent need to recognise the systemic integration of the ecosystem and consequent need for defragmentation. Resource management within this broad landscape is sectoral. This book documents the challenges associated with fragmented sector-based management by assembling contributions from several authors who reviewed various aspects associated with the functioning of the Lake Kariba ecosystem and its surrounding environment.

1.2. Natural resources management in Lake Kariba and its environs

Natural resources are a direct source of livelihood for most rural people in Africa and provide very important ecosystem goods and services. Lake Kariba and its environs offer important ecological and socio-economic functions. Ecosystem services include storage of freshwater for humans and wildlife, natural flood-control through water retention and as habitat for a wide range of aquatic flora and fauna. The ecosystem also serves as an important natural sink for carbon and pollutants such as sulphur from acid rain and heavy metals.

The ecosystem offers diverse livelihood and food security alternatives to the local people and serves broader national/regional needs. The ecosystem is a major source of timber and non-timber forest products that include medicinal plants, firewood, fruits, worms, and raw materials for building and craft making. Apart from subsistence agriculture, most people living around Lake Kariba depend on natural resources through wildlife hunting, fishing and harvesting of waterfowls. They utilise these resources to help buffer themselves against the brutal effects of poverty.

Figure 1: Map showing the location of Lake Kariba

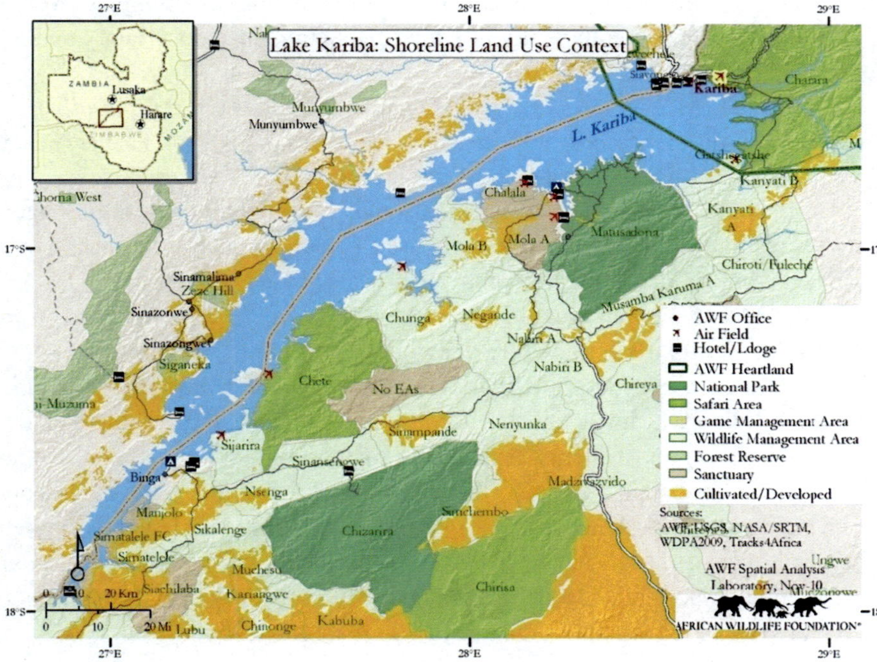

Source: African Wildlife Foundation

Effective management of these natural resources is important for long-term sustainable development in the area. Efforts in most of the riparian countries within the Zambezi basin have been directed towards reducing the threats posed to resources by population growth, the effects of climate change and unsustainable resource extraction practices (Murphree 1993, Chitiga & Nemarundwe 2003, Nyikahadzoi 2006). However, these efforts have failed to maintain ecosystem integrity because the management systems are fragmented (Timberlake 2000). Currently, such resource regimes are typically failing to motivate co-ordinated action among different stakeholders.

The DARMA (Defragmenting African Resources Management) project, which is the basis for this book, has identified four major forms of natural resources management fragmentation.

First, the *technical expertise for natural resources management is fragmented* across different government ministries, departments and agencies, non-governmental organisations (NGOs), universities and other research centres. This piecemeal management structure means that diverse regulatory authorities end up managing sets of narrow and discrete, but often overlapping, resource interactions. In most cases, they either ignore or give little consideration to these overlaps. According to Camacho (2011), such resource management regimes fail to take advantage of significant opportunities for inter-jurisdictional learning, as well as information sharing and collaboration, which can help reduce uncertainty and improve management efficacy.

Second, DARMA also recognises that *management actions are spatially fragmented* across different geographical scales. In this context, authorities in one resource sector are not required to consider the impact of their activities on users of other resources or on the well-being of other resources. For example, agencies with regulatory authority over land-based resources have little incentive to consider the impact of their action on users of water-based resources.

Third, DARMA notes that management efforts of *the commons are fragmented across sectors*. For example, researchers working in fisheries know other researchers and stakeholders in fisheries, while researchers working in wildlife know their colleagues involved in wildlife management and/or research. However, these wildlife and fisheries researchers may be unfamiliar with each other across sectors. With this approach, they view natural resource sectors in isolation and as 'islands' in the ecosystem in which they exist. A fragmented system is the result, consisting of many regulatory authorities, each with different goals and strategies supported by sectoral laws, and with each authority managing only specific aspects of the resources contained within a broader ecosystem.

Finally, *natural resource management is fragmented across national boundaries*. Therefore shared trans-boundary resources such as water, fish and wildlife can be overexploited if their management is fragmented in this way. Fragmented and inadequately co-ordinated political and management jurisdictions compromise the sustainable use of such resources. Metcalfe (1999) argues that such resources cannot be managed unilaterally because they straddle international borders.

1.3. Background to the study area

As mentioned earlier, Lake Kariba was created by damming the Zambezi River in 1958 for the purpose of generating hydropower for the Federation of Rhodesia and Nyasaland (today Zambia, Zimbabwe, Malawi). Over time, a number of other economic activities based on the utilisation of resources within the area emerged; some of the historical developments of these economic activities are contained in ensuing chapters of this book. The terrestrial ecosystem includes grassland and forest/woodland habitats, and supports wildlife, while the aquatic ecosystem includes aquatic resources, such as, fish, crocodiles, hippos and waterfowls.

During the pre-colonial era, chiefs, using traditional laws, were responsible for the management of natural resources. According to Chigwenya & Manatsa (2007), beliefs and taboos formed codes of behaviour that ensured sustainable natural resource management. Some of these traditional beliefs, values and practices still remain very important for the integrity of natural resources in most African countries. Later, during the colonial period, the state used various statutory instruments to guide the conservation of natural resources. This was the genesis of fragmented natural resources management systems (Chigwenya & Manatsa 2007). In both Zambia and Zimbabwe, successive colonial governments introduced sectoral laws such as the Game and Fish Act of 1929 in Zimbabwe, which empowered governors of game reserves to form institutions for managing fish and game in isolation from other resources. This brought about spatial fragmentation with the introduction of game reserves, as well as the fragmentation of technical expertise, with wardens and rangers being introduced to manage game reserves. Several other such acts were promulgated in both countries that enhanced the sectoral approach to natural resources management. Key among these were the Parks and Wildlife Management Act (1949), Natural Resource Act (1942) and Forestry Act (1948) in Zimbabwe. Similar sectoral laws enacted in Zambia included the Water Act (1949) and the Fisheries Act (1974).

Despite these historical enactments, sustainable utilisation of resources remains problematic to this day. Malasha (2005) attributes this situation to the failure of natural resource management regimes to acknowledge the key cross-sectoral interrelationships among the different systems. When they attained independence from their colonial overlords, the post-colonial governments of Zambia and Zimbabwe inherited the colonial management structures for natural resources, which perpetuated fragmentation and largely unco-ordinated management.

Given the diverse range of opportunities offered by the lake and lakeshore resources, a co-ordinated governance system is critical for sustainable livelihoods based on a functional ecosystem. However, there are multiple uses and tenurial systems that govern the lake and lake resources. Finding optimal institutional arrangements that cater for the diverse needs of users and the ecological requirements of the resources remains a great challenge.

1.4. Property rights and land fragmentation

Land fragmentation is the division of contiguous habitats into smaller units that often result in the loss of the original character, connectivity and functionality of the land and its ecosystems. The process interrupts ecological processes necessary for the long-term sustainability of the ecosystem. There are three distinct property right regimes in the Lake Kariba area: communal areas, state land and large-scale, private commercial farms. Communal tenure property includes individual property rights over arable land and homestead sites, as well as common property rights with respect to grazing, woodlands and water (Murombedzi 1991). However, most people have limited or no access to arable land. At the same time, expropriation of access to the lake and lakeshore resources by the powerful elites alienates local level resource management systems, and also continues to increase pressure on the resources. Programmes have been launched to help the disadvantaged, such as the Communal Areas Management Programme for Indigenous Resources (CAMPFIRE) in Zimbabwe and Administrative Management Design (ADMADE) in Zambia, which are designed to ensure that local communities benefit from wildlife resources found in the lakeshore area. Management of such resources is vested in local rural district authorities in Zimbabwe and in traditional authority in Zambia.

In the region, national parks, other categories of wildlife areas, forest reserves and water belong to the state, and national governments have direct management responsibilities. There are various laws that have been enacted to control and manage resources under this property regime, which are discussed in detail in follow-up chapters of this book. There are also private commercial farms for crop production, crocodile farming and hunting concessions.

The three different property regimes identified here embody different philosophies and approaches. However, they do interact, as any decision that is made in one regime can impact on other regimes and resource users, as well as affect the proper functioning of the ecosystem.

1.5. Institutions and policies: Managing the lake and lakeshore resources

A broad range of social, economic and environmental policies and institutions – domestic and international – were found to have a significant impact on the conservation and utilisation of Lake Kariba's aquatic and lakeshore resources.

Kariba is divided between Zimbabwe and Zambia, so the lake and its lakeshore resources are governed by separate legal and planning structures and different administrative systems. Both riparian countries have different policies and legislation that seek to protect certain resources within the ecosystem. On the Zimbabwean side, the shoreline is administered by two rural district councils, one municipality, the Forestry Commission and the Zimbabwe Parks and Wildlife Management Authority. Laws administered by different government departments with jurisdiction over different resources and a mandate to protect and manage them on a sustainable basis are in place. On the Zambian side most of the shoreline area and the resources therein are under the governance of traditional leaders. There are also local authorities in Siavonga and Sinazongwe.

These legal instruments, though quite comprehensive, tend to conceptualise the different stakeholders in isolation and adopt a narrow, sectoral approach to natural resource management. In both countries, the legal instruments are uncoordinated and hence ill equipped to deal with resource use that requires a holistic management approach for their sustainability. For example, when managing wildlife, managers do not take into consideration their impact on other resources or economic activities. While elephants are protected for tourism, the animals tend to encroach on human settlements, crop fields and communal forests, destroying crops and competing with humans over use of forests and forest products. Managers tend to marginalise such interactions when they design management options for different sectors. Timberlake (2000) views agro-ecosystems and socio-economic systems as interrelated in space and time.

At regional level, the management approaches used for the different lake and lakeshore resources is spatially fragmented, despite the existence of a number of trans-national regional policies and agreements that, if properly co-ordinated, could protect these resources for local communities (see Box 1). At present, there is no specific policy or protocol that exclusively guides the governance and management of the lake and lakeshore resources. Neither is there a policy framework that co-ordinates the regional policies and agreements to maintain ecosystem integrity. In fact, the regional protocols, just like the national policies and legislation, tend to be sectoral in their approach. They fail to acknowledge and appreciate the links among systems and how actions in one sector impact other sectors within the broader ecosystem.

Box 1: Regional policies and agreements relevant to Zambezi Basin management

- The Southern African Development Community (SADC) Wildlife and Law Enforcement Protocol was signed in 1991 to establish common regional approaches to conservation and sustainable use of wildlife resources. It promotes the conservation of shared wildlife through supporting the establishment of trans-boundary conservation areas. It encourages the facilitation of community-based wildlife management. All the Basin countries have ratified the protocol with the exception of Zimbabwe and Angola.
- The SADC Shared Watercourse Protocol was signed in 2000 to provide sustainable and co-ordinated management, protection and utilisation of shared watercourse systems. It recognises those communities living with the resource as legitimate stakeholders in the watercourse. Among the Basin countries, Zimbabwe, Zambia and Angola still have to ratify it for the purpose of it coming into force.
- The SADC Fisheries Protocol was signed in 2003 to promote the responsible use of fish and other living aquatic resources in the region to enhance food security and livelihood among fishing communities. All countries, except Zimbabwe, have ratified the protocol.
- The SADC Forestry Protocol, signed in 2003, seeks to promote the development, conservation, sustainable management and utilisation of all types of trees and forests in a way that maintains the forest's ecological functions. It further seeks to alleviate poverty and enhance the economies of SADC member states through the promotion of trade in forestry products and by encouraging the participation of local communities in the management of forest resources. It is not yet in force because the prerequisite two thirds of member states have not yet ratified it.
- The SADC Protocol on Tourism was signed in 2003. It encourages non-consumptive wetland resources utilisation by optimising resource usage and aims to increas the region's competitive advantage by aggressively promoting regional tourism and improving tourism services and infrastructure. It also obligates member states to pursue sound, sustainable polices on the utilisation and management of natural and cultural resources and the environment. Of the Basin countries, Malawi and Zambia have yet to ratify the protocol and Angola still has to sign and ratify it.
- The Zambezi River Basin Water Commission (ZAMCOM), signed in 2004 by the eight riparian countries, seek to promote equitable and reasonable utilisation of water resources within the shared river basin.
- Southern Africa Vision for Water, Life and the Environment in the 21st Century (2009) seeks to improve the availability of fresh water in the region. It encourages the participation of NGOs, community-based organisations and researchers to accelerate and finalise their water sector legislative and instrumental reforms.

1.6. Threats to lake and lakeshore resources

If current levels of unco-ordinated planning, population growth and unemployment continue, along with a development impetus that promotes 'unchecked' and extensive crop production, tourism, urbanisation and mining, Kariba's lake and lakeshore resources will continue to be degraded. It is generally true that a high value is attached to tourism within the region for employment creation and overall national economic development. The negative environmental impact of tourism activities (e.g. boating) is mainly through the release of pollutants. In Chapter 3, Mhlanga et al. show how tourism and other activities have impacted the aquatic biota. They report that the promotion of tourism activities like house-boating and offshore fishing for the Lake Tanganyika freshwater sardine (kapenta) has impacted negatively on water quality through pollution from oil spills and direct waste discharge. The number of boats on Lake Kariba has increased, resulting in oil and fuel pollution caused by accidental leakages or spillage from engines and/or deliberate waste oil dumping. The local authorities do not prioritise the proper management of industrial, agricultural and domestic waste. Much interest is rather placed on housing and employment creation. The increasing nutrient enrichment in rivers from partially treated sewage effluent discharged from urban areas, as well as fertiliser-rich runoff from agriculture, is promoting excessive growth of invasive aquatic plants. Examples include the water hyacinth (*Eichhornia crassipes*), water lettuce (*Pistia stratiotes*), Kariba weed (*Salvinia molesta*) and water fern (*Azolla sp.)*, all of which have negative ecological and physical impacts. They cause blockages to water channels, contribute to fish mortality and provide habitat for successful breeding of bilharzia-carrying snails and malarial mosquitoes.

Most people living in the Lake Kariba area depend on natural resources for their livelihoods. The vicious cycle of poverty results in situations where lake and lakeshore resources are the only source of livelihood for local communities in terms of food, water and shelter. It is estimated that about 80% of the population in the basin depends on wetland resources such as land, fish, wood and water (Laisi 2000). Concerns have been raised about over-fishing and even the possible extinction of some fish species.

As the human population continues to grow, the amount of land available per capita is shrinking rapidly and this is likely to force more and more people into ecologically fragile areas. Pressure on lake and lakeshore resources to support more agricultural activities is increasing and development of upland agriculture has resulted in extensive land clearing. This has degraded land through soil erosion, which reduces the soil's water retention capacity and results in poor water quality.

Legally, the imposition of state control has left many indigenous common property resources under a *de facto* open access regime. Under the open access regime the rule of capture drives each individual to get as much as possible from the resource before others do. As their situations worsen due to regional economic decline, they will put more and more pressure on the dwindling resource in order to survive (Mukamuri *et al.* 2003). Their actions have resulted in localised over-exploitation of certain resources. For example, there is clear evidence of over-harvesting of large and increasingly rare indigenous trees that are exploited for carving curios and crafts. Nyikahadzoi (1998) and Malasha (2001) report isolated cases of over-fishing in the gill net inshore fishery along Lake Kariba. Such unco-ordinated sectoral approaches to resource management and unplanned developments at policy level added to the rationale for writing this book.

1.7. Methodological approach

An ecosystem-based approach is based on the understanding and recognition that any particular ecosystem is influenced heavily by surrounding systems and that all land and water is found inside an ecosystem (IUCN 2008). Around Lake Kariba the land and water interlock and interact with one another. In order to explore the interconnections, a number of steps and approaches were utilised in the development of this book.

The first step involved identifying scientists who have worked in the Lake Kariba area for over 10 years. These individuals constituted the initial core network of scientists that led the larger network. A core team of six experts initiated the process of writing cross-disciplinary reviews. The authors of the book recognised early on that an ecosystem approach to the management of natural resources around Lake Kariba is never an easy task because the common pool resource has complex dynamics with many and diverse resource users, managers and interest groups. A resource-based approach was consequently used in this book in order to adequately elucidate key interactions, and resources were categorised as either terrestrial or aquatic. Within these two broad categories, six resource sectors were identified. From the aquatic ecosystem the resources included (i) water resources, (ii) fish resources and (iii) other aquatic organisms (including crocodiles and hippos), and from the terrestrial ecosystem, resources included (iv) forests and grasslands, (v) land and (vi) wildlife resources. These are shown in Box 1 in Figure 2 below. The task of each review was to elucidate the cross-sectoral interactions (depicted by double-ended arrows in Box 1 in Figure 2).

Each of the six resource sectors forms a chapter in this book. In each chapter the author(s) describe the status and nature of the specific resource with respect to the current scientific knowledge and the ecological interactions with other resources. The reviews provide the historical development of resource use and factors that have led to the fragmentation of resource management. The chapters also describe the different resource users and goods and services supported by each resource sector. Thereafter the chapters provide the current institutional arrangements, focusing on resource ownership, pattern of interactions and existing governance regimes for the resource (shown in Box 3 in Figure 2). They then attempt to predict the long-term impact on the resource and also on users if current resource use and governance patterns continue.

Figure 2: Conceptual Framework for Analysing the impact of fragmentation

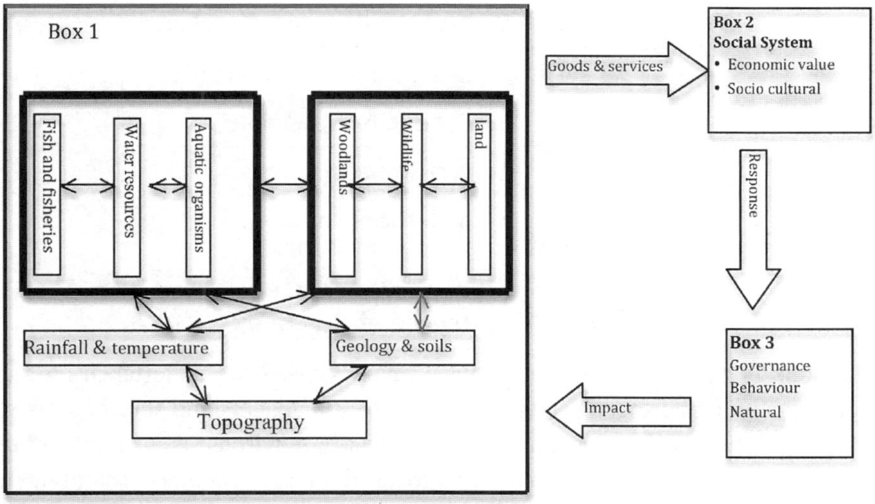

The sector-based reviews were presented to the larger network and stakeholders at a workshop.

For each of the five likely results of the interaction between the five identified resource sectors, participants were asked to rate them using a likert scale 1 to 5 (1 being very low and 5 high). After a lengthy discussion a mutually agreed upon score was assigned as a measure of how bad or good the interaction between resource sectors was in terms of the five dimensions shown in Table 1. The scores were then added together to find an aggregate score that characterised the resource interactions between any given two resources sectors. Results of this process are discussed in Chapter 8. During the same workshop a matrix was developed that showed how different departments are involved in the management of the different resource sectors. This is presented as Table 20 in Chapter 8.

Table 1: Dimensions of measuring inter-sectoral interactions

Dimensions of interaction	Likert scale (1–5)
Severity of impact	1 = not very severe 5 = very severe
Value (i.e. ecosystem cost)	1 = low cost to ecosystem 5 = very high to ecosystem
Scope (geographical spread)	1 = very localised 5 = over a wide geographical area
Irreversibility	1 = damage is easily reversible 5 = damage is irreversible
Social costs	1 = very low social costs 5 = high social costs

1.8. The purpose of this book

The book is based on cross-disciplinary reviews that were undertaken by a network of natural and social scientists, government managers and stakeholders who understand ecosystem issues around Lake Kariba environs as an initial step of defragmenting knowledge. The reviews focused on discussing ecosystem interactions that relate to the exploitation of commons within the Lake Kariba environs from which critical ecosystem interactions that relate to the common exploitation of the common pool resource were drawn. The information in the book can be used to develop future research and monitoring needs and can also be used in conflict mitigation.

1.9. Outline and organisation of the book

The book has eight chapters. The overall conclusion drawn from the contributions is that the cross-sectoral challenges associated with Lake Kariba and its environments cut across six key resources (see Figure 2). Contributors identifed sustainable resource utilisation and protection with respect to the socio-economic cultural and political influences as a major management issue. With this realisation, future research on Lake Kariba should consider the interrelatedness among these key resources.

In Chapter 2, Mandima & Nyikahadzoi illustrate that the Lake Kariba area represents a context where the land resource is the basis for all the other related biodiversity and natural capital including water, wildlife, fish, woodlands and grasslands. There is an inherent association at the ecosystem level between land and other resources. The key land uses – mining, agriculture, tourism, urban development, fishing and aquaculture – keep requiring more land to remain viable, leading to increasing pressure on land and shrinking the land available for wildlife movements and dispersal, especially on the Zimbabwean side, where wildlife population density is high. Generally land resources are highly threatened by numerous competing uses administered by different land authorities on the basis of multiple statutory provisions that are applied with little or no co-ordination. This ultimately threatens the sustainability of other resources, which are highly dependent on the status of the land resources.

In Chapter 3, Mhlanga *et al.* emphasise the role of water with regards to its institutional setting, and as a central resource within the Lake Kariba area and in the Zambezi River Basin ecosystem in general. Water is important for hydropower generation for Zambia and Zimbabwe. The authors note that there is competition for water for diverse local ecosystem services and human needs to meet their livelihoods. Different interests in water resources are reflected in different institutions and legal frameworks and increasing pluralism in the management of water.

In Chapter 4, Mhlanga & Mhlanga highlight several intra-resource and inter-resource interactions in fish resources on Lake Kariba. They also discuss the various climatic factors that influence the fishery resource. After describing the various institutions responsible for the exploitation of the fisheries resources, they go on to show how the integrity of the resources is being compromised by land based activities such as mining, agriculture and the use of pesticides.

In Chapter 5, Phiri & Mhlanga examine the ecological, social and economic importance of aquatic organisms other than fish communities in Lake Kariba. These organisms include phytoplankton and zooplankton, macrophytes (aquatic vegetation), macroinvertebrates and aquatic vertebrates. The authors evaluated their socioeconomic importance for communities in both Zambia and Zimbabwe. They found a paucity of information on the distributions, population status and trends, habitats and ecology of most aquatic organisms in Lake Kariba. However, sustainable utilisation of these resources requires an appreciation of the links among the different components of the ecosystem, as well as enacting of programmes that address the livelihood development goals of local communities.

In Chapter 6, Mhlanga & Mhlanga discuss the inter-sectoral rconnections in the management of woodland commons along the lakeshore of Lake Kariba in order to show the importance of an integrated ecosystem approach for management of common pool resources in this diverse and complex ecosystem. Woodland resources are threatened by increasing demand for agricultural land due to the natural rate of human population increase, as well as in-migration. And where elephants occur in large numbers, they modify woodland vegetation by reducing the number of trees. Woodlands are also threatened by fires and increasing demands for firewood.

In Chapter 7, Dzingirai & Mhlanga show that the management of wildlife is inadequately co-ordinated among the various organisations and legislative instruments that govern wildlife management. Within the Lake Kariba environs wildlife is central to tourism development. Although it is also an important source of income for local inhabitants, the authors found that they are economically marginalised and never get to accumulate any wealth from tourism. Management and wildlife-related development initiatives have tended to operate in a fragmented manner and managers are not cognisant of the intertwined and complex relationship between wildlife and other components of the environment. The authors illustrate how multiple institutions, legislation and policies governing wildlife resources and their utilisation have resulted in fragmented and compartmentalised control and management of wildlife resources.

In the concluding chapter, Chapter 8, Nyikahadzoi *et al.* summarise the critical ecosystem interactions among the six resources within Lake Kariba environs and put forward recommendations to promote and implement the defragmentation of natural resources management in the area. They present a matrix, consisting of the six resource types and their respective governance arrangements and legislation, to illustrate the overlaps among sectors and the ensuing conflicts due to fragmented legislation. The authors propose that management of the area should move toward defragmented decentralisation, arguing that sustainable management can only occur under a defragmented and decentralised system.

References

Camacho A. E. 2011. 'Transforming the means and ends of natural resource management'. Center for Progressive Reform, University of California.

Chigwenya A. & Manatsa D. 2007. 'The history of natural resources management in Zimbabwe: A chronicle of how sustainable resource management has remained an elusive concept', *Journal of Sustainable Development in Africa* ***9(2)****: 102–115.*

Chitiga M. & Nemarundwe N. 2003. 'Policies and gender relationship and roles in the miombo woodland region of southern Africa.' In: Kowero G., Campbell B.M. and Sumaila U.S. (eds) Policies and Governance Structures in Woodlands of Southern Africa. *Centre for International Forestry Research, Indonesia.*

IUCN 2008. The Ecosystem Approach: Learning from Experiences. *Ecosystem Management Series No. 5. IUCN, Gland, Switzerland.*

Laisi E. 2000. Water and Wetland Resources. *SADC/IUCN/ZRA/SARDC, Harare.*

Magadza C.H.D. 1986. 'Conflicts of resource use on the Lake Kariba environs', *Nature and Resources* **XXII(4)**: 1 –12.

Malasha I. 2001. 'Fisheries co-management: A comparative analysis of the Zambian and Zimbabwean inshore fishery of Lake Kariba.' *D Phil thesis*. University of Zimbabwe, Harare.

Malasha I. 2005. 'Contested fishing grounds: Examining the possibility of a transboundary management regime in Lake Kariba.' Commons Southern Africa Occasional Paper Series No. 13. Programme for Land and Agrarian Studies (PLAAS), University of Western Cape, Cape Town.

Metcalfe S. 1999. *Study on the Development of Transboundary Natural Resources Management Areas in Southern Africa: Community Perspectives.* Biodiversity Support Programme, Washington DC, USA.

Mukamuri B., Campbell B.M. & Kowero G. 2003. 'Local organisations and natural resource management in the face of economic hardship: A case study from Zimbabwe.' In: Kowero G., Campbell B.M., Sumaila U.S. (eds) *Policies and Governance Structures in Woodlands of Southern Africa.* Centre for International Forestry Research, Indonesia.

Murombedzi J. 1991. *Wetland Conservation under Common Property Regimes in Zimbabwe.* CASS Publications, University of Zimbabwe, Harare, Zimbabwe.

Murphree M.W. 1993. *Communal Land Wildlife Resources and Rural District Council Revenues.* CASS Publications, University of Zimbabwe, Harare.

Nyikahadzoi K. 1998. 'A socio-economic evaluation of management techniques used for controlling fishing effort in the Lake Kariba gill net fishery on Lake Kariba on the Zimbabwean side.' *M Phil thesis.* University of Zimbabwe, Harare.

Nyikahadzoi K. 2006. 'An investigation of the impact of bio-ecological approach in the management of kapenta fishery at Lake Kariba: An economic and institutional perspective.' *D Phil thesis.* University of Zimbabwe, Harare.

Timberlake J. 2000. *Biodiversity of the Zambezi Basin.* Biodiversity Foundation for Africa (BFA) Occasional Publications in Biodiversity No. 9. BFA, Bulawayo.

Kariba landscape showing human habitation. Photo: Mohammed Hashim

2. Fragmentation of land resources in the Lake Kariba environs

Jimmiel MANDIMA and Kefasi NYIKAHADZOI

2.1. Introduction

Before colonisation in Zambia and Zimbabwe, land ownership, use and access rights in the Zambezi Valley were traditionally held under the authority of chiefs They allocated usufruct rights to their subjects so they could grow crops in the alluvial soils of the receding river banks during the low season. Inheritance of land was largely patrilineal with men having more land rights, a trend that still dominates to this day in most of the chiefdoms surrounding Lake Kariba. However, the transition into structured colonial rule resulted in the alienation of some land from traditional authority, particularly those sites that were allocated to white settlers. African people were further disenfranchised during the white-ruled 10-year era of the Federation of Rhodesia and Nyasaland (1953-1963), when Lake Kariba was created and close to 57,000 Valley Tonga people were resettled from the valley to the escarpment /plateau area, in the process losing access to prime land and resources (Scudder & Colson 2002).

In the transition to independence, the land around Lake Kariba remained under state ownership as per policies enacted during the colonial era, with the difference that chiefs in parts of the area still retained the power to allocate land, though the dual authority over land (where the state land commissioner had a say) complicated land tenure, resource use and access rights.

Thus, the land resources are clearly largely under the jurisdiction of the states in various forms and administered by multiple ‘land and planning authorities’, different institutional and legislative authorities that are described in detail in later sections of this chapter. It is clear that while the overall use of the resource and the respective management is influenced to a greater extent by the physical and ecosystem characteristics of the area, the prevailing institutional and jurisdictional authorities and their mandates have a strong bearing on the defragmentation that characterises the area.

2.2. Different land property regimes

This section describes the different uses of the land resources by a diverse group of users guided by different governance structures, including traditional, customary and public state-run institutions.

Different land uses and land users

The land resources around Lake Kariba are subject to diverse uses that are mainly influenced by the agro-ecological characteristics of the area. Noteworthy is the fact that terrestrial use of the land was strongly connected to the Zambezi River before damming, and since the lake was formed, the shoreline area has retained this dependency on the land-water nexus. Consequently, it comes as no surprise that there is considerable fragmentation of governance and conflict for resource use in the area (Mhlanga 2009). The main economic activities along the Lake Kariba shoreline are agriculture, fishing and tourism, with farming being the largest livelihood source for the inhabitants of the lakeshore in Zambia. Agricultural production is primarily for subsistence purposes. On the Zambian side rural communities depend primarily on agriculture supplemented by fishing. A small proportion is employed within the tourism industry (Ngalande 2006).

Agriculture

Most rural communities depend on subsistence agriculture, cultivating grain crops that are adapted to low rainfall, like sorghum, millet and maize, as well as vegetables, groundnuts and, in a few areas, cotton as a cash crop. Droughts are frequent, which means that farmers tend to rely on illegal stream bank and lakeshore cultivation, even though productivity levels are characteristically very low. Low rainfall is the main limitation to viable agriculture so in areas where soils are suitable for cultivation, crop production under irrigation is carried out. In Zimbabwe, pioneer schemes may be found in Gache Gache and Cheziya in Nyami Nyami district, and advanced plans exist for irrigation in areas of Binga district as part of the national strategy for food security. These irrigation schemes rely on water abstraction from the lake, generating another dimension of conflict over and fragmentation of shared watercourses.

On the Zimbabwean side, farming is only carried out along the lakeshore Communal Areas since it is prohibited within all protected areas along the lakeshore. There is a 5 km buffer zone around the whole shore, where agriculture is prohibited. While crop farming is the main source of livelihood for the rural population, it is relatively insignificant along the Zimbabwean side, where the rugged terrain of the shoreline, its poor soils, low and erratic rainfall and crop damage by wild animals make the area unsuitable for agricultural production. This fact is demonstrated by the situation in Binga District, where the six wards within the lakeshore area are characterised by the lowest levels of agricultural production and the highest levels of poverty. Food supplies in a normal year last only six to eight months, while sales of cash crops are negligible because the amount of farmland available to communities is limited, with most land reserved for public and private wildlife use. These communities depend for survival on livestock sales, wage employment, beer brewing, craft sales and remittances. Most individuals are part-time farmers and part-time fishers who depend on a combination of agriculture and fishing.

On the Zambian side, in Siavonga, Gwembe and Sinazongwe districts, agriculture used to be dominated by cash cropping of cotton and wheat by the multinational Gwembe Valley Development Company (GVDC), complemented by livestock production and agribusiness for marigolds. However, these land uses have transitioned to subsistence crop cultivation on the escarpment and on the valley floor by local shoreline communities. The main occupation of these communities is agriculture, but frequent droughts mean that they are usually only able to harvest enough food to last a few months (three to five months) and then they have to survive on government handouts for the rest of the year.

Livestock husbandry is significant for lakeshore communities, with several hundred thousand cattle grazing on the escarpment and within the valley floor on the Zambian side. Cattle are kept primarily to provide draught power and as a source of social security during adverse situations such as droughts or other emergencies. More recently, farming in the area has increasingly focused on small livestock production. Local NGOs in the Siavonga district are working in partnership with local communities, the district agricultural and veterinary departments, and chiefs to promote the production of small livestock with a deliberate focus on improved goat varieties.

Fishing and aquaculture development

Fishing is mainly confined to the lakeshore area and the main tributary rivers, consisting of *inshore fishing* for commercial and subsistence purposes by mainly small-scale fisher folk, *offshore kapenta fishing* by large-scale commercial operators and recreational sport fishing, mainly competitive fishing for *Hydrocynus vittatus* (tiger fish). The Kariba tigerfish tournament has over the years become an internationally renowned competition that attracts thousands of sport fishermen from all over the world every year. These different fishing activities require land facilities along the shoreline for fishing camps, landing sites and boat mooring, often resulting in conflicts between the different user categories.

Aquaculture development occurs in two main forms in the Lake Kariba area: fish farming in cages in the lake as well as in land-based pond systems, and crocodile farming. The main commercial fish farms are owned by Lake Harvest Aquaculture (LHA), the largest farmer of Nile tilapia in sub-Saharan Africa. LHA is developing a similar venture in Siavonga, Zambia. The Zambia Development Agency has also invited investors interested in a joint venture with Aqua Harvest Fish Farm in Siavonga, where tilapia will be intensively farmed in cages covering 90 ha within the lake and land based activities on 4.5 ha on the shorelines of

Lake Kariba. All this will further fragment land resources in the area. Crocodile farming is capital intensive, so it is beyond the reach of the average entrepreneur and it results in land fragmentation and conflict. Only a few private operators are involved in crocodile ranching and there are at least 10 crocodile ranches within the whole lakeshore area on both sides of the lake, with local communities risking further land alienation as many more sites are being allocated for this economic activity. Padenga Holdings Limited operates three farms located on the shores of Lake Kariba in Zimbabwe, and is one of the largest Nile crocodile farming operations in Africa, supplying about 33% of the world's demand for large, high-quality skins.

Wildlife

The land in National Parks and Safari Areas, Forest areas and intact communal forests is endowed with rich wildlife resources that are used for consumptive and non-consumptive purposes. In terms of biodiversity richness, the protected wildlife areas in the area incorporate some of the most outstanding terrestrial and riverine wildlife viewing and scenic landscape in Southern Africa. The land is typified by extended riverine habitat that hosts large elephant herds (*Loxodonta africana*), hippopotamus (*Hippopotamus amphibius*), crocodile (*Crocodilus niloticus*), lion (*Panthera leo*), leopard (*Panthera pardus*), buffalo (*Syncerus caffer*), a diversity of antelope, including kudu (*Tragelaphus strepsiceros*), many smaller mammals, reptiles and insects, and until very recently, the black rhino (*Diceros bicornis*). The area also has an abundant avifauna with over 300 bird species recorded. In addition, the Zambezi River and Lake Kariba are an important reservoir for freshwater fish resources that include the tiger fish (*Hydrocynus vittatus*), lungfish (*Protopterus annextens*), and a wide variety of cichlid (tilapias) and cyprinid species, some of which are local endemics and rare species.

In Zimbabwe, these land resources support a vibrant safari hunting industry in Safari Areas and designated parts of communal land as part of the Communal Areas Management Programme for Indigenous Resources (CAMPFIRE), while in Zambia such use is confined to Game Management Areas (GMAs) under the auspices of Community Resources Boards (CRBs). CAMPFIRE is centred on the practice of community-based natural resource management (CBNRM), which aims to generate revenue for the country's underdeveloped rural districts through sustainable use of their local wildlife and habitat (Metcalfe 1994). There is a plethora of literature that details the expressed logic of CBNRM programmes as a way of incentivising local communities to coexist with wildlife on their land resources (Hulme & Murphree 2001, Lewis *et al.* 1988).

In principle, these CBNRM programmes allow private investors to lease hunting concessions from local communities throughout the district. The guidelines for quota setting and benefit sharing for these programmes is provided for by the Zimbabwe Parks and Wildlife Management Authority (ZPWMA) and administered by CAMPFIRE.

Game viewing on the other hand, is not restricted like hunting and may be done anywhere, but it is mainly confined to the National and Recreational Parks where private investors run operations based on a permit granted by the 'land authority' in the area – either the district authority or National Parks. Like in the case of hunting described above, photographic safaris are conducted by private investors, and the local communities or Parks authority benefit from income derived from bed night levies charged to tourists who use the camps and also from the fees for the facilities and concessions leased by the operators.

Forestry

There is no commercial exploitation of timber within the forest area along the Zimbabwean side as consumptive use of timber is prohibited in forest areas and in all protected areas trees are protected to serve as wildlife habitat. On the Zambian side, indigenous forests along the lakeshore are exploited for charcoal and timber. Forests in Siavonga and Sinazongwe districts are being extensively exploited for commercial charcoal production. Hardwoods, mainly *Pterocarpus angolensis*, *Afzelia quanzeis*, *Sterculia quinqueloba* and *Colophospermum mopane* are selected for timber extraction. Communities on either side of the lake utilise non-timber forest products through access for livestock grazing, collection of firewood, medicines and thatching grass. In Zambia, the area around Siavonga district along the shoreline of the Eastern basin has local forests (Lukwechele) and further downstream and outside the plan area (but with ecological connections), the Mutulan'ganga Forest. As the local human population increases and the demand for land increases, the forested areas have become highly threatened by pressure for settlement and crop cultivation (slash and burn agriculture), and logging for charcoal production.

Worth noting though is the fact that in Zimbabwe these areas are administered by the Forestry Commission yet they provide habitat for wildlife resources that are under the jurisdiction of the Parks and Wildlife Management Authority. Similarly, on the Zambian side, the Zambia Forestry Department (ZFD) administers the forests that serve as habitat for wildlife resources that are under the jurisdiction of the Zambia Wildlife Authority (ZAWA).

Mining and quarrying

The land on the immediate outskirts of the Kariba urban area and within the Charara Safari area is used for quarrying of muscovite quartzite (glitterstone), which is used in construction. No other mining is currently under way but the potential remains high for the exploitation of coal in the Sengwa area, as well as for other related minerals (i.e. uranium, beryl, graphite, diamonds). There are known reserves of coal at Sengwa in Gokwe where in the 1990s Rio Tinto started exploration with plans for the Sengwa Colliery development to utilise an estimated 1.3 billion tons of coal, of which 600 million tons are proven reserves. This colliery, if developed in the coming years, is seen as the ideal feed for an on-site thermal power station. Though no commercially viable deposits were found from earlier exploratory processes, it is worth noting that the potential for future exploration and mining remains very high and this would change the natural and social ecosystem landscape of the whole area with regards to fragmentation of land resources.

In Zambia, there is one main mining operation of bituminous coal at Maamba in Sinazongwe district. Deposits of various minerals – mainly tin, mica, beryl, uranium, tungsten, tantalum, fluorite, graphite, zinc, copper and lead – have been reported in the hinterland of the lake on the Zambian side, and although not currently exploited they may be of economic value in the future.

Thermal power generation

Recent reports in the Zimbabwean government print media confirm that the mining firm RioZim has been granted a licence to build a 2 400-megawatt independent thermal power plant in Gokwe in a development that could more than double national power supply (Kadzere 2010). The multi-billion dollar power plant will be commissioned in phases, with the first unit being expected on grid by 2014 while completion of the thermal station is expected by 2020 (*Ibid*). These developments will change the landscape in this area and also influence other developments associated with urbanisation in the mine and power station centres, exacerbating fragmentation of land resources.

On the river, discussions to resuscitate earlier intentions for hydropower generation at Batoka Gorge have recently been newsworthy and seem to have gained momentum in 2012. This will be associated with developments similar to those that have characterised Kariba downstream, impacting on the demand for land resources and also creating associated resource use conflicts. The Batoka Dam will inundate the only known nesting sites for the Taita falcons, *Falco fasciinuche*, in the gorge (Du Toit 1984), a dire ecological consequence.

Tourism

While tourism was not taken into account during the planning phase for Kariba Dam, it is now a significant source of income around the lake. Hotels have been built, especially on the Zimbabwe side, where game viewing and recreational fishing are important economic activities. In both Kariba and Siavonga urban centres on the eastern Sanyati basin, the demand for land for additional lodges, camping sites and large-scale hotels is on the increase. The number of bed nights in these hotels is estimated to be more than 90 000 per annum (Nathalie & Dayer 2006). An income of US$14 million per annum has been estimated for tourism activities in the entire Zambezi valley (Nathalie & Dyer 2006). Common ancillary activities, which include boat cruises, fishing, diving, relaxing and camping on islands, add to land resource fragmentation. However, benefits are again largely distributed to entrepreneurs and the central governments. Apart from the few Tongas employed in unskilled and semi-skilled jobs in hotel and safari operations, local people do not really profit from tourism (Scudder 2005, Kaluba & Mukupe 2000).

Pressure for tourism infrastructure is growing fast on the Zambian side. The Chipepo Development Trust (CDT), through the local traditional leadership, is inviting investors for the Lake Kariba Waterfront in Gwembe District, which will see the development of integrated tourism facilities on 2 000 ha of land along the shoreline. These facilities are to include hotels, lodges, housing estates, lakeside golf course, retail shops and other ancillary services.

Mlibizi, Binga, and Chalala on the Zimbabwe side are all likely to experience increased demand for land to develop shoreline tourism facilities in the near future now that the Zimbabwean socio-political environment seems to be stabilising.

Current tourism-based use of the land resources and the growing demand for land to develop further tourism infrastructure are driving fragmentation and have the potential to outcompete other uses of the lakeshore area, namely fishing villages, landing sites and so on.

Land tenure, institutional governance of use and access to the land resources

The land resources in the plan area fall under three tenure categories: state land, communal land and private land.

State land consists mainly of the Parks and Wildlife Estate on the Zimbabwe side (the Parks and Safari Areas) and the forests. These areas are governed in terms of provisions of the Parks and Wildlife Management Act and the Forestry Act respectively.

Communal land is still state land but use rights are bestowed on the local communities indefinitely but with no freehold title. In Zimbabwe, the local government ministry (at national level) and local district authorities (in the plan area) administer this land through the Urban, Town and Country Planning Act, and the Rural District Councils Act. In contrast, Zambia's legal framework provides for dual land authority shared by state and chief, with the chiefs having enough authority to allocate land to private investors. Although land still belongs to the state, since the introduction of the new land Act of 1995, chiefs and state authorities have been able to grant leasehold titles for 99 years. The granting of titles has resulted in the alienation of most communal land from the state to the private sector.

As private investment in large-scale agribusiness has growns, this gradual shift to security of tenure through title deeds reflects a similar growing phenomenon across most of Africa. Multinationals are acquiring more and more land for the mass production of biofuel and genetically modified crops. These large scale land acquisitions have implications for sustainable development and biodiversity conservation (Anon 2010).

Private land is land alienated from local communities through outright purchase or long-term lease (99-years) from the local district or the chief. Like most of sub-Saharan Africa, land tenure has gradually evolved from simple traditional processes to modern complex systems; from the communal types to those where there is more tight control over allocation of land, suggesting more individual control of land (White 1959). From the foregoing, traditional land tenure in the Kariba area in both countries reflected a mix of the three possible systems. In the first system, an individual obtains land rights by residence, without allocation through a hierarchy of estates, an approach possible where land is generally plentiful and the populations are sparse. In the second system, land is held under the control of lineages, whereby access to agricultural land is exclusively reserved for use by those members who can trace their heritage from a common ancestry. In the third system, chiefs exercise direct control over allocation of land with a descending hierarchy of estates.

The traditional land ownership systems outlined above evolved with the imposition of colonial rule in many parts of Africa, especially in sub-Saharan Africa, which resulted in land alienation and the settlement of European commercial farmers who were granted individual freehold or leasehold tenure on what became crown or state land. This resulted in the creation of two different legal systems, namely the long-established customary land law and English land law (Mvunga 1980). European settlers soon influenced the agrarian systems of the Tonga subsistence farmers, who adopted new technologies such as hybrid maize and ox-drawn ploughs, and over time traditional attitudes towards land ownership gave way to pressures for the individualisation of land tenure.

As a consequence of the colonial influence and land apportionment, on the Zimbabwean side, the terrestrial land resources are all state land under the jurisdiction of three different 'planning authorities', namely the rural district councils, as provided for by the Communal Lands Act and Town and Country Planning Act, the Parks and Wildlife Management authority, as provided for by the Parks and Wildlife Act, and the Forestry Commission.

This state land is under the jurisdiction of two types of institutional authorities.

First, all communal land on the Zimbabwean side of the lake is under the jurisdiction of district authorities notably Kariba, Nyami Nyami, Binga and Hwange district councils. Chieftaincy still exists and has power, as provided for in the Traditional Leaders Act (Chapter 29:17), which institutionalises the governance of communal land and resettlement areas. In Zambia, state land is mainly under the jurisdictions of Sinazongwe, Siavonga and Gwembe district councils. These local districts have planning authority over the land resources in both countries but in Zambia traditional chiefs still wield power over land that often supersedes that of local district authorities, and their unilateral decisions often result in land being alienated to the private sector. Second, state land is under the the jurisdiction of Parks and Wildlife Management Authority in Zimbabwe, which administers the Matusadona National Park and the related Safari Areas (Hurungwe, Charara, Sibilobilo and Chete) as well as the Lake Kariba Recreational Park. The Forestry Commission administers the Kavira and Sijarira Forest Reserves in the South West in Binga District.

What emerges clearly is how the institutional arrangements and management of land have evolved from traditional systems of 'communal rights to use and access' to post-colonial systems of freehold and top-down control of land resources by the state, which has created serious fragmentation of resource use.

Legal framework for conservation and land use

A broad range of broad social, economic and environmental policies and programmes – both national and international – have a bearing on the conservation and use of land resources in the Lake Kariba area.

The Zimbabwe Environmental Management Act Chapter 20:27 of 2002 provides for the sustainable management of natural resources and protection of the environment, and the prevention of pollution and environmental degradation. It also provides for the preparation of a National Environmental Plan and other plans for the management and protection of the environment, as well as the establishment of an Environmental Management Agency and an Environment Fund.

The Tourism Act (2001) is the primary government document guiding the tourism sector in Zimbabwe. The Act established the Zimbabwe Tourism Authority (ZTA), which manages and markets Zimbabwe as a tourist destination. It also established the Zimbabwe Tourism Fund to develop the tourism sector under the management and control of the Minister of Tourism. The Fund is a primary source of revenue for the ZTA. Tourism infrastructure and service facilities are also required to be registered or graded under the Act.

The Zimbabwe Traditional Leaders Act Chapter 29:17 of 1998 provides for the appointment of village heads, headman and chiefs, and the establishment of Councils of Chiefs and village, ward and provincial assemblies. It defines their functions, particularly regarding institutionalising the governance of communal land and resettlement areas.

Zimbabwe's Forestry Act Chapter 19:05 (1990) governs the establishment of the Forestry Commission, which is the state agency responsible for regulating gazetted forests in Zimbabwe, and the Communal Land Forest Produce Act (1987) for communal areas. In privately owned areas the Forestry Commission is involved in setting and monitoring the timber quotas but the Forestry Produce Act governs the management and marketing. In communal areas, rural district councils draw up concession agreements on the advice of the Forestry Commission, which then supervises them. Zambia has a comparable Forestry Act (1999), which government revised in 2011 to incorporate Joint Forestry Management (JFM) as a model for co-management for local forests with local communities while government retains overall jurisdiction over national forests.

The Mines and Minerals Act Chapter 21:05 (1965) is the principal act governing mining in Zimbabwe. It provides security of tenure and has clear provisions for acquisition, maintenance and relinquishing of mining titles. The Zambian equivalent, the Mines and Minerals Development Act (2008), is undergoing further revisions in 2012 to incorporate environmental aspects and provisions that allow access rights to mining for small holders.

The Zimbabwe National Museums and Monuments Act Chapter 25:11 of 2001 governs the management, protection and utilisation of national sacred sites and attractions falling under the Ministry of Home Affairs.

The Wildlife-based Land Reform Policy of 2006 was promulgated in Zimbabwe to rationalise the ownership, access and use rights of wildlife resources. It aimed to correct the imbalance that prevailed before independence, where most of the wildlife resources were under the private sector while local communities living in the same landscapes had no opportunities to participate in the wildlife industry.

As in Zimbabwe, similarly large legislative framework governing land resources exists in Zambia, such as the Lands Act (1995) and the Chiefs Act (1965). For this reason, their governments have developed a Lakeshore Combination Master Plan to reconcile the legislative frameworks and allow for co-ordinated and integrated management between the two countries, including the lake. However, the provisions of the Master Plan have yet to be implemented on the ground.

The multiple statutes and regulatory frameworks that relate to the use of land resources create sectoral silos that result in duplication, inefficiencies and general confusion for the intended stakeholder beneficiaries. In both countries, government departments and the other entities with planning authority, like rural districts and urban councils, have divergent visions with each seeking to advance its own narrowly defined values and priorities in a bid to remain viable and justify their existence. In the process, most people from the local communities that depend exclusively on the land for their livelihoods become the victims of this conundrum of confusion and conflict dynamics. At the same time, local actors and the state legitimise fragmented and inequitable access to land, creating insecurities in management and differential options for all entities involved – local farmers, local elites, business operators and local-level state and national-level state authorities.

It is clear that government's failure to establish critical links and co-ordination between sectors to synergise management efforts of the different land resources can only be a reflection of its disregard of the relationships that exist in the terrestrial ecosystem.

2.3. Impact of fragmentation on the land resource and livelihoods

The Lake Kariba environs represent a landscape context where the land resource forms the basis for all the other related biodiversity and natural capital with regard to water, wildlife, fish, woodlands and grasslands, as discussed in the ensuing chapters. So there is an inherent association at the ecosystem level. As such, key interactions are commonly connected to the increased demand for land for competing uses of all natural resources available on the land. Of particular note is the fact that all other key land uses described earlier, like mining, agriculture, tourism, urban development, fishing and aquaculture, increasingly require more land to remain viable. Consequently, there is an ever-growing demand for land, resulting in shrinkage of the land available for wildlife movements and dispersal. This problem is more significant on the Zimbabwean side, where wildlife population numbers and densities are high. The infrastructure and facilities developed for the new and expanding uses are associated with attendant pollution impacts on the water systems and the environment in general. Predictably, the likely deterioration in water quality will in due course negatively affect ecosystem integrity, thereby compromising the delivery of ecosystem services by land resources.

Key threats to land resources in the area include incompatible, inadequate and unco-ordinated land use planning; incompatible expanding human settlements; urban development; incompatible tourism infrastructure development; and lack of policy harmonisation. With regard to land use planning, the respective planning authorities do not have plans with provisions relevant to contemporary land demand issues, and even where plans are in place, their provisions are not enforced. One consequences of this situation has been the expansion of developments in Kariba town, where incompatible industrial and residential uses are juxtapositioned. Likewise, in Siavonga, Zambia, there is no updated land use plan that restricts crop cultivation to suitable zones or governs riverbank tourism infrastructure, resulting in expanding habitat degradation from slash and burn agriculture, destruction of wildlife habitat and illegal off-take of resources in the form of wildlife poaching and timber for charcoal production. These short-term uses have a medium- to long-term negative impact on the sustainability of livelihoods and food security.

Urban growth has outpaced the provision of service infrastructure, with serious consequences for water and sanitation services in Zimbabwe and Zambia. Both countries suffer from regular plant failures and the discharge of semi-treated raw effluent into public waters that is accompanied by attendant pollution and public health challenges. A similar threat is also growing on the open waters where houseboats discharge raw waste into the lake while on charter.

The Lakeshore Master Plan, which was meant to be the vehicle for harmonisation between the two countries, has never been operationalised. This has resulted in growing land fragmentation and increased conflict among competing land users in the Lake Kariba area.

2.4. Conclusion

In view of the foregoing, it is clear that land resources in the plan area are highly threatened. There are numerous competing uses administered by different land authorities on the basis of multiple statutory provisions that are applied with little or no co-ordination. The sustenance of other resources (fish, woodlands and grasslands, wildlife, water and other aquatic organisms) is highly dependent on the status of the land resource.

The Valley Tonga remain grieved, feeling short-changed, and the livelihood strategies they continue to pursue from the uplands are detrimental to the ecosystem health of the plan area (Magadza 2010, Tumbare 2008). Worth noting is that efforts to promote CBNRM, through programmes like CAMPFIRE in Zimbabwe's Nyami Nyami and Binga districts and ADMADE in Zambia's Game Management Areas, have not yielded the desired result of improving land access to local communities (Hulme & Murphree 2001, Lewis *et al.* 1988). In the Zimbabwean case, it has become clear that devolving power to the local district authority still keeps the power within the state, and thus does not unlock it to locally based grassroots institutions, as in historical times when traditional chiefs had unquestionable power over land resources (White 1959). Professional staff working at most of the local districts are brought in from outside the area, as most locals lack the formal training, capacity and skills to hold such office; priorities tend to be on a tangent and not always aligned with local needs. In Zambia, the ADMADE model was abandoned due to challenges of accountability and the new community resource boards are dogged by issues of corruption, lack of transparency and accountability. Where chiefs continue to wield the power to make decisions regarding private sector investments, cases have been characterised by rampant corruption and underhand deals that have resulted in further alienation of communal land.

2.4. Conclusion

Our findings agree with observations by Agrawal & Ribot (1999) that, ironically, decentralised structures of administration effectively tend to centralise power, as observed in regional and district committees where government officials make decisions while the local representatives sit silent, and in village councils where local people might be able to participate but have no resources to allocate. In response, new land management models have emerged that seek to establish legally recognised, community-based institutions in Kariba's communal areas to democratise the power base and voice the interests of the local community on issues related to land resources and their use.

References

Agrawal A. & Ribot J.C. 1999. 'Accountability in decentralisation: A framework with south Asian and west African cases', *Journal of Developing Areas* **33**:473-502.

Anon 2010. 'Rising global interest in farmland and the importance of responsible agricultural investment.' In:*Agriculture and Rural Development & Development Economics, Joint Notes: Land Policy and Administration.* World Bank Series Issue 54. World Bank, New York.

Du Toit R. F. 1984. 'Some environmental aspects of the proposed hydro-electric schemes on the Zambezi River, Zimbabwe', *Biological Conservation* **28**: 73-87.

Hulme D. & Murphree M. (eds) 2001. *African Wildlife and Livelihoods: The Promise and Performance of Community Conservation.* James Currey, Oxford.

Kadzere M. 2010. 'RioZim Power Boost', *The Zimbabwe Herald, 8 October 2010, Business Section.*

Kaluba K. & Mukupe H. 2000. 'Socio-economic benefits of the Kariba Dam.' In: Tumbare M.J. (ed.*) Management of River Basins and Dams: The Zambezi River Basin.* A.A. Balkema, Rotterdam.

Lewis D.M., Kaweche G.B. & Mwenya A.N. 1988. *Wildlife Conservation Outside Protected Areas: A Lesson from an Experiment in Zambia.* ADMADE Research Publication No. 2. Associated Printers, Lusaka.

Magadza C. H. D. 2010. 'Environmental state of Lake Kariba and the Zambezi River Valley: Lessons learned and not learned', *Lakes & Reservoirs: Research & Management* **15**: 67-192.

Metcalfe S. 1994. 'The Zimbabwe Communal Areas Management Programme for Indigenous Resources (CAMPFIRE).' In: Western D. & Wright R. M. (eds.) *Natural Connections: Perspectives in Community-based Conservation.* Island Press, Washington D.C.

Mhlanga L. 2009. 'Fragmentation of resource governance along the shoreline of Lake Kariba, Zimbabwe', *Development Southern Africa* **26**: 585-596.

Mvunga M.P. 1980. *The Colonial Foundations of Zambia's Land Tenure System.* NECZAM, Lusaka.

Nathalie V. & Dayer R. 2006. Science and politics of large dam projects. Case Study – Kariba Dam In: Bernhauer T., Wehrli B. & Wüest A. (eds) *The Science and Politics of Large Dams.* EAWAG/ ETHZ, Switzerland.

Ngalande P. 2006. Socio-Economic Assessment of Resource Utilisation Along the Coastal Zone of Lake Kariba. In: University Lake Kariba Research Station. *Lake Kariba. A Case for Integrated Coastal Zone Management.* Southern Africa Network for Training and Research on the Environment. University Lake Kariba Research Station. Kariba, Zimbabwe.

Scudder T. & Colson E. 2002. 'Long term field research in the Gwembe Valley, Zambia.' In: Van Kemper R. & Royce A. (eds) *Longitudinal Research in Anthropology.* Alta Mira Press Walnut Creek, CA, USA.

Scudder T. 2005. *The Kariba Case Study.* California Institute of Technology (CIT) Social Science Working Paper. CIT, USA.

Tumbare M. J. 2008. 'Managing Lake Kariba sustainably: Threats and challenges', *Management of Environmental Quality* **19**: 731-739.

White C.M.N. 1959. 'Survey of African land tenure in northern Rhodesia', *Journal of African Administration* **11**: 171-178.

Marineland Harbour on Lake Kariba. Photo: Mohammed Hashim

3. Challenges surrounding water management within the Lake Kariba environs

Lindah MHLANGA, Crispen PHIRI and Portia CHIFAMBA

3.1. Introduction

In developing countries, especially in Africa, dams and the resulting artificial lakes are always a major strategy to alleviate shortages of water for irrigation and to meet the growing need for electricity (Magadza 1986). Lake Kariba was created solely for the purposes of generating hydroelectric power for what was then the Southern and Northern Rhodesian colonies of Britain, now Zimbabwe and Zambia respectively. The intensification of copper mining activities in Northern Rhodesia between 1920 and 1945 and the rapid expansion of the manufacturing sector in Southern Rhodesia had brought about the need for a cheap and stable source of electric power in the two countries (WCD 2000). In response, the dam was constructed from 1955-1960, and unexpectedly provided new resources for communities to exploit. Infrastructure from the primary development for hydroelectric power generation made the area more accessible and secondary activities emerged (Magadza 1986). Today a wide range of economic activities, which are based directly and indirectly on land and water resources, have developed on both the Zambian and the Zimbabwean sides of the lake. These include fisheries, animal husbandry, irrigation, transport and recreation. Lake Kariba has become a multi-sectoral and multi-stakeholder natural resource.

Water within the lake is an important hydropower resource for the Zambian and the Zimbabwean governments. However, hydroelectric power generation competes with local ecosystem services and with the livelihood needs of local human groups. In this chapter, we discuss water with regard to institutional settings and show how it is a central and critical resource within the Lake Kariba environs. We argue that water is a political and economic good that requires political goodwill and shared common vision to avoid political conflicts associated with its use and management. However, co-operation remains a challenge, as illustrated by the different interests reflected in different institutions and legal frameworks, as well as increasing pluralism in the management of water in the area at national, bilateral and regional levels. This fragmentation of resource management is impacting negatively on Lake Kariba and its resources.

3.2. State of the resource

Lake Kariba is one of the world largest reservoirs with a maximum surface area of 5 577 km^2 and a total storage of 180.6 km^3 (WCD 2000). The discharge capacity of the flood gates is 9 500 m^3 per second. The hydroelectric generation capacity of Lake Kariba is 1 266 MW. The major source of water flowing into the lake is from the Zambezi River, which contributes 77.2% of the inflow, while the rest is from smaller affluent rivers (15.8%) and rainfall (7%) (Coche 1974). The main secondary rivers on the Zimbabwean side in order of importance are Gwaai, Sanyati and Sengwa, which are 47 140 km^2, 43 500 km^2 and 5 200 km^2 respectively. Rivers situated in Zimbabwe drain 95 840 km^2, or 63.6% of the lake catchment area (Balon & Coche 1974). Zambian rivers have a comparatively smaller catchment area, the major ones being Chimene, Zongwe, Lufua and Chezya, which are 2 567 km^2, 2 290 km^2, 2 274 km^2 and 850 km^2 respectively (*Ibid*). The hydrographs of the secondary rivers are characterised by many high peak floods of short duration that form local floods and superimpose themselves on the base flood, which travels from the Victoria Falls and the subsequent gorges before reaching the lake (*Ibid*).

The Zambezi River is perennial but its flows are variable throughout the year. High flows occur between February and May during the rainy season. The river's water discharge is 450 $m^3 s^{-1}$ during the dry season and 1 770 $m^3 s^{-1}$ to 1 080 $m^3 s^{-1}$ during the rainy season. High discharge fluctuations are characteristic of rivers in a semi-arid tropical climate. Other rivers flowing into Lake Kariba are semi-annual and dry out during the period of low water discharge. The downstream flows are dictated by power generation and this has altered natural flow patterns (WCD 2000).

3.3. Institutional arrangements and management of water resources

Water resource management is fragmented in Zambia and Zimbabwe, with 14 organisations exercising a legal mandate to manage Lake Kariba and the Zambezi River with its tributaries (Tumbare 2008). Table 2 provides details of the main institutions responsible for managing Lake Kariba's waters. These waters are shared by Zambia and Zimbabwe, two states with separate national legislation and interests. To more harmoniously manage the part of the Zambezi River they share, the two countries entered into a bilateral agreement. They signed the Inter-ministerial Council Bilateral Treaty under the provisions of the Southern African Development Community's Protocol on Shared Water Courses, after which they formed the Zambezi River Authority (ZRA) in October 1987.

The ZRA is the over-arching institution for the bilateral management of these shared waters. The activities of this intergovernmental body are governed by the

Zambezi River Authority Act of 1987, a bilateral Act that empowers the ZRA to administer the waters of Lake Kariba on behalf of Zambia and Zimbabwe and safeguard the interests of two nations in hydroelectric power generation. The mission of the ZRA is to co-operatively manage and develop these shared water resources in an integrated and sustainable manner. The ZRA Act recognises the need to preserve biodiversity by putting in place measures that protect species and meet water requirements for different ecosystems. While the principal function of Lake Kariba is generation of hydroelectric power, ZRA endeavours to ensure that the requirements of other users are not compromised, including the needs of the environment itself. To this end, the ZRA monitors the operation and maintenance of the dam wall and related installations, and is also responsible for pollution monitoring. It has no mandate, however, to prosecute offenders or enforce the law.

Table 2: Institutions responsible for managing Lake Kariba's waters

Institutions	Responsibilities	Relevant egislation
	Zambia	
Zambia Environmental Management Agency	- Integrated environmental management - Protection and conservation of the environment and the sustainable management and use of natural resources - Protection of the environment and pollution control	Environmental Management Act No. 12 of 2011
Department of Water Affairs	Ownership, control and use of water resources	Water Act, Cap 312 (1949)
Department of Fisheries	Management of aquatic resources	Fisheries Act No. 22 of 2011
Siavonga, Sinazongwe and Gwembe district authorities	- Management of natural resources within local areas - Preparation and implementation of development plans	- Town and Country Planning Act No. 16 of 1995 - Local Government Act No. 22 of 1991
Zambia Electricity Supply Corporation Limited (ZESCO)	Generation of electricity on the Kariba North Bank Power Station	Energy Regulation Act No. 16 of 1995

3.3. Institutional arrangements and management of water resources

Institutions	Responsibilities	Relevant egislation
	Zimbabwe	
Ministry of Water Resources Development and Management (MWRDM)	Provide overall policy guidelines on the development, exploitation and utilisation of water resources	Water Act (Chapter 20:24) of 1998
Zimbabwe National Water Authority (ZINWA)	- Water resources planning, management and development - Water quality, pollution control and environmental protection - Hydrology and hydrogeology - Dam safety - Water pricing	Zimbabwe National Water Authority Act (Chapter 20:25) of 1998
Ministry of Environment & Natural Resources Management: Environmental Management Agency	- Sustainable management of natural resources and protection of the environment - Prevention of pollution and environmental degradation - Preparation of environmental plans for management and protection of the lake	Environmental Management Act (Chapter 20:27) of 2002
Ministry of Environment & Natural Resources Management: Zimbabwe Parks and Wildlife Management Authority	Administration of Lake Kariba Recreational Park	Parks and Wildlife Act (Chapter 20:14) of 1996 Revised Edition
Ministry of Transport Communication and Infrastructural Development	Regulation of shipping on Lake Kariba	Inland Waters Shipping Act (Chapter 13:06) of 1971

Institutions	Responsibilities	Relevant egislation
Ministry of Tourism & Hospitality Industry: Zimbabwe Tourism Authority	- Controlling and regulating tourism - Issuing permits for all forms of tourism activities on and around Lake Kariba	Tourism Act (Chapter 14:20) of 1996
Ministry of Energy and Power Development: Zimbabwe Electricity Supply Authority (ZESA)	Generation of electricity at Kariba South Bank Power Station	Electricity Act (Chapter 13:19 of 2002)
Ministry of Local Government Rural and Urban Development: Rural district councils (Binga, Hwange, Nyaminyami) and Town Councils (Kariba, Victoria Falls)	- General administration and development of the communal land and general state land - Preparation of general development plans	- Rural District Council Act of 1988 - District Development Fund Act (Chapter 29:06) of 1988 - Regional Town & Country Planning Act (Chapter 29:12) of 1998 - Housing Standards Control Act (Chapter 29:08) of 1997
Bilateral and regional institutions		
Zambezi River Authority (ZRA)	- Monitoring and maintaining the Kariba Complex - Maintaining the water levels in the dam in consultation with ZESCO and ZESA - Collecting and processing hydrological data	Zambezi River Authority Act (Chapter 20:23) of 1987
SADC Water Division	Promotion of environmentally sustainable development	SADC Policy and Strategy for Sustainable Development
	Considers the environment as a legitimate user of water	Regional Strategic Action Plan on Integrated Water Resources Development and Management

3.3. Institutional arrangements and management of water resources

Institutions	Responsibilities	Relevant egislation
Global Water Partnership	Calls for a desirable future in which the region's environment is conserved and sufficient water is allocated to maintain ecosystem integrity	Southern Africa Vision for Water, Life and Environment: Chapter 7
Zambezi Watercourse Commission (ZAMCOM)	- Practising integrated water resources management (IWRM) in the Zambezi River Basin - Ensuring sustainable use of natural and water resources - Promotion of equitable and reasonable utilisation of natural and water resources - Mitigation of flood damage - Harmonisation of water quality and effluent standards at basin level	Zambezi Watercourse Commission (ZAMCOM) Agreement of 2004

Water resources management institutions in Zimbabwe

The principal legislation governing water resources in Zimbabwe is the Water Act (Chapter 20:24) of 1998, which stipulates that the power over all water in the country is vested in the president. The Ministry of Water Resources Development and Management (MWRDM) administers the Water Act. The main mandate of the MWRDM is to provide overall policy guidelines on the development, exploitation and utilisation of water resources. According to the Water Act, with regards to Lake Kariba waters, the MWRDM has to ensure the availability of water to people for primary purposes and to meet the needs of aquatic and associated ecosystems. The ministry's major technical arm is the Zimbabwe National Water Authority (ZINWA).

ZINWA is a parastatal that was established in 2000 through the Water Act (Chapter 20:24) of 1998. Its operations are stipulated in the Zimbabwe National Water Authority Act (Chapter 20:25). through the MWRDM, ZINWA formulates policies and standards for Lake Kariba's waters in five areas: (i) water resources planning, management and development; (ii) water quality, pollution control and environmental protection; (iii) hydrology and hydrogeology; (iv) dam safety; and

(v) water pricing. Subject to the Water Act, ZINWA also assists and participates in or advises on any matter pertaining to the planning of the development, exploitation, protection and conservation of water resources in Lake Kariba. Under the provisions of the Water Act, ZINWA should also ensure that the exploitation, conservation and management of Lake Kariba waters ensure equitable accessibility and efficient allocation, distribution, use and development.

It also has a responsibility to encourage and assist local authorities to discharge their functions with regard to the development and management of water resources in areas under their jurisdiction, in particular the provision of potable water and the disposal of waste water. On Lake Kariba, ZINWA may further undertake research, develop a database on hydrological issues, and conduct hydrological and geographical surveys. Finally, the authority is mandated to promote mechanisms for the co-operative management of international water resources, of which Lake Kariba is a typical case.

The Environmental Management Agency (EMA), a parastatal under the Ministry of Environment and Natural Resources Management, is also involved in the management of water resources on Lake Kariba. EMA was established under the Environmental Management Act (Chapter 20:27) and operationalised in March 2003 through Statutory Instrument 103 of 2003. On Lake Kariba, its primary responsibilities are to ensure sustainable management of natural resources and protection of the environment, prevent pollution and environmental degradation and prepare environmental plans for the management and protection of the lake.

On the Zimbabwean side, Lake Kariba is a Recreational Park under the jurisdiction of the Zimbabwe Parks and Wildlife Management Authority (ZPWMA). The ZPWMA controls fishing, and administers and manages the Lake Kariba Recreational Park. The Zimbabwe Electricity Supply Authority's (ZESA) main responsibility on Lake Kariba is the generation of electricity at Kariba South Bank Power Station. On the Zimbabwean side, there are two district councils and one municipality that have an interest in and influence on the management of water resources in Lake Kariba. In addition, the Ministry of Transport is responsible for regulating shipping services on Lake Kariba. The ministry is primarily involved in the provision of boat transport and navigation control and ensuring safety for lake users.

The governance of water resources as laid out in the Water Act (1998) and the ZINWA Act (1998) provides for the involvement of users of water in the decision-making process through catchment and sub-catchment councils. Catchment councils are statutory bodies created as platforms for different stakeholders to consult and collectively manage water resources in a catchment area (Manzungu & Kujinga 2002). There are seven catchment councils in Zimbabwe, namely Save, Sanyati, Mazowe, Runde, Mzingwane, Gwayi and Manyame. Lake Kariba falls under two catchment councils, Gwayi and Sanyati. There is a provision by

ZINWA through councils for local water users to participate in deciding how to manage water. Although this provision is there however local communities do not participate in water resources management around Lake Kariba.

Water resources management institutions in Zambia

The lead institution in environmental management in Zambia is the Zambian Environmental Management Agency (ZEMA), which was instituted by the Environmental Management Act No. 12 of 2011. The act continued the existence of Environmental Council of Zambia (ECZ) by re-naming it ZEMA. It provides for integrated environmental management and the protection and conservation of the environment and the sustainable management and use of natural resources. It also provides for the prevention and control of pollution and environmental degradation. The act allows for public participation in environmental decision-making. ZEMA is headed by a Director-General who is the Chief Executive Officer of the agency. The Director-General reports to the Board, which oversees the implementation and successful operation of the policy and functions of the agency. Under the agency is an inspectorate, which consists of technical staff and facilities required to administer, monitor and enforce measures to protect the environment and prevent pollution.

The Ministry of Energy and Water Development is responsible for water resource management in Zambia through the Water Act, CAP 312 (1949), which provides for the ownership, control and use of water. The technical arm under this ministry is the Department of Water Affairs whose responsibility is water resource assessment and development. All public water in Zambia is vested in the president. The Zambia Water Act, however, does not apply to the Western Province and the Zambezi River.

The Department of Fisheries (DoF) has a mandate with regards to the management of fisheries resources on Lake Kariba through the provisions of the Fisheries Act No. 22 of 2011. A detailed description of the institutions that have been developed through institutionalisation of co-management on the Zambian shore is described in the fisheries chapter (Chapter 4). This increases the multiplicity of institutions with an influence on water resources management on Lake Kariba. Three rural district councils – Siavonga, Sinazongwe and Gwembe – have jurisdiction over Lake Kariba's waters.

International and regional agreements

The Zambezi River basin in which Lake Kariba is located covers 1,359,000 km^2 and spans eight riparian states, namely Angola, Zambia, Namibia, Botswana, Zimbabwe, Malawi, Tanzania and Mozambique. These states have signed various regional agreements regarding the management of the Zambezi River basin that, together with their own national policies and legislation, have implications for the management of Lake Kariba. Refer to Table 2 earlier in this chapter for details of the major regional agreements impacting on the management of Lake Kariba's waters.

The water resources within Lake Kariba must be viewed in the context of the Zambezi River basin and the Southern Africa region. Generally, the region has limited water resources, which makes the Zambezi River a major source of water for all the riparian countries. Conflict on sharing and access to the water resource can arise from issues such as determining the hierarchy of uses of the waters of a shared river, prioritising between prior and new needs or uses and even agreeing on the criteria to determine who gets water and how much water (Mutembwa 1998). This situation is complicated further because the eight riparian countries have different levels of interest in the Zambezi waters. For example, Zambia has the largest share of the Zambezi basin, yet it has other major water resources. In contrast, Namibia and Zimbabwe suffer from water scarcity. The share of each of the eight countries of the Zambezi basin and their respective precipitation contributions are shown in Table 3.

Table 3: Share of Zambezi basin in terms of surface area and precipitation

Countries	Basin area (%)	Precipitation (%)
Angola	18.2	19.7
Botswana	1.5	0.9
Malawi	7.5	9.1
Mozambique	11.6	12.4
Namibia	1.1	0.7
Tanzania	2.2	2.7
Zambia	41.9	42.3
Zimbabwe	15.9	12.2

Source: Beck & Bernauer 2011

In order to alleviate potential water conflicts the riparian states have put co-operative mechanisms in place for the management and development of the Zambezi River. These mechanisms are based on the Convention on Non-navigational Uses of International Watercourses, which was adopted by the General Assembly of the United Nations in 1997. They are also based on the Revised Protocol on Shared Watercourses in the Southern African Development Community, which was adopted in August 2000. The protocol resulted from efforts initiated in the mid 1980s to put in place a Zambezi Watercourse Commission (Tumbare 2008). The purpose of the commission was to practise integrated water resources management in the basin whilst promoting more efficient, equitable and reasonable utilisation of the Zambezi water resources by the riparian states for their sustainable economic development (Tumbare 2008).

Prior to setting up the commission and developing the protocol the member states formulated and agreed to 19 projects under the Zambezi River Action Plan (ZACPLAN). The ZACPLAN project commenced in 1987 to meet the need for multi-national management for the Zambezi River basin. Under ZACPLAN a Zambezi River Basin Water Commission (ZAMCOM) was instituted, based on the Helsinki Rules of 1967. According to the agreement, each basin country has the right to a reasonable and equitable share of the water in the basin and that such benefits should be achieved with minimum disadvantage to the other basin states. Before ZAMCON, issues of equity and the allocation of water for each country were determined nationally, except for Lake Kariba. Although ZAMCOM was established, only seven of the eight Zambezi basin riparian states except Zambia signed the agreement in July 2004 (Tumbare 2008). The agreement stipulates that at least six of the eight riparian states have to ratify the ZAMCOM agreement to enable it to come in force. The agreement came into force on 26 June 2011.

The fact that Zambia did not sign the agreement limits ZAMCON's effectiveness. We identified a number of reasons for lack of consensus on sharing water resources through the agreement. It appears those countries that stand to gain most from further development of their water resources may have perceived the agreement as a threat to their sovereignty. Downstream members who are affected negatively by upstream management are usually keen on endorsing co-operation whilst upstream members who perceive a net loss would be reluctant. As illustrated in Table 2 the eight riparian states have different shares of the Zambezi river basin, generating an imbalance between major shareholders and minor shareholders, who may not agree on the desired relative influence of shareholders. Despite these limitations, ZAMCOM provides a platform for dialogue among riparian states and it can also facilitate basin wide programmes, projects and flood/drought management.

There are four levels of authority within ZAMCOM:

- The ZAMCOM Council of Ministers from the eight riparian states is the highest level, which makes the ultimate decisions.
- The ZAMCOM Technical Committee, which consists of senior officials from the eight riparian states, is the second level of authority and provides technical advisory support to the Council of Ministers.

- The third level is the ZAMCOM Secretariate, who manages the Commission's daily affairs, sources funds and executes projects.
- Finally, Zambezi River Basin National Steering Committees have been set up in each riparian state to provide opportunities for stakeholders to participate (Tumbare 2008).

Competition and conflicts over water are likely to increase within the Zambezi basin as human population growth and recurrent droughts drive the demand for water. The population in Southern Africa was 137.1 million in 1995 and in 1998 was projected to be 196.8 million by 2010 (Mpande & Tawanda 1998). On average the population in the region is expected to double in the next 27 years, creating an immediate demand for more food and land. In water-scarce countries, greater demand for agricultural production translates into an increased demand for arable land and an intensification of agricultural practices, largely through irrigation, which in turn creates greater demand for water. In 1995, levels of irrigation development were reported in the SADC Fact Sheet to be about 46% in Zimbabwe whilst those of Botswana, Malawi, Mozambique and Zambia were lower than 1% (Mpande & Tawanda 1998). The type of crop grown also determines the amount of water used. In 1995 it was anticipated that the SADC countries will be competing for water within the next 25 years (*Ibid*). However, there is no co-ordination to address these challenges and agreements on the allocation of the Zambezi waters will need to be reached soon.

The SADC Protocol on Shared Water Course Systems is the main instrument of regional co-operation in water resources management of the shared water systems of the SADC region. The thrust of the protocol is to treat river basins as entities and it emphasises the need for the equitable distribution of water. With regards to Lake Kariba, other than hydroelectric generation, the protocol recognises the need for equitable utilisation of the resources of the Zambezi water course system for agriculture, domestic, industrial and navigational purposes. All basin states are obliged to maintain a balance between resource development and conservation to ensure sustainability.

Management challenges

The management of Lake Kariba's water resources is fragmented, with the involvement of a multiplicity of institutions at national level in Zambia and Zimbabwe. In addition, the Zambezi River straddles eight, countries so its management at international level is also fragmented. Efforts have been made to use an integrated water resource management approach in order to ensure sustainability. However despite the existence of regional institutions like ZRA and ZAMCOM, there are still too many institutions at national level involved in management of Lake Kariba's waters.

A number of challenges and disadvantages may be associated with having multiple legal provisions that are managed by a number of different organisations (Tumbare 2008), such as duplication of efforts resulting in resource wastage, loss of synergy, difficulty in accounting for responsibility in case of problems, confusion among resource users about who is the relevant authority to approach and delays in disaster management and mitigation response. To reduce the effects of having many players in pollution management on Lake Kariba, ZRA formed an Environmental Monitoring Working Group made up of all the stakeholders. They have entered into a Memorandum of Understanding to manage Lake Kariba and its catchment in a more efficient and environmentally sound manner (Tumbare 2008).

The challenges of having many planning authorities and fragmentation of water resources governance on both the Zambian and Zimbabwean shorelines was noticed in the 1990s. To address this, Lakeshore Combination Master Plans were developed under the Zambia/Zimbabwe SADC Fisheries project for both the Zambian and the Zimbabwean lake shore. The Zimbabwe Ministry of Local Government, Rural and Urban Planning (MLGRUP), through the Department of Physical Planning (DPP), developed a statute to implement a Kariba Lakeshore Combination Master Plan (KLCMP). This established a "combination authority" with representatives from Hwange, Binga, Nyaminyami Rural District Councils and Kariba Municipality and Zimbabwe Parks and Wildlife Management Authority to ensure that lakeshore planning is well co-ordinated (Magadza 2006, Nyikahadzoi & Songore 1999). Unfortunately, the plan has not been implemented on Zimbabwe's side, as the country has been hit by an economic crisis. However, Zambia has reported some progress and success (see Chapter 4).

3.4. Ecosystem interactions and competing water uses

Water within Lake Kariba environs is a multiple use resource, with competing interests from different users. The uses of water can be direct or indirect, consumptive or non-consumptive. Consumptive uses reduce water while non-consumptive uses often change the quality of the water.

Although Lake Kariba is recognised as a multi-purpose water body, water resource management focuses on maximising electricity generation. The lake's other uses include aquaculture, agriculture, tourism, inland shipping, domestic and industrial purposes. It also supports the aquatic and terrestrial ecosystems that provide other direct and indirect ecosystem services such as sewage dilution and processing, watering riparian forests and plants. Less than 1% of the Zambezi River water is used for irrigation, water supply and other uses, excluding power generation (Mukono & Mwiinga 2000). Power generation uses the largest amount of water (see Table 4). There is approximately 185 billion m^3 in Lake Kariba at maximum retention. Sixty-five billion m^3 is live storage, of which 40% is used for hydropower generation in Kariba North and Kariba South Bank Power Stations.

Aquaculture and crocodile farming are economically important small users of water. Boating, transport and fishing are non-consumptive water uses. While at present the amount used for irrigation is small, it is however likely to increase in response to drought and population increase and the need for increasing food production. It has been estimated that, because of the general water scarcity in the SADC region, 10 billion m^3 will be diverted from the Zambezi River by 2030. This will significantly increase competition for water.

Table 4: Amounts of Zambezi River water used by different sectors

Sector	Water (million m^3/year)
Municipalities	24
Coal mining	7
Agriculture	16
Electricity: Kariba	26000
Electricity: Hwange thermal	34

Source: Mukono & Mwiinga 2000

Irrigation and hydroelectricity generation are conflictive users because irrigation is a consumptive use that reduces water available for power generation. Tilmant *et al.* (2010) carried out a simulation of the economically efficient balance between irrigated agriculture and hydropower generation in the Zambezi basin and concluded that most of the planned irrigation schemes in Zambia, Zimbabwe, Namibia, Angola and Botswana will not be economically sound if the power stations that are in an advanced planning phase are implemented.

Power generation causes fluctuation in Lake Kariba's shoreline, which affects subsistence farming at the water's edge. The Zambian lakeshore area that falls within the draw-down zone is important for the Zilili system of cultivation. Zilili cultivation is carried out during the dry season from May to October using residual moisture within the previously inundated areas (Losse 1998). The crop is either grown entirely on residual soil moisture or irrigated. The amount of land available for this type of agriculture depends on the extent of flooding. The high water of 1998 –2000 drastically reduced the amount of shoreline available for Zilili cultivation. Zilili farming is practiced along the Zambian shoreline wherever suitable land is available. Approximately 70%, 65% and 80% of the villages in Siavonga, Munyumbwe and Sinazongwe respectively engage in this form of cultivation (Losse 1998, Anon 1992). The sizes of the gardens range from 0.2 to 1 ha per family. The harvest from zilili cultivation supplements low yields from dry land agriculture. Few farmers have these gardens when the harvest is good hence the shoreline area is very important for food security in dry years.

On the Zimbabwean shoreline cultivation is prohibited. Utilisation of the streambanks for gardening and livestock grazing is against regulations and yet the gardens are important for livelihood. A study of households in the Zambezi Valley in Zimbabwe showed the importance of riverine resources (Lynam *et al.* 1998). Households depend on the river water for domestic use, livestock and small-scale irrigation. They also obtain vegetation and animal products such as fish, construction material and clay for making pots from rivers. Households generally cluster along rivers and most have winter gardens along the rivers. Intensive use, however, leads to soil erosion in the riverine areas, resulting in siltation of the lake. While there is need to protect rivers, at the same time, authorities also need to ensure that people's livelihoods are supported.

In Zambia irrigated agriculture is practised on a small scale. There is an irrigation scheme in Siavonga of about 92 ha and of about 40 ha in Sinazongwe (Anon 1992). Livestock, mainly cattle, goats and sheep graze along the drawdown zone throughout the year. Communities that are upland also graze their cattle along the lakeshore during the dry season.

The environment is an important user of water. In recognition of this fact, the Chapter 7 of the Southern Africa Vision for Water, Life and Environment calls for a desirable future in which the region's environment is conserved and there is sufficient allocation of water to maintain ecosystem integrity. The lake's ecosystem depends on water flow in terms of quantity and timing of flow and seasonality. The ecosystem is therefore affected by water table fluctuations. Water quality is also important, with poor quality endangering ecosystems. Land and water resources management must ensure that these vital ecosystems are maintained.

3.5. Ecosystems interactions

Within Lake Kariba and its environs, links between the lake and the land result in interactions among the main competing uses of water, which include hydropower generation, urban and rural water supply, fisheries, aquaculture, agriculture and industrial production, sewage and waste water disposal, recreation, navigation and support for aquatic and terrestrial wildlife. All these uses impact on the quality and quantity of water in the lake.

The various resources on Lake Kariba as defined in this book (land, water, fish, other aquatic resources, woodland and grassland, wildlife) are managed in sectors. This approach does not depict the reality of an ecosystem, where there are connections among all the resources and the people who use and manage them. Water is a vital factor that connects biotic and abiotic processes in an ecosystem. The ecosystem interactions between water and the other resources are discussed below to illustrate why we need an ecosystem approach for the integrated management of land, water and living resources. The ecosystem approach can promote conservation and sustainable use in an equitable way.

3.6. Impact of damming the Zambezi River

What impact has the construction of Lake Kariba on the Zambezi River had and what lessons can be learnt? The dam's environmental, economic and social impacts were studied and documented in 2000 by the World Commission of Dams (WCD 2000). What emerges from their research is the catastrophic impact that the dam had on the communities who were displaced from the Zambezi Basin in an insensitive manner (Scudder 1960). There was no assessment of the number of people affected and their living conditions prior to resettlement. The conditions in the resettlement areas were unacceptable with inadequate water, poor soils and social facilities such as schools and clinics.

These socio-environmental issues were never adequately addressed mainly because the dam was constructed without an environmental and social impact assessment (WCD 2000, Tumbare 2008) and inadequate financial resources were provided to mitigate these impacts before and after construction. Changes in land tenure and water resource use rights, an increase in competing uses and users for space along the lakeshore and the designation of land as protected areas and the lake as a recreation park have altogether alienated the local Tonga communities from the natural resources they used to depend on.

Efforts to address the plight of the displaced people have been minimal. A recent project is the Zambezi Valley Development Fund, which has provided funding to drill boreholes, provide grinding mills, electrify clinics and schools, and purchase school science laboratory equipment (Tumbare 2008). The fund has also been used to finance the construction of an irrigation scheme in each of the seven districts where the Tonga/Korekore people were resettled. While these schemes are intended to help in poverty alleviation and to improve the health and living conditions, their value has yet to be realised.

Table 5 summarises the main social and ecological impacts of the creation of Lake Kariba as described by the study of the World Commission of Dams (WCD 2000). According to the Commission the losses experienced by displaced communities were economic (land), political (autonomy), social and psychological (the social fabric was torn apart and people were separated from relatives) and cultural (loss of shrines or cultural property in general). The benefits, which include schools, clinics and infrastructure, were outweighed by the losses. The design of the dam did not include a provision whereby the displaced communities would benefit.

Table 5: Social and ecological impacts of the creation of Lake Kariba

Types of impact	Impacts
Social	– Abandonment of riverine life – Trauma and loss of property and livestock in transit – Compensation not provided or grossly inadequate – Settlers were not accorded customary rights – Endless food insecurity and poverty – Loss of land and reduction of agricultural productivity – Separation from relatives – Loss of cultural property
Ecological	– Development of a kapenta fishery – Creation of habitats with increased biological diversity – Blocking of upstream and downstream fish migration – Development of a tourism industry – Accumulation of pollutants in the lake – Alteration of river flow regimes downstream of dam wall

3.7. Intra-resource connections in water resources

Rainfall provides water that supports the terrestrial and aquatic ecosystems. Intra-resource connection can be assessed in terms of the flow of water on the landscape through the social and ecological systems. The use of water can either be direct or indirect. Water use can also be considered in terms of the ecological system that it supports. Green water supports the growth of rain fed crops, timber, pastures as well as grass, forest and biodiversity. Blue water is the fraction used for irrigation, industry and other activities. Ecosystem function is affected by the extent of water abstraction for direct use such as domestic and industrial purposes.

Lake Kariba is characterised by low rainfall and frequent droughts, which have implications on water use. At Livingstone, rainfall declined from 954 mm per annum in 1980 to 551 mm in 1994. This reduction in rainfall was accompanied by a reduction in runoff from 1 186 m^3/s to 442 m^3/s (Mukono & Mwiinga

2000), resulting in low lake levels. The decline in rainfall affected the delivery of water throughout the whole water cycle. Persistent periods of low lake levels caused by drought reduced hydropower generation between 1977 and 1997 from the expected power output of 6 720 GWh per annum to an average output of 6 400 GWh per annum (WCD 2000). This reduction illustrates the intricate link between climate, lake levels and hydroelectric power generation.

Due to climate change-related temperature increases there has been a decline in precipitation in the area and an increase in water loss through evaporation. Magadza (2010) has projected that lake temperature will rise by approximately 4°C by the end of the century. The higher temperatures and higher evaporation rates will reduce water availability for the various uses and will increase competition for water. The quantity of rainfall will consequently influence fish production, an issue that is discussed later in this chapter.

Many rivers connect Lake Kariba to a very large catchment area, which spans eight riparian states. The river systems transport materials, water and pollutants into the lake. The upstream activities impact downstream waters due to this hydrological connectivity. Land-based upstream activities that generate pollutants decrease the water quality of the rivers and ultimately of the lake. Pollutants are also transported through ground water seepage into the rivers and into the lake.

The rivers draining mining areas bring into Lake Kariba water of high conductivity and high concentrations of metals. For example, high levels of sulphur were detected in the Deka, Kunzinze, Ume and Sengwa Rivers due to anthropogenic activities within their catchments (Pettersson & Kaniki 2002). The Deka and the Kunzinze Rivers drain the coal mines of Hwange in Zimbabwe and Maamba in Zambia respectively, while the Ume and Sengwa Rivers on the Zimbabwean side bring in pollutants from mining areas far upstream. Once in the lake these metals bio-accumulate in fish and plants (Berg *et al.* 1995). It has been observed that the concentrations of metals tend to be higher during high water discharge in rivers draining mining areas compared to low water discharge periods (Pettersson *et al.* 2000).

Upstream–downstream interactions affect both natural systems and human beings alike and can result in loss of lives and property. The scale and nature of upstream activities can negatively affect downstream users, particularly when there is insufficient water and excessive amounts of water are being abstracted for irrigation by upstream users. In periods of high rainfall, when there is excess water, the flood-gates on Lake Kariba are opened and excess water is discharged into the Zambezi River, causing flooding downstream from Muzarabani in Zimbabwe up to Cabora Bassa in Mozambique.

3.8. Interactions of water with the fishery

The availability of water is linked to the presence of fish, and the types of fish depend on the type of aquatic system. Flowing water in the rivers is associated with a particular type of fish species assemblage. In Lake Kariba, the distribution, abundance and productivity of the fishery depends on the characteristics of the water. Riverine fish species dominate in river mouths. In contrast, damming created a deep water environment that was suitable for kapenta, a pelagic fish introduced from Lake Tanganyika. This fish forms the basis of an economically important pelagic fishery.

The quantities of nutrients found in Lake Kariba are regulated by in-flowing rivers. The extent of the flood determines the quantities of nutrients brought into the lake and thus available at overturn (Marshall 1997). Kapenta catches are strongly linked to total inflow and rainfall (Chifamba 2000), with poor rainy seasons resulting in a decrease in the productivity and biomass of pelagic communities. Generally, the productivity of the fishery correlates with the quantities of nutrients brought into the lake (Karenge & Kolding 1995, Chifamba 2000). The interaction between rainfall and water nutrient levels can be used to predict fish catches and the effect of climate change on the fishery.

The safety of the dam and the need to maximise power generation requires effective management of the amount of water stored. Hydrological management requires flood forecasting data for which there is a network of rainfall stations and telemetry flow meters in the Zambezi River. The frequency of anticipated spilling is every three to five years (Allison 1970). Sudden discharges have ecological impacts and also affect human communities living downstream of the dam. Macrophyte beds, invertebrates and fish nests may be affected by the rapid drawdown. These changes influence fish production. The use of the lake water for power generation results in cyclic flooding and exposure of the shoreline. Exposure of shoreline allows the increase of grazing for both domestic animals as well as wildlife. Upon subsequent flooding, plant materials and animal droppings release nutrients into the lake thereby increasing fish yields.

3.9. Interactions of water with other aquatic organisms

The lake has been affected by use of dichlorodiphenyltrichloroethane (DDT) within its hinterland from 1970 until 1984 for tsetse fly control and agricultural purposes. DDT has bio-accumulated and bio-magnified within the trophic structures with high levels in crocodiles, tiger fish and cormorants (Berg *et al.* 1992).

The growth of Kariba and Siavonga towns in Zimbabwe and Zambia respectively, as well as the establishment of many fishing camps with minimum town planning, has resulted in localised foreshore microbial pollution, as well as the attraction of water borne disease vectors, such as bilharzias-transmitting snails. Higher incidents of bilharzias were detected in Siavonga compared to Kariba due to differences in sanitation levels between the two towns (Chimbari *et al.* 2003).

Organic pollution and nutrient enrichment is currently not a major problem except for localised enrichment in river estuaries (Mhlanga 2001). In the late 1980s, enrichment of water in river mouths resulted in the proliferation of water hyacinth (*Eichhornia crassipes*) (Mhlanga 2001). It dramatically increased within the Sanyati basin until 1996, when it covered all sheltered estuaries, bays and shallow waters of the lake as a response to localised enrichment but has since declined. In 1998, the chemical poison 2,4-Dichlorophenoxyaetic acid (2.4 D) was used to control the potential spread over the whole lake, although the weevil *Neochetina eichhorniae* had also been introduced (Mhlanga *et al.* 1999). Infestation with weeds affects navigation, fishing and can interfere with fish migration.

Animals such as hippopotamus (*Hippopotamus amphibius*) are important in estuarine areas. They graze along the shoreline and spend long periods in the water thus they bring in nutrients from the terrestrial ecosystem into the lake. These create muddy conditions favoured by some fish species and these areas tend to have high fish production. Flooding of the shoreline during high water levels enriches the shallow areas following decay of the submerged plant material. The wild animals that graze along the shoreline during low water also deposit dung that is also an important source of nutrients.

3.10. Interactions of water with mining

The mining activities that are close to Lake Kariba are Maamba Collieries in Zambia and the glitterstone quarry near Kariba in Zimbabwe. There are other mining areas in Zambia and Zimbabwe located in sub-catchments that drain into Lake Kariba. These include coal mines in Hwange (Zimbabwe), gold, platinum and nickel mines in the Kadoma and Kwekwe area (Zimbabwe) and several other iron, chromium, copper and antimony mines spread out on the Zimbabwean side of Lake Kariba (ZACPLAN 1998). Zimbabwe also has numerous closed nickel, copper, antimony and gold mines.

Mining within the catchment of Lake Kariba has had an impact on the aquatic biota over the past two decades, aggravated by the fact that affluent rivers were observed to bring in metals adsorbed to particulate matter (Legget 1994). A study done in 1990 and 1991 found that the levels of chromium, cadmium, copper, lead, manganese, nickel, zinc and selenium in sediments of Lake Kariba were similar or lower compared to temperate and tropical water bodies (Berg *et al.* 1995). Apart from lead, the concentrations of the most heavy metals in Lake Kariba water were also generally similar or lower than in temperate and tropical freshwater systems (*Ibid*). In 2008, almost twenty years later, researchers found much higher concentrations of both chromium and nickel in sediments from the lake (Nakayama *et al.* 2010).

The study by Berg *et al.* showed that the concentrations of lead and cadmium in aquatic plants (*Lagarosiphon ilicifolius*, *Vallisneria aethiopica* and *Potamogeton* spp) and fish (*Tilapia rendalli*, *Oreochromis mortimeri*, *Labeo altivelis*, *Limnothrissa miodon*, *Hydrocynus vittatus*) from Lake Kariba were higher compared to unimpacted temperate and tropical aquatic systems. Nakayama *et al.* (2010) also found that the concentrations of chromium, nickel and lead in fish (*Oreochromis niloticus* and *Serranochromis thumbergi*) and crayfish (*Cherax quadricarinatus*) from Lake Kariba were higher than those from Lake Itezhi-tezhi (Zambia), which they suggested was probably due to the higher numbers of boats that use leaded petrol, and the greater use of anti-fouling paints, which contain chromium-nickel compounds, on Lake Kariba. High levels of mercury, ranging between 66 and 395 mg/kg dry weight, have also been detected in Fish Eagles (*Haliaeetus vocifer*), while mercury concentrations of 2.4, 4.5 and 4.9 mg/kg dry weight have been detected in muscle, kidney and liver tissues respectively of Reed Cormorants (Douthwaite 1992). Mercury bioaccumulation has been observed along the fish food chain with the highest concentration in the top predator, *Hydrocynus vittatus*, and which decreased in the order *Hydrocynus vittatus* > *Limnothrissa miodon* > *Sargochromis codringtonii* (Mhlanga 2000).

The increase in Lake Kariba of the trace metals zinc, nickel, lead, molybdenum, vanadium and mercury indicate a need to monitor the levels of these metals (Legget 1994). Spatial and seasonal differences found in the concentration of metals suggested rivers were the source of the metals, an effect illustrated by higher concentrations of metals in the water in the Mlibizi basin and Sanyati basin in comparison to the other middle basins, Binga and Sengwa. These middle basins do not receive inflow from major rivers. The amount of zinc, lead and nickel changed with season, with concentrations being higher during the wet season. The concentration of the labile fraction during the rainy season was almost double that of the dry season. When the rivers are flowing they bring in large quantities of particulate matter containing the metals; the labile fraction increases due to dissociation of the bound metals.

Mercury levels could pose a public health risk in Lake Kariba, as they have been reported to be higher than the World Health Organisation's (WHO) acceptable levels for drinking water (Legget 1994, Chifamba 2007). Chifamba (2007) also detected high levels of lead in rainwater in the town of Kariba and high levels have been alleged to have caused trunk paralysis in elephants.

3.11. Interactions between water and land

Land activities within the hinterland of Lake Kariba affect the water quality in the lake. Various land uses around Lake Kariba impact on water quality, including sewage and solid waste disposal, agriculture, aquaculture and industrial activity.

Pollution of water from sewage waste arising from the inadequate processing of sewage, leakage of pipes and breakdown of equipment is most apparent near large settlements, mainly Kariba, Siavonga and Binga (Magadza & Dhlomo 1996, Sanyanga & Masundire 1999). The towns of Livingstone in Zambia and Victoria Falls in Zimbabwe discharge inadequately treated water from pond systems or wastewater directly into the Zambezi River. Livingstone discharges approximately 8 000 m^3 of waste water into the river because the sewage works are overloaded and frequently breakdown. Due to its huge capacity, Lake Kariba has so far had a diluting effect; however, if loads from sewage disposal are excessive, localised enrichment can occur, resulting in the proliferation of aquatic weeds.

DDT has been used to control tsetse fly and mosquitoes within the hinterland of Lake Kariba and within the Zambezi Valley (Berg 1995). This has resulted in DDT accumulation in crocodile fat and crocodile eggs (Phelps *et al.* 1989, Phelps & Billings 1972). Wessels *et al.* (1980) found high pesticide levels in crocodile eggs from Basin 1 of Lake Kariba compared to other areas. The spread of DDT has provided proof of the critical links between the aquatic and terrestrial ecosystems around Lake Kariba, including humans. Other than direct use of water, humans eat fish harvested from Lake Kariba. As a result high levels of DDT and DDE were found in human milk of nursing mothers in Kariba, which raised fears of negative health impacts on breast feeding babies (Chikuni *et al.* 1997a, b). Similarly high levels in eggs of the Zambezi Parrotfish (*Hippopotamyrus discorhynchus*) suggested possible negative impacts on recruitment (McCarton & Mhlanga 1994).

Leaching of metals from solid waste disposal sites affect both surface and ground water (Chifamba 2007). During the rains, heavy metals (lead and mercury) from disposal sites leach into the lake thereby contaminating the water. Waste from industries is also a source of environmental concern around Lake Kariba. There is no formal disposal mechanism for industrial fluid waste such as used diesel, oil and other lubricants. A large amount of these are produced in Kariba and Siavonga when boats and motor vehicles are serviced (Sanyanga & Masundire 1999). The waste is disposed onto soils and eventually some of the materials then get washed into the lake. In addition, two towns, Livingstone and Victoria Falls, discharge industrial effluents to the Zambezi River upstream from Lake Kariba. Other effluents discharged within the area originate from agricultural activities.

The availability of relatively clean water and the high temperature throughout the year in Kariba are ideal for fish farming. There are two types of farming systems used: the pond system along the lakeshore area and cages on the lake itself.

There is potential for these farming units to pollute the water, particularly from the waste feed and fish excreta. A study of sediments near fish cages, which was done at a low level of fish farming (four tons of fish per year), indicated an effect on the levels of carbon, nitrogen and phosphate in the water (Troell & Berg 1996). Over the last two decades, fish production from cages has increased considerably, which may have resulted in a greater impact on both the water and sediments.

3.12. Interactions of water with forests and grasslands

A large proportion of rainwater supports rivers and forests. A model of the amount of water that goes to support the forest and grasslands within the Lake Kariba area has not been developed. According to the first global assessment of Green and Blue water flows, grasslands utilise about 11% while forests utilise approximately 17% (Keys *et al.* 2012). The extent of degradation around Lake Kariba is not known. What is known, however, is that catchment degradation due to deforestation, overgrazing or cultivation can cause siltation in water bodies. Generally, the Zimbabwean shoreline is protected as a nature reserve but on the Zambian side, agriculture occurs even along the lakeshore area. The Gwaai River, which joins the Zambezi just above Lake Kariba, can transport as much as 1.8 million tons of silt a year (Chikwanha & Ward 1979), and the rate of degradation around Lake Kariba should have increased significantly in the last 20 years (WCD 2000). Even though Tumbare (2008) argues that loss of storage due to siltation is minimal, there is an urgent need to properly investigate and quantify the current rates of siltation into the lake.

3.13. Interactions of water with wildlife

Many type of wildlife utilise the shoreline area by taking advantage of the better grazing and ready access to drinking water. Animals exert a positive effect on the ecosystem through dung deposited on the shoreline that releases nutrients when submerged. Dung releases potassium and phosphorus more rapidly compared to dry grass (McLachlan 1970). In their daily activities, hippopotamus also transfer nutrients from the terrestrial system to the aquatic system.

3.14. Conclusion

Water is a central and critical resource within the Lake Kariba environs and in the Zambezi River Basin. The waters of Lake Kariba are primarily used for hydroelectric power generation but this use of the resource is competing with local ecosystem services and the needs of local residents to meet their livelihoods. The different and varied interests of water users are reflected in the prolific number of institutions and legal frameworks governing the waters of Lake Kariba and the Zambezi River at national, bilaterial and regional levels. The region has witnessed increasing pluralism in water resources management.

In order to reduce fragmentation and conflicts, efforts have been made towards instituting an Integrated Water Resource Management (IWRM) framework for the management of the Zambezi River. IWRM is a holistic approach based on the acknowledgement of the interdependence of many different users and the interaction between water and other resource uses. The adoption of the IWRM framework is significant because it makes it possible to address the effect of defragmentation, which has implications for ecosystem sustainability. This framework still has to be fully operationalised.

IWRM allows participatory decision-making by all stakeholders, which enables them to influence strategies for water resource development and management in their own areas. Participation is intended to promote local self-regulation in relation to issues such as water conservation and catchment protection. This approach is more effective than central regulation and surveillance. IWRM can also ensure sustainable development, allocation and monitoring of water resources within Lake Kariba environs in the context of social, economic and environmental objectives. It removes the sectoral approach and introduces cross-sectoral links that help reduce conflicts and wastage and promote sustainable systems.

In order to ensure sustainability, co-ordination and collaboration among the individual sectors at national, bilateral and regional levels is required. There is a need to foster stakeholder participation, transparency and cost-effective local management. If effectively implemented IWRM offers the prospect of greater efficiencies, water conservation and demand management that are equitably shared among all water users, including hydroelectric power generation.

A large proportion of the population within the Lake Kariba environs is poor and dependent on the status of the ecosystem for their livelihoods. Application of the ecosystem approach to water resource management will ensure ecosystem sustainability. Ecosystem management, enabled by pro-poor governance, can reduce chronic poverty in the area. The ecosystem approach was recommended as necessary support towards the Millennium Development Goals and if instituted for Lake Kariba and the Zambezi Valley it may address the issues of environmental sustainability and poverty alleviation within the basin.

References

Allison G.F. 1970. 'The hydrological management of Lake Kariba', *Rhodesia Science News* **4(2)**: 49–60.

Anon 1992. 'Lakeshore development planning: Lake Kariba-Zambia: Part I: Current socio-economic activities, resources and infrastructure.' *Unpublished manuscript.* Agrindco International (Z) Ltd.

Balon E.K. & Coche A.G. 1974. *Lake Kariba: A Man-made Tropical Ecosystem in Central Africa.* Dr. W. Junk b.v. Publishers, The Hague.

Beck L. & Bernauer T. 2011. 'How will combined changes in water demand and climate affect water availability in the Zambezi river basin?' *Global Environmental Change* **21**: 1061–1072.

Berg H. 1995. 'Modelling DDT dynamics in Lake Kariba: A tropical man-made lake and its implications for the control of tsetse flies', *Annales Zoologici Fennici* **32**: 331–335.

Berg H., Kiibus M. & Kautsky N. 1992. 'DDT and other insecticides in Lake Kariba ecosystem, Zimbabwe',*Ambio* **21(7)**: 444–450.

Berg H., Kiibus M. & Kautsky N. 1995. 'Heavy metals in tropical Lake Kariba, Zimbabwe', *Water, Air and Soil Pollution* **83**: 237–252.

Chifamba P.C. 2000. 'The relationship of temperature and hydrological factors to catch per unit effort, condition and size of the freshwater sardine, *Limnothrissa miodon* (Boulenger), in Lake Kariba',*Fisheries Research* **45**: 271–281.

Chifamba P.C. 2007. 'Trace metal contamination of water at a solid waste disposal site at Kariba, Zimbabwe', *African Journal of Aquatic Science* **32**: 71–78.

Chikuni O., Nhachi C.F.B., Nyazema N.Z., Polder A., Nafstad I. & Skaare J.U. 1997a. 'Assessment of environmental pollution by PCBs, DDT and its metabolites using human milk of mothers in Zimbabwe', *Science of the Total Environment* **199**: 183–190.

Chikuni O., Polder A., Skaare J.U. & Nhachi C.F.B. 1997b. 'An evaluation of DDT and DDT residues in human breast milk in the Kariba Valley of Zimbabwe', *Bulletin of Environmental Contamination and Toxicology* **58**: 776–778.

Chikwanha R. & Ward P.R.B. 1979. *Sediment from Rhodesian Rivers (1977–1978). Joint Report by Ministry of Natural Resources and the Department of Water Development and Civil Engineering.* University of Zimbabwe, Harare.

Chimbari M.J., Dhlomo E., Mwadiwa E. & Mubila L. 2003. 'Transmission of schistosomiasis in Kariba, Zimbabwe, and a cross-sectional comparison of schistosomiasis prevalences and intensities in the town with those in Siavonga in Zambia', *Annals of Tropical Medicine and Parasitology***97**: 605–616.

Coche A.G. 1974. 'Limnological study of a tropical reservoir.' In: Balon E. K. & Coche A. G. (eds) *Lake Kariba: A Man-made Tropical Ecosystem in Central Africa.* DR W Junk b.v. Publishers, The Hague.

Douthwaite R.J. 1992. 'Effects of DDT on the fish eagle *Haliaeetus vocifer* population of Lake Kariba in Zimbabwe', *Ibis* **134**: 250–258.

Karenge L. & Kolding J. 1995. 'On the relationship between hydrology and fisheries in man-made Lake Kariba, central Africa', *Fisheries Research* **22**: 205–226.

Keys P., Barron J. & Lannerstad M. (2012) Releasing the pressure: Water Resource efficiencies and gains for ecosystem services. United Nations Environment Programme, Nairobi.

Legget K. 1994. 'Trace metal concentration in Lake Kariba', *ULKRS Bulletin* **1/94**: 1–10. University Lake Kariba Research Station, Kariba, Zimbabwe.

Losse G.F. 1998. *The Small-scale Fishery on Lake Kariba in Zambia.* Schriftenreihe der GTZ No. 265 Wiesbaden Universum Verlagsantalt, Germany.

Lynam T.J.P., Chitsike J., Howard M., Hodza P., Khumalo M.A. & Gunda S.W. 1998. 'Assessing the contributions of renewable natural resources to the livelihoods of communal area households in the Zambezi Valley of Zimbabwe.' In: Christoffersen N., Campbell B. and du Toit J. (eds) *Communities and Sustainable Use: Pan-African Perspectives*. IUCN–The World Conservation Union, Harare.

Magadza C.H.D. 1986. 'Conflicts of resource use on the Lake Kariba environs', *Nature and Resources* **22(4)**: 2–12.

Magadza C.H.D. 2006. 'Kariba Reservoir: Experience and lessons learned', *Lakes & Reservoirs: Research & Management* **11**: 271–286.

Magadza C.H.D. 2010. 'Environmental state of Lake Kariba and Zambezi River Valley: Lessons learned and not learned', *Lakes & Reservoirs Research and Management* **15(3)**: 167–192.

Magadza C. H. D. & Dhlomo E. J. 1996. 'Wet season incidence of coliform bacteria in Lake Kariba inshore waters of Kariba town area', *Lakes and Reservoirs: Research and Management* **2(1/2)**: 89–96.

Manzungu E. & Kujinga K. 2002. 'The theory and practice of governance of water resources in Zimbabwe', *Zambezia* **29(2)**: 191–212.

Marshall B.E. 1997. 'A review of zooplankton ecology in Lake Kariba.' In: Moreau J. (ed) *Advances in the Ecology of Lake Kariba*. University of Zimbabwe Publications, Harare.

McCarton B. & Mhlanga W. 1994. 'Fish.' In: Douthwaite R.J. & Tingle C. C. (eds) *DDT in the Tropics: The Impact on Wildlife in Zimbabwe of Ground Spraying for Tsetse-fly Control*. Natural Resources Institute, Chatham, U.K.

McLachlan S.M. 1970. 'The influence of lake level fluctuations and the thermocline on water chemistry in two gradually shelving areas of Lake Kariba, Central Africa', *Archiv fur Hydrobiologie* **66**: 499–510.

Mhlanga L. 2001. 'Water quality of the Eastern basin of Lake Kariba, Zimbabwe in relation to the encroachment of *Eichhornia crassipes*', *Verhandlungen der Internationale Vereinigung für theoretische und angewandte Limnologie* **27**: 3595–3598.

Mhlanga L., Magadza C.H.D., Mandima J. & Chifamba P.C. 1999. 'Water hyacinth in Lake Kariba, Zimbabwe', *ULKRS Bulletin* **1/99**. University Lake Kariba Research Station, Kariba, Zimbabwe.

Mhlanga W. 2000. 'Mercury in tigerfish (*Hydrocynus vittatus*, Castelnau), Greenhappy (*Sargochromis codringtonii*, Boulenger) and Kapenta (*Limnothrissa miodon*, Boulenger) from Lake Kariba, Zimbabwe', *African Journal of Ecology* **38**: 224–229.

Mpande R.L. & Tawanda M. 1998. 'Population dynamics and the emerging competition for water use in the Zambezi River Basin.' In: de Sherbinin A. & Dompika V. (eds)*Water and Population Dynamics: Case Studies and Policy Implications*. IUCN, PRB, USAID. Paisanbooks, Philadelphia, USA.

Mukono S.N. & Mwiinga F. 2000. 'Environmental aspects of water use in arid regions: The Lake Kariba case.' In: Tumbare M. J. (ed) *Management of River Basins and Dams: The Zambezi River*. AA Balkema Rotterdam, The Netherlands.

Mutembwa A. 1998. 'Water and the potential for resource conflicts in southern Africa.' *Global Security Fellows Initiative (GSFI) Occasional Paper No. 3*. GSFI, University of Cambridge, U.K.

Nakayama S.M.M, Ikenaka Y., Muzandu K., Choongo K., Oroszlany B., Teraoka H.,

Mizuno N. & Ishizuka M. 2010. 'Heavy metal accumulation in lake sediments, fish (*Oreochromis niloticus* and *Serranochromis thumbergi*), and crayfish (*Cherax quadricarinatus*) in Lake Itezhi-tezhi and Lake Kariba, Zambia', *Archives of Environmental Contamination and Toxicology* **59**: 291–300.

Nyikahadzoi K. & Songore N. 1999. 'Introducing co-management arrangements in Lake Kariba inshore fishery: progress, opportunities and constraints.' *Paper presented at an International Workshop on Fisheries Comanagement, Penang Malaysia 23–28 August 1999.*

Pettersson U.T. & Kaniki C. 2002. *A Metal Survey of Water Draining the Lower Catchement of Lake Kariba: Zambezi River Authority Report.* Zambezi River Authority, Kariba, Zimbabwe.

Pettersson U.T., Ingri J. & Andersson P.S. 2000. 'Hydrogeochemical processes in the Kafue River upstream from the Copperbelt mining area, Zambia', *Aquatic Geochemistry* **6(4)**: 385–411.

Phelps R.J. & Billings K.J. 1972. 'Pesticide levels from animals in Rhodesia', *Transactions of the Rhodesian Scientific Association* **55**: 6–9.

Phelps R.J., Toet M. & Hutton J.M. 1989. 'DDT residues in the fat of crocodiles from Lake Kariba, Zimbabwe', *Transactions of the Zimbabwe Scientific Association***64(2)**: 9–14.

Sanyanga R. A. & Masundire H.M. 1999. Waste Management in the Zambezi Valley:which way forward. In: Yap N.T. (ed) *Cleaner Production and consumption in Eastern and Southern Africa:challenges and opportunities.* Weaver Press, Harare.

Southern Africa Research and Documentation Centre (SARDC). 1995. 'Fact sheet 1995.' SARDC, Harare, Zimbabwe.

Scudder T. 1960. *The Ecology of the Gwembe Tonga.* Kariba Studies II. Manchester University Press, U.K.

Tilmant A., Kinzelbach W., Beevers L. & Juizo D. 2010. *Optimal Water Allocation in the Zambezi Basin.* International Environmental Modeling and Software Society (iEMSs), Ottawa, Canada.

Troell M. & Berg H. 1996. 'Cage fish farming in tropical Lake Kariba: Impact and biogeochemical changes in sediment.' In: 'Persistent pollutants and aquaculture in tropical Lake Kariba-managing fisheries sustainability'. *PhD dissertation.* University of Stockholm.

Tumbare M.J. 2008. 'Managing Lake Kariba sustainably: Threats and challenges', *Management of Environmental Quality: An International Journal* **19(6)**: 731–739.

Wessels C.L., Tannock J., Blake D. & Phelps R.J. 1980. 'Chlorinated hydrocarbon insecticide residues in *Crocodylus niloticus* Laurenti eggs from Lake Kariba', *Transactions of the Zimbabwe Scientific Association* **60(3)**: 11–17.

World Commission on Dams (WCD). 2000. *Kariba Dam Case Study.* WCD, Cape Town, South Africa.

ZACPLAN. 1998. *Water Consumption and Effluent from Urban and Rural Areas, Manufacturing and Service Industries and Mining Industry. Final Report. Zambezi River Authority.* SADC, Danida and Denconsult. Ref. No. 104.SADC.31.

Aquaculture fish cages on Lake Kariba. Photo: Wilson Mhlanga

4. Cross-commons interactions of the fish resources in Lake Kariba

Wilson MHLANGA and Lindah MHLANGA

4.1. Introduction

Lake Kariba is a man-made lake that was created in the late 1950s. The primary objective for the construction of the dam was hydro-electric power generation. However, several important secondary economic activities emerged, including tourism and fishing. The fishery was initially based on the species that occurred in the Zambezi River prior to dam construction but the introduction of a freshwater sardine, known locally as kapenta (*Limnothrissa miodon*) gave rise to a very important commercial industrial fishery.

The introduction of kapenta from Lake Tanganyika is one of the few planned introductions that occurred on the lake based on sound ecological principles. Following the creation of Kariba dam, the riverine environment now had a vacant ecological niche of deep offshore (pelagic) waters in which none of the Zambezi River fishes occurred, making the introduction of kapenta ideal.

The introduction of the pelagic plankton-feeding sardine took place in 1967 and 1968 (Bell-Cross & Bell-Cross 1971). The 1968 introductions also included the Lake Tanganyika shrimp (*Limnocaridina tanganicae*), which was meant to form part of the food source of the introduced sardine. The total number of *L. miodon* introduced into Lake Kariba was estimated at 362 400; 237 600 fry were introduced between July and November 1967 and 124 800 were introduced between August and September 1968. A total of 12 160 *Limnocaridina tanganicae* were introduced in September and October 1968 (*Ibid*).

Prior to the kapenta introduction, there had been some introductions of local species between 1959 and 1962. An estimated 26 tons of *Oreochromis macrochir* and *Tilapia melanopleura* fingerlings were stocked into the lake (Bell-Cross & Bell-Cross 1971). These fish were brought from the Chilanga Fish Farm in Zambia, but failed to establish viable populations in the lake. Possible reasons given for the failure of these introductions were the inability of the fingerlings to adapt to a lacustrine environment and heavy predation by tigerfish (*Hydrocynus vittatus*).

Prior to the construction of Lake Kariba, the riparian Tonga communities utilised the Zambezi river fishes on a subsistence basis. Consequently, access to the fishery resources was not governed by any regulations from central government. Malasha (2003) noted that at the time that Kariba was constructed, the laws governing the fishery resources in both Zambia and Zimbabwe did not cover the

Zambezi River, and hence Lake Kariba. He also noted that in Zambia, the Fish Conservation Ordinances and subsequent laws were only applicable to fisheries that had been prescribed by the Director responsible for fisheries, and the Zambezi River did not fall into this category. For Zimbabwe, the Game and Fish Preservation Act did not apply to the Zambezi River. Consequently, the two governments had to come up with new regulations for the Lake Kariba fishery.

So for Lake Kariba, there was no history of fisheries management prior to dam construction; fisheries regulations and formal fisheries management institutions evolved afterwards. The introduction of kapenta formed the basis of a totally new fishery that had not existed before the dam was built.

The creation of Kariba resulted in the uprooting and relocation of those communities who lived on land that was to be inundated by the lake's waters (Bourdillon *et al.* 1985). It is estimated that a total of 57 000 Tonga and Goba inhabitants were resettled, of whom 22 000 were in Southern Rhodesia (now Zimbabwe) and 35 000 in Northern Rhodesia (Zambia) (*Ibid*). These communities did not benefit directly from the electricity that was generated.

In Zambia, most of the communities were resettled along the new shoreline or relocated to areas on the Northern side of the Zambezi Valley between Kariba and Chirundu. The rocky southern shoreline of the newly created lake precluded the creation of new settlements. Consequently, in Zimbabwe resettlement often involved relocation to new sites that were far from the shoreline. Most of these settlements were 30 to 60 km from the shoreline. The only exception was at the western end of the lake between Tobwe and Devil's Gorge (*Ibid*). These differences in the settlement patterns were to have significant impacts on both land use patterns as well as the evolution of the artisanal (inshore) fishing settlements on the two sides of the lake.

A number of interventions were carried out prior to the damming of the Zambezi River. These interventions included the translocation of some terrestrial wildlife species to higher ground, including areas designated as National Parks (i.e. wildlife-protected areas), such as Matusadonha National Park. This translocation was dubbed "Operation Noah". The other intervention was the bush clearing carried out in some areas that were to be flooded. According to Balon & Coche (1974) a total of 953.8 km^2 were cleared on the northern shore (Zambia) and 443.8 km^2 were cleared on the southern shore (Zimbabwe). The rationale was that these cleared areas would form an integral part of the fishing grounds for the artisanal gill-net fishers who would utilise the fishery resource once the lake was full.

4.2. The fishery resource

Following the creation of the lake, most of the fish species were those that had been in the Zambezi River in the pre-impoundment period. At least 41 fish species have been recorded in Lake Kariba. These include the introduced Lake Tanganyika sardine (*Limnothrissa miodon*). Table 6 lists these species.

Table 6: Fish species recorded in Lake Kariba

Family	Scientific name	Common name
Anguillidae	*Anguila bengalensis labiata*	African mottled eel
Clupeidae	*Limnothrissa miodon*	Lake Tanganyika sardine
Mormyridae	*Cyphomyrus discorhnycus*	Zambezi parrotfish
	Marcusenius macrolepidotus	Bulldog
	Mormyrops anguilloides	Cornish jack
	Mormyrus longirostris	Eastern bottlenose
Characidae	*Brycinus imberi*	Imberi
	Brycinus lateralis	Striped robber
	Hydrocynus vittatus	Tigerfish
	Micralestes acutidens	Silver robber
Distichodontidae	*Distichodus mossambicus*	Nkupe
	Distichodus shenga	Chessa
Cyprinidae	*Barbus fasciolatus*	Red barb
	Barbus lineomaculatus	Line-spotted barb
	Barbus paludinosus	Straightfin barb
	Barbus poechii	Dashtail barb
	Barbus unitaeniatus	Longbeard barb
	Labeobarbus marequensis	Large-scale yellowfish
	Labeo altivelis	Hunyani labeo
	Labeo congoro	Purple labeo
	Labeo cylindricus	Red-eye labeo
	Opsaridium zambezense	Barred minnow
Schilbeidae	*Schilbe intermedius*	Silver catfish

Family	**Scientific name**	**Common name**
Clariidae	*Clarias gariepinus*	Sharptooth catfish
	Heterobranchus longifilis	Vundu
Malapteruridae	*Malapterurus shirensis*	Electric catfish
Mochokidae	*Synodontis nebulosus*	Clouded squeaker
	Synodontis zambezensis	Brown squeaker
Cyprinodontidae	*Aplocheilichthys johnstoni*	Johnston's topminnow
Cichlidae	*Oreochromis andersonii*	Three-spot tilapia
	Oreochromis macrochir	Greenhead tilapia
	Oreochromis mortimeri	Kariba tilapia
	Pharyngochromis acuticeps	Zambezi happy
	Pseudocrenilabrus philander	Southern mouthbrooder
	Serranochromis macrocephalus	Purpleface largemouth
	Serranochromis robustus	Nembwe
	Sargochromis carlottae	Rainbow happy
	Sargochromis codringtonii	Green happy
	Sargochromis giardi	Pink happy
	Tilapia rendalli	Northern redbreast tilapia
	Tilapia sparmanii	Banded tilapia

Note: Family and scientific names are after Skelton (2001)
Schilbe intermedius was previously known as *Schilbe mystus* and *Eutropius depressirostris* (Skelton 2001)
Sources: Kenmuir 1983, Zengeya & Marshall 2008, personal observation

Since the publication of the list by Kenmuir (1983), a number of additional species have been observed in Lake Kariba. These include the large-mouth bass (*Micropterus salmoides*) and the Nile tilapia (*Oreochromis niloticus*). The specimen of large-mouth bass was brought to Lake Kariba Fisheries Research Institute by an angler who had been spear-fishing in the Sanyati Basin just off Andora Harbour in Kariba Town (Mhlanga W. *pers. obs.*). Prior to 1990, the exotic Nile tilapia (*Oreochromis niloticus*) was not recorded in studies carried out by various workers as well as in the artisanal fishery community. Chifamba (1998) observed that during 1993/1994, *O. niloticus* occurred only in an area near a fish farm that was culturing this species. However, in 1997 to 1998, Mhlanga (2000a) noted that this species had established itself in the Sanyati River and constituted 0.4% of the fish caught in experimental gill nets. In 1998, there were no *O. niloticus* in the artisanal (inshore) gill-net fish catches on the Zimbabwean side (Songore *et al.* 1999). However, in the 2003 annual artisanal fish catches on the Zimbabwean side, *O. niloticus* constituted 2% (7.2 metric tons) of the artisanal fish catches (Lake Kariba Fisheries Research Institute, unpublished data).

Zengeya & Marshall (2008) conducted a fish survey in May 2006 along the Zimbabwean shore of Lake Kariba. Samples were taken at 11 sites, using an electrofisher and rotenone poisoning, and 52 880 fish belonging to 33 species in 10 families were collected. *Barbus unitaeniatus* (59% of the total sample) was the only abundant cyprinid and was the most numerous inshore species, whilst other members of this fluvial family were poorly represented. Amongst the remainder, the Cichlidae (30% of the specimens) were the dominant family, with three notable changes having occurred over the years. The first was the appearance of *Tilapia sparrmanii* – absent in the early years of the lake – which has increased following the establishment of submerged vegetation in the lake. The second was the spread of *Serranochromis macrocephalus* and the third was the establishment of the alien Nile tilapia, *O. niloticus*.

Zengeya & Marshall (2008) noted that pre-impoundment studies listed between 28 and 31 fish species in the Middle Zambezi River whereas 45 species have now been recorded from Lake Kariba (Marshall 2006). However, seven of these were reported to have either disappeared or were very rare.

The fishery resources on Lake Kariba can be classified into two broad sectors, namely the capture fisheries and aquaculture. The capture fisheries are based on harvesting fish from the wild, while aquaculture involves the culturing of fish in ponds or cages.

The aquaculture sector is based on a few commercial fish farms. Some fish farms are reported to have been set up in the Siavonga area in the Sanyati Basin on the Zambian side. On the Zimbabwean side of the Sanyati Basin (Basin 5), the major fish farm is the Lake Harvest Cage Culture Project. Annual production from this farm is approximately 8 000 metric tons. Production is based exclusively on one species, namely the Nile tilapia (*Oreochromis niloticus*). The aquaculture production on the Zambian side is reported to be based on several species including Three-spot tilapia (*O. andersonii*) and Nile tilapia.

The capture fishery sector is made up of several sub-sectors: the kapenta (pelagic) fishery, the inshore (artisanal) gill-net fishery and recreational fishery.

The kapenta (pelagic) fishery

The pelagic fishery is a single-species fishery that is based on the introduced freshwater sardine, *Limnothrissa miodon* (kapenta). Mtsambiwa (1996) studied some management aspects of the pre-recruitment ecology of *Limnothrissa miodon* in Kariba. He noted that the kapenta recruited to the fishery at a total length of 41mm. He also concluded that the mean size of kapenta in the catch was greater than the observed size at maturity, thus indicating that the fish had a chance to spawn at least once before being harvested. From the larval ecology study, food availability was identified as the only possible limiting factor with respect to growth and survival. Mtsambiwa (1996) concluded that due to the occurrence of larvae in most of the shoreline areas sampled, the kapenta in Lake Kariba utilise most of the shoreline as nursery grounds.The kapenta fishing licence holders employ fishing crew who carry out the fishing. The kapenta are usually salted and sun dried before they are packaged. The dried kapenta are then transported mainly to the urban centres where there is a high demand for this product, especially among the low-income urban population.

The major by-catch of this fishery is tigerfish (*Hydrocynus vittatus*). This is a commercial fishery and entry into the fishery is regulated by a licensing system in both Zambia and Zimbabwe. Initial capital investment is high. The fishing gear is a lift-net mounted on a pontoon. Fishing is done at night using mercury vapour lights (Fish Aggregating Device) that are usually powered by a diesel generator. In 1993, average costs for a company with one fishing vessel were 1 800 000 Zimbabwe dollars (Zw$), at the time equal to US $277 000 (Mwamoto *et al.* 1993). Most companies own at least two or more fishing vessels. Annual fishing licenses with a designated number of "fishing units" are issued to privately owned companies and kapenta fishing co-operatives. Each fishing unit corresponds to one fishing vessel.

In 1990, total kapenta catches from the Zimbabwean side were estimated at 21 751 metric tons (Sanyanga *et al.* 1992), with an estimated value of Zw$65 million (approximately US$10 million). At this time there were 45 kapenta fishing companies (Mwamoto *et al.* 1993). In 1996, kapenta catches on the Zimbabwean side totalled 15 423 tons (Chitembure *et al.* 1997). The retail price of dry kapenta at the time was Zw$ 21/kg (21 Zimbabwe dollars per kilogram), this catch was valued at Zw$ 107,961,000 (approximately US$11,824,863). On the Zambian side, total catch was estimated at 5 728 tons. The price of dry kapenta was 1,750 Zambian Kwacha (ZKw) per kg (Anon 1997). Thus the estimated value of the catch from the Zambian side was ZKw 3,341,333,275 (approximately US$ 634,872). Table 7 shows the trend in annual catches of kapenta from 1991 to 1996.

In 1996 there were 73 companies operating with 292 fishing vessels (rigs) on the Zimbabwean side, while in Zambia there were 50 companies operating with

Table 7: Annual Kapenta catches (tons) on Lake Kariba: 1991 to 1996, 2000, 2004 and 2009

	1991	1992	1993	1994	1995	1996	2000	2004	2009
Zambia	7,284	7,672	8,526	7,178	6,738	5,728	8,863	6,574	9,993
Zimbabwe	19,306	18,931	19,957	19,232	15,280	15,423	10,500	8,735	9,728
Total	26,590	26,603	28,483	26,410	23,016	21,151	19,636	15,309	19,721

Source: Adapted from Chitembure *et al.* 1997, Mbewe *et al.* 2011 and Tendaupenyu 2012

230 fishing rigs (Chitembure *et al.* 1997). By 2001, there were 92 fishing companies with 288 rigs on the Zimbabwean side (Nyikahadzoi & Raakjaer 2009). For management purposes, the major kapenta fish landing sites are Siavonga, Chipepo and Sinazongwe on the Zambian side, while on the Zimbabwean side the main bases are Sanyati (also referred to as Kariba), Bumi/Chalala, Sengwa and Binga/Mlibizi.

A bio-economic study of the kapenta fishery was conducted in 1996 (Anon 1997). Table 8 shows the results of running a Beverton and Holt model with a set of specific input parameters.

Table 8: Results of running the Beverton & Holt Model on the kapenta fishery

Biological and economic parameters combined			**Biological parameters only**	
Optimum rent (Zw$)	Effort (No. of rigs at optimum rent)	Effort (No. of rigs at zero rent)	Maximum Sustainable Yield (MSY) (tons)	Effort (No. of rigs at MSY)
60 000 000	461	875	25 000	1 125

Note: In 1996, the exchange rate was 1 US$ = 9.3 Zimbabwean dollars (Zw$)
Biological and economic parameters used: natural mortality = 3.5/yr; q = 0.004; fishing mortality = 2.1; cost/rig = Zw$300 000; age at first capture = 4 months; retail price = Zw$21/kg of dry weight
Source: Anon 1997

The abundance of kapenta in Lake Kariba has also been studied using hydroacoustic techniques (Mhlanga *et al.* 1995). In studies carried out in July 1994 and February 1995, mean kapenta densities were estimated at 27,000 fish per hectare and 48,000 fish per hectare respectively. Fishing effort was also negatively correlated with fish density.

Lindem (1988) conducted a hydroacoustic survey of kapenta in September 1988. Mean fish densities ranged from 13,000 fish per hectare to 38,000 fish per hectare. The estimated biomass varied between 16 kg/ha and 120 kg/ha with an average of 37 kg/ha. The total pelagic biomass of kapenta was estimated to be in the range of 16,000 tons to 25,000 tons in September 1988. Further long-term studies need to be conducted in order to assess whether these acoustic estimates can be used in management for predictive purposes.

Management of the kapenta fishery, including licensing and enforcement of regulations, is undertaken by the Department of Fisheries in Zambia, which falls under the Ministry of Agriculture and Livestock, and the Zimbabwe Parks and Wildlife Management Authority, which falls under the Ministry of Environment, and Natural Resources Management.

The artisanal (inshore) gill-net fishery

The inshore fishery is based on the exploitation of the riverine mid-Zambezi fish species as well as the introduced Nile tilapia (*Oreochromis niloticus*). Fishing is carried out from boats using gill-nets. When this fishery was set up, it was hoped that it would create employment for some of the families who had been displaced by the construction of the dam. The fishers usually sell their fish to traders, mostly women who come to buy the fish in the fishing camps. The fish are usually salted and dried before they are transported mainly to the urban centres.

Various types of boats are used and these include fiberglass and metal boats as well as dug-out canoes (*pers. obs.*) Most of these boats are non-motorised. Entry into this fishery is also regulated through a licensing system on both shores. The low capital investment required to carry out fishing, coupled with limited enforcement of regulations, makes it easier for unlicensed fishers to harvest the resource.

Apart from regulation of entry, fishing effort is also regulated. In both Zambia and Zimbabwe, there is a minimum mesh size regulation. The minimum mesh size in Zambia is 3 inches (76 millimetres) while in Zimbabwe it is 4 inches (102 millimetres). On the Zimbabwean side, each licensed fisher is allowed to use a maximum of five fishing nets of varying mesh sizes above the stipulated minimum mesh size. The enforcement of these regulations is a challenge given the wide-ranging distribution of the fishing villages along the 2 164 km of shoreline.

Bourdillon *et al.* (1985) chronicle the rise and fall of the number of fishers during the early years. A survey conducted on the northern shore (Zambia) in August 1959 recorded 407 fishers with 784 gill nets and 93 boats, which were mainly dug-out canoes. By 1962, it was estimated that there were 2 500 fishers on the Zambian side producing about 3 000 tons of fish (Scudder 1965). The gill net fishery on the southern side (Zimbabwe) only started in 1962 with only 208 licensed fishers (Minshull 1973).

The fall in catches from 3 000 tons in 1962 to 1 100 tons in 1967 resulted in a marked decline in the number of fishers on the Zambian side. It is estimated that by 1967, there were less than 500 fishers active on the Zambian side (Scudder 1967). The number of fishers on the Zimbabwean side peaked at just over 1 000 in 1966, and then declined to less than 500 in 1971 (Minshull 1973). During the period 1970 to 1974, the estimated number of fishers on the Zimbabwean side was between 210 and 280 (Marshall *et al.* 1982).

The liberation war in Zimbabwe in the late 1970s marked a decline in the number of fishers, especially on the southern shore. When Zimbabwe gained independence in 1980, the fishery along the southern shore was re-established at levels of activity similar to those prevailing in the 1970s (Bourdillon *et al.* 1985).

Table 9 shows the estimated annual catch and the average price of fish from the artisanal fishery on the Zimbabwean side from 1981 to 1984.

Table 9: Annual catch and average price of fish on the Zimbabwean side: 1981-1984

	1981	1982	1983	1984
Total catch (tons)	807	344	328	455
Average price (Zw$/ton)	287	637	879	–

Source: Bourdillon *et al.* 1985

After Zimbabwe's independence, the inshore fishery continued to increase steadily on both shores, as shown in Table 10.

Table 10: Number of fishers, boats, nets and villages, 1990–2011

Years	No. of fishers		No. of boats		No. of nets		No. of villages	
	Zam	Zim	Zam	Zim	Zam	Zim	Zam	Zim
1990	2 167	746	1 835	409	21 568	1 478	256	39
1993	2 283	1 229	1 861	586	15 823	4 899	278	41
2011	4 653	1154	2 451	583	26 695	4 501	63	41

Note: Zam = Zambia; Zim = Zimbabwe
Sources: Chitembure *et al.* 1995, Songore *et al.* 1998, Mbewe *et al.* 2011 and FAO 2011

By 1998, on the Zimbabwean side there were 1 404 fishers; 98% were male and only 2% were female (Songore *et al.* 1998). A few years later, in 2011, the number of fishers and nets on the Zimbabwean side had decreased slightly from the previous years, while in Zambia the number of fishers, boats and nets had increased significantly.

As part of the Zambia/Zimbabwe SADC Fisheries Project on Lake Kariba, co-management was initiated on both shores (*pers. obs.*). While there were no major settlement changes on the Zimbabwean side, this initiative had a significant impact on the Zambian side. The introduction of the co-management approach resulted in the regrouping of fishers into fewer villages. This reduction in the number of fishing villages on the Zambian side was reflected in the 1996 Fisheries Statistics for Lake Kariba (Chitembure *et al.* 1997). The regrouping exercise which was undertaken in 1995 resulted in the changes shown in Table 11 below.

Table 11: Percentage changes in the inshore fishery on Lake Kariba, 1990–1995

	Percentage change		
	Zambia (1990 to 1993)	**Zambia (1993 to 1995)**	**Zimbabwe (1990 to 1993)**
Fishers	5.35	-41	64.75
Villages	9	-76	5
Boats	1	-30	43
Nets	-27	-17	229

Source: Chitembure *et al.* 1997

Management of the artisanal fishery is through the Department of Fisheries in Zambia. This department collaborates with stakeholders in a co-management arrangement where there are Village Management Committees and Zonal Management Committees. In Zimbabwe, the artisanal fishery is managed by the Zimbabwe Parks and Wildlife Management Authority, through Lake Kariba Fisheries Research Institute. The artisanal fishery co-management arrangements that were initiated during the Zambia/Zimbabwe SADC Fisheries Project on Lake Kariba were more successful on the Zambian side than on the Zimbabwean side. One of the few remaining Sub-Area Fishers Associations (SAFA) on the Zimbabwean side is the Gache-Gache Fishers Association (Manzungu *pers. comm.*).

Several factors may have contributed to the poor adoption of co-management arrangements on the Zimbabwean side. The fishery sector in Zimbabwe tends to be overshadowed by issues related to terrestrial wildlife since the sector is part of the Zimbabwe Parks and Wildlife Management Authority. The marked staff turn-over that occurred during the early stages of the co-management programme resulted in a loss of momentum, as there was no smooth transition when new staff members came on board. The economic challenges that Zimbabwe faced also reduced financial resources for the fisheries sector.

The recreational (sport) fishery

The recreational fishery is the third sub-sector of the capture fishery on Lake Kariba. A major difference between this sector and the other two is that it is primarily not commercial, i.e. fishing is carried out as a sport. The main fishing gear in this fishery is the rod and line, while spear-fishing is carried out to a limited extent by a few individuals. The sport fishery supports tourism developments on the lake. For example, the annual Kariba International Tigerfish Tournament is the major annual event in this fishery. It attracts participants from Southern Africa (Namibia, South Africa and Zambia), Europe (United Kingdom), North America (Canada), Australasia (Australia and New Zealand), as well as the Middle East. Quantitative data on production (i.e. catch statistics) from this fishery are not readily available as they have not been collected systematically – apart from angling tournaments – and no economic valuation of the sector has been carried out recently.

Over the last few years, the number of subsistence fishers has increased, especially in major settlements such as Kariba Town (*pers. obs.*). The harsh economic environment in Zimbabwe is likely to have significantly contributed to this influx. No licence is required for the recreational fisher (angler). On the Zimbabwean side, the angler only has to pay a daily or annual levy to the Zimbabwe Parks and Wildlife Management Authority (ZPWMA).

4.3. Institutional arrangements

The institutional arrangements for the management of the fishery resource are linked to the legislation governing the fishery resource. The institutional arrangements are at both national and bi-lateral levels, given that the lake is shared between Zambia and Zimbabwe.

At the national level the Department of Fisheries (DoF) is responsible for fisheries management on the Zambian side, and the Zimbabwe Parks and Wildlife Management Authority (formerly the Department of National Parks and Wildlife Management) is responsible for fisheries management on the Zimbabwean side, through the Lake Kariba Fisheries Research Institute. The Department of Fisheries falls under the Ministry of Agriculture and Livestock (MAL), while the Zimbabwe Parks and Wildlife Management Authority falls under the Ministry of Environment and Natural Resources Management (MENRM).

The Department of Fisheries is headed by a Director, with two Deputy Directors, one responsible for Capture Fisheries and the other responsible for Aquaculture. Four Chief Fisheries Research Officers are each responsible for Capture Fisheries Research, Capture Fisheries Extension, Aquaculture Research and Aquaculture Extension.

In Zimbabwe, the Parks and Wildlife Management Authority is headed by a Director General. Three Directors are each responsible for Conservation, Commercial Services and Finance, Human Resources and Administration. The head of station at Lake Kariba Fisheries Research Institute reports to the Chief Ecologist (Scientific), who in turn reports to the Director of Conservation.

The introduction of fisheries co-management led to the formation of Village Management Committees (VMCs) and Zonal Management Committees (ZMCs) on the Zambian side. Representation includes government (DoF), local authorities, kapenta fishers and artisanal fishers. On the Zimbabwean side, Sub-Area Fishers Associations (SAFAs) were established in the inshore fishery. These associations primarily represent the artisanal fishers with no representation from the kapenta fishers. The evolution of fisheries co-management arrangements has been comparatively faster on the Zambian side than on the Zimbabwean side. This is because both the government authorities and the stakeholders (especially the kapenta operators) were determined to see the programme succeed. The kapenta operators saw the village regrouping exercise as an opportunity to resolve conflict with the artisanal fishers living on the islands (Malasha 2003).

At the bi-lateral level, Zambia and Zimbabwe have signed a Protocol on the Management of the Shared Fisheries Resources on Lake Kariba, which was facilitated through the Zambia/Zimbabwe Joint Permanent Commission (JPC). It provides the legal framework for joint management of the fishery resource. Two major bodies fall under this Protocol, namely the Joint Fisheries Management Committee (JFMC) and the Joint Fisheries Technical Committee (JFTC). The JFMC is the decision-making body while the JFTC is the scientific/technical body.

In Zimbabwe, the major legal instrument used to manage the fishery is the Parks and Wildlife Act (Chapter 20:14) of 1975 as amended on 1 January 1982. This Act was further amended in 2001 through the Parks and Wildlife Amendment Act of 2001. The Amendment Act provided *inter alia* for the transformation of the Department of National Parks and Wildlife Management from a fully-fledged government department funded by central treasury, to a self-financing authority (quasi-government) headed by a Director-General appointed by a board and with the approval of the Minister. The Director-General is appointed on a fixed-term contract basis.

In Zambia, the Fisheries Act (Chapter 314) of 1974, now known as Chapter 200, was enacted to replace the old Fisheries Conservation Ordinance (Department of Fisheries 2008). From a legal and fisheries management perspective, no major changes were introduced in the Act of 1974 (*Ibid.*) Some of the major changes that were introduced in the Act of 1974 were the establishment of the Department of Fisheries and the removal of the power of the Barotse Royal Establishment to control fishing in the Western Province, particularly the Upper Zambezi. The Act of 1974 was repealed and replaced by the Fisheries Act 22 of 2011. The new Act provides for the establishment of Fisheries Management Committees, which include stakeholders in fisheries management and development. These stakeholders include six representatives of the fishers as well as one representative each of the local authority, the chief, NGOs, commercial fishing operators, the aquaculture industry and two other members. The Act also establishes a Fisheries and Aquaculture Development Fund (Government of Zambia 2011).

At the policy and strategy level, Zimbabwe still has to develop a sector-specific fisheries policy and strategy. In the meantime, the Parks and Wildlife Act guides policy and strategy interventions. It should be noted that fisheries extension in all water bodies outside the Parks and Wildlife Estate falls under the Ministry of Agriculture. This has a bearing on policy development.

Zambia has a National Fisheries Policy to guide development in this sector (Department of Fisheries 2008). The aim of the policy is to provide an overall national vision for the development of the fisheries sector. The policy also prescribes the institutional arrangements for the management of the fisheries and aquaculture sector and identifies relevant stakeholder institutions that will support implementation to address current concerns (*Ibid*). Apart from the Fisheries Policy, Zambia also has a National Aquaculture Strategy (Department of Fisheries 2006). The strategy aims to guide development in the sector and is part of the Zambian government's plan to alleviate poverty, increase income generation and improve the economy through foreign exchange earnings of fish exports. The strategy proposes various interventions to address critical issues related to aquaculture development. These issues are input supply (i.e. production and delivery of fish feed and fish seed), availability of farm credit access to extension support and access to markets. The summary of the institutions governing the fishery resource is shown in Table 12.

4.4. Ecological interactions

Interactions in the fishery resource on Lake Kariba encompass inter-resource as well as intra-resource interactions. Inter-resource interactions include interactions with sectors such as water, land (agriculture, mining, pest control), wildlife, forests and grasslands. Intra-resource interactions occur with other aquatic organisms such as phytoplankton, zooplankton, insects, crocodiles, hippopotami, aquatic vegetation (macrophytes) and fish-eating birds. Climatic factors such as

Table 12: Institutions involved in governing the fishery resource on Lake Kariba

Responsibilities	Institutions and institutional arrangements	
	Zambia	Zimbabwe
Artisanal fishery		
Licensing (issuing fishing permits)	Dept. of Fisheries (DoF) in consultation with VMCs and ZMCs	Parks and Wildlife Management Authority in collaboration with Nyami-Nyami and Binga Rural District Councils
Management	Co-management	Parks and Wildlife Management Authority
Kapenta fishery		
Issuing fishing permits	Department of Fisheries	Parks and Wildlife Management Authority
Management	Co-management	Parks and Wildlife Management Authority
Recreational fishery		
Fishing (processing angling fees)	Department of Fisheries	Parks and Wildlife Management Authority
Aquaculture		
Issuing fish farming (aquaculture) licences	Department of Fisheries	Parks and Wildlife Management Authority

temperature (water and air), river inflows, rainfall, floods and droughts also influence the fishery resource.

In the kapenta fishery, water stratification and river inflows affect the productivity of the fishery. Masundire (1989) observed that local floods caused local increases in zooplankton abundance. Zooplankton is the major food source for kapenta. This effect was observed to be most marked in the Sanyati Basin (Basin 5).

In all the basins, zooplankton is most abundant in June and August (*Ibid*). At this time the lake is completely mixed and isothermal. Chitembure *et al.* (1997) noted that there were two peaks in kapenta catches during the year: March and August/September. The peak in March coincided with the inflows of the local rivers, while the peak in August/September coincided with the complete mixing of the lake waters, after the breakdown of stratification between May and July. The mixing brings up nutrients from the lower water layer into the upper layer where they are used by the phytoplankton and zooplankton, thereby promoting greater kapenta production.

Chifamba (2000) observed that kapenta catches (expressed as catch per unit of effort) were strongly associated with minimum temperature, total inflow and rainfall. She suggested that water temperature was likely to influence natural mortality, with high temperature associated with high natural mortality. Air temperature also influences kapenta production through nutrient cycling. These observations show that increases in temperatures through climate change are likely to affect kapenta production negatively. The high temperatures would result in high natural mortality and this would result in fewer fish being available for harvesting (i.e. reduced recruitment into the fishery).

The impact of climate change on the kapenta fishery was studied by Ndebele-Murisa *et al.* (2011) and Magadza (2011). Ndebele-Murisa *et al.* (2011) concluded that both climate (maximum temperature in particular) and nutrients, which are influenced by water levels, are the primary determinants of Lake Kariba's kapenta production. Magadza (2011) reported that observation data indicated that, over the last 35 years, the Zambezi Valley in the vicinity of Lake Kariba has been warming at a rate of more than 2^0C per 100 years. He proposed that this warming had affected the food chain and productivity of the lake, precipitating a decline in the pelagic fishery yield.

Marshall (2012) has argued that there is little evidence that climate change has affected the inshore fish stocks. While the kapenta fishery is influenced by river flow, which is a reflection of the climate in the huge catchment area above the lake, and by the seasonal cycle of stratification, these factors do not explain all the variations in catches of this species. He points to reported declines in the catch per unit effort through periods when river flows were both high and low, proposing that the impact of fishing is the only factor that can explain this anomaly. In view of this ongoing debate, it is therefore important to study the impact of climate change on both the artisanal and kapenta fishery.

Fishing effort has a direct impact on the abundance of kapenta, as higher fishing effort (i.e. higher fishing pressure) will result in lower fish abundance. In a study of kapenta abundance in four of the lake's five basins, Mhlanga *et al.* (1995) noted a negative correlation between fishing effort and fish density (fish abundance). Further studies using the same techniques (i.e. hydro-acoustics) need to be conducted to validate this observation through a long time-series of data.

The decline in kapenta catches is further compounded by 'leaks' from the fishery, in the form of kapenta fishing crew illicitly selling fish while still on the lake. The fish sold on the lake are not accounted for in the official catch statistics and some kapenta operators estimate losses of more than 50% of their catch through these clandestine fish sales conducted on the lake.

The decline in fish catches is likely to be due to the factors highlighted above as well as additional factors such as the use of smaller mesh sizes on kapenta fish nets. From these observations, a multidisciplinary study should be conducted to assess the relative impact of each of the different factors on fish production.

Karenge & Kolding (1995) studied the relation of several hydrological indices (mean annual lake levels, lake level fluctuations, and amplitude of fluctuations) and recruitment indices and mean annual condition factor of four inshore fish species. These species were Tigerfish (*H. vittatus*), Kariba bream (*O. niloticus*), Pink happy (*S. codringtonii*), and Eastern bottlenose (*M. longirostris*).

For Tigerfish, they found significant correlations between recruitment and lake level, between recruitment and delta lake level and between condition factor and lake level. For Kariba bream, they observed significant correlations between recruitment and lake level, recruitment and delta lake level, recruitment and amplitude, condition factor and lake level and condition factor and delta lake level. For Pink happy, they found that only one correlation was significant, between condition factor and lake level. For Eastern bottlenose, the only significant correlation was that of catch per unit effort and lake level. The absolute lake levels were most important for Tigerfish, which migrates upstream to breed. The rate of change of lake levels (delta lake level) appeared to govern the tilapias, which spawn in the shallow (littoral) zone of the lake. High lake levels in general denoted strongly running rivers.

In light of the above, fish life cycles can be further influenced by two major human-induced interventions. First is the draw-down caused by the opening of the flood-gates on Kariba's dam wall, either to regulate the volume of water in the lake, or to generate hydro-electric power. The second intervention would be the construction of new dams upstream of the lake, such as the proposed Batoka Dam. The regulation of water releases from any upstream dam would affect water level fluctuations in Lake Kariba.

The Zambezi River supplies 80% of the inflow into the lake while the Sanyati River (the second largest river) supplies about 8% (Marshall 1988). The Zambezi River flows through Zambia, Angola, and Namibia before it reaches Lake Kariba. The outbreak of any fish disease upstream is likely to impact the fish in the lake. Kibria *et al.* (2009) reported that the first confirmed outbreaks of EUS on the African continent occurred in 2007 in Botswana, Namibia and Zambia. According to Mwera (2012), there have been no outbreaks of EUS in commercial fish farming operations in the Eastern Basin of Lake Kariba on the Zimbabwean side. Mudenda (*pers. comm.*) also reported that there have been no outbreaks of EUS on the Zambian side of the lake. While there have been no outbreaks of EUS in Lake Kariba, it is imperative that regular monitoring of potential disease outbreaks be carried out.

Invasive alien species of both fauna and flora can also affect a fishery. In Lake Kariba, the major invasive alien plant species is the water hyacinth (*Eichhornia crassipes*), while the major invasive alien fish species is the Nile tilapia (*O. niloticus*). Recently there have been sightings of the Australian red claw crayfish (*Cherax quadricarinatus*), with samples having been collected from the Sanyati Basin (Phiri *pers. comm.*).

The origin of water hyacinth on Lake Kariba is unknown. It had been observed in pot plants in some of the houses in Kariba Town and in some fishing camps in the 1980s (Mhlanga *et al.* 1998). Since its construction in the late 1950s, no reports of the outbreaks of this weed in Lake Kariba had been received up to 1993. The first reports of the occurrence of water hyacinth (*Eichhornia crassipes*) in Lake Kariba were received in 1994 (*Ibid*). By 1995 the weed had started spreading from the Nyaodza River mouth and was creating navigational problems for the artisanal fishers in the Nyaodza area. In the Nyaodza and Gache Gache Rivers, the water hyacinth later proliferated to such an extent that it blocked navigation channels and had an adverse impact on the artisanal and recreational fishers. The proliferation of this weed in these areas was most likely due to the high nutrient levels in these rivers.

Following this outbreak, attempts were made to use biological control methods (weevils) and chemical control methods (Roundup, a glyphosate herbicide) in 1996 and 1997. Despite these attempts, the weed continued to proliferate and a decision was then made to control the weed using aerial spraying of 2,4D. Aerial spraying was carried out in the Gache Gache and Nyaodza Rivers on the Zimbabwean side. No spraying was carried out on the Zambian side as earlier aerial reconnaissance had shown that there were no large water hyacinth mats.

The exotic Nile tilapia (*O. niloticus*) is a popular species in fish farming. Some farm dams in Zimbabwe have been stocked with this species, while in Zambia it is also cultured on some fish farms. On the Zimbabwean side, the fish escaped and was observed in the Sanyati River in 1997 and 1998 (Mhlanga 2000a). At this time it had not yet started appearing in the artisanal catches (*pers. obs.*). By 2003, it constituted 2% (7.2 tons) of the annual catch from the inshore fishery on the Zimbabwean side (Lake Kariba Fisheries Research Institute, unpublished data).

The Nile tilapia is known to hybridise with indigenous species such as Kariba bream (*O. mortimeri*). The extent of hybridisation on Lake Kariba has not yet been studied, nor has the current occurrence of pure strains of Kariba bream been documented. This hybridisation has implications on the conservation of pure strains of the indigenous Kariba bream. It can have significant effects on conservation of biological diversity. Studies are urgently required to assess the current status of Nile tilapia and Kariba bream in Lake Kariba and to identify those areas where pure strains of the indigenous bream can be found.

The Zambezi Valley, in which Lake Kariba is located, has a wide variety of insects, some of which cause diseases in both humans and livestock. Two major pests are the tsetse fly (*Glossina* species) and mosquitoes. The control of these insects has involved the use of persistent organochlorine pesticides such as DDT. Although use of DDT was discontinued in tsetse fly control, it is still used for residual spraying in households to control mosquitoes. The DDT finds its way into the aquatic ecosystem, affecting non-target organisms such as fish and fish-eating birds. In a study of DDT levels in fish on the Zimbabwean side of Lake Kariba, McCarton & Mhlanga (1994) observed that residue burdens in individual fish particularly Tigerfish (*H. vittatus*) and Sharptooth catfish (*C. gariepinus*) from the headwater streams were high enough to provide a source of contamination for fish-eating birds.

Mining activities can also negatively impact fish production especially through the use of chemicals in the extraction process. Alluvial gold panning has been occurring for some time in the Sanyati River (*pers. obs.*). The gold-panners are known to use mercury to process the ore. Mhlanga (2000b) observed the occurrence of mercury in Tigerfish, (*H. vittatus*), pink happy (*S. codringtonii*) and kapenta (*L. miodon*) from Lake Kariba. Although the observed total mercury concentrations (less than 0.095 mg/kg wet weight) did not pose a human health risk, the gold panning has continued since 1992 when this study was carried out. Mercury is known to biomagnify along the food chain and there may have been significant increases in its occurrence in fish. It is therefore necessary to carry out more studies in order to assess the current levels of mercury occurring in fish.

Douthwaite (1992) reported high levels of mercury in the fish eagle (*Haliaeetus vocifer*), a fish-eating bird, with total mercury concentrations in the liver at 66–395 mg/kg dry weight.

Apart from heavy metal contamination, gold panning also destroys fish habitats and this can result in reduced spawning and breeding of the fish, especially for species such as Tigerfish, which migrate upstream to breed. An assessment of the habitat degradation due to gold panning activities needs to be carried out, especially on the Sanyati River.

Deforestation in the river catchment area can also lead to habitat degradation. Deforestation is occurring in the catchment area. During the rainy season, the Sanyati waters carry a lot of sediment and floating logs are sometimes a hazard especially for small boats (*pers. obs.*). Studies are further required to determine the sediment load of affluent rivers such as the Sanyati.

Fisheries management measures can influence the distribution and abundance of fish. These management measures may include the creation of areas that are closed to fishing. On the Zimbabwean side, areas closed to gill-net fishing include the river mouths and those sections that are in Wildlife Protected Areas (i.e. National Parks and Safari Areas). In a study of fished and unfished areas, Sanyanga *et al.* (1995) observed a significant reduction in mean length of commercially fished species in the fished areas, with size distribution curves that were skewed, lacking the small and large length classes. Non-commercial fish species were abundant in the fished areas, with the Squeaker (*S. zambezensis*) being the most abundant.

Mabaye (1994) studied the behaviour and ecology of *Serranochromis codringtonii*, *Tilapia rendalli* and *Oreochromis mortimeri* using radio telemetry. He noted that all three species exhibited lateral, horizontal and vertical movements. Lateral (upstream–downstream) movements were spontaneous and sporadic and they involved excursions along the longitudinal axis of the lake. The maximum distance covered by tagged individuals was four kilometres. Mabaye concluded that the lateral movement appeared to be associated with fish searching for potential breeding grounds and more profitable foraging sites. In contrast, horizontal (inshore–offshore) movements were synchronised and cyclic in nature. Whole colonies of each species were reported to move offshore during autumn and return inshore during late spring. Vertical movements involved fish moving into deep water as water temperatures decreased in autumn. They moved to the middle levels during the coldest time of the year, which is also the period of homothermy (July/August) in this monomictic lake. From Mabaye's results, it is likely that during the lateral movements, the species that were studied may have moved from unfished areas to fished areas.

While water quality monitoring is being conducted in the Sanyati Basin, there is need for a lake-wide study to assess the overall impact of cage farming on water quality. Cage culture also alters the abundance of fish species in the area around cages. Wild fish are attracted to the cages either to prey on the fish in and around the cages (e.g. *H. vittatus*) or to feed on the excess food (pellets) from the cages (e.g. *Brycinus lateralis*). Crocodiles have also been observed near the cages. However, the impact of fish cages on the fauna in the area around the cages still needs to be studied and documented.

Moreau *et al.* (1997) analysed biomass flows in Lake Kariba to reach a better understanding of the ecosystem, using the ECOPATH model and software. The ECOPATH model allowed the researchers to integrate (and to incidentally give credit to) heterogenous data coming from surveys operated by specialists of the different groups that were considered (*Ibid*). The model takes an ecosystems approach to include ecology and trophic relationships and interactions.

4.5. Institutional and social interactions

The fishery sector is influenced by various institutional and social interactions. These interactions sometimes affect the resource utilisation patterns.

Commercial exploitation of the fishery is influenced by central government policy. Government's efforts to limit entry into the fishery are meant to ensure sustainable utilisation of the resource, especially the kapenta fishery, whose entry is more regulated than entry into the inshore fishery. Zimbabwe conducted a Kapenta Permit redistribution exercise in 2005 and 2008 due to the government policy on indigenisation.

On both sides of the lake, the kapenta landing sites are located in areas with some levels of infrastructure development, which is necessary for this sector. Conversely, the location of artisanal fishing villages is not influenced by levels of infrastructure development. In fisheries, the landing sites and the fishing villages are under the jurisdiction of local authorities while the fishery resource is under the jurisdiction of a different institution. This split has major implications on resource management and infrastructure development. An example is in the artisanal fishery in Zimbabwe. The local authorities (Binga Rural District Council and Nyami-Nyami Rural District Council) do not see the fishing villages as priority areas for infrastructure development. Consequently, these villages lack basic social services such as potable water, schools and clinics.

Service provision in the artisanal fishery on the Zambian side is comparatively better, especially after the introduction of the co-management arrangement (regrouping exercise). The slow progress in implementation of the co-management arrangement on the Zimbabwean side may have been strongly influenced by both social and economic factors.

Most artisanal fishers on the Zimbabwean side are seasonal. This is due to the fact that during the rainy season, the fishers return to their rural homes (where their families reside), reportedly to grow crops to supplement their income from fishing. To come up with appropriate management interventions, the role of economic factors (low returns from fishing) and social factors (lack of basic services in the fishing camps) have to be ascertained first. The planning authorities (parks, local authorities and central government) have to liaise more in the planning process.

The set-up of fishing villages (for example on the Zimbabwean side) gives rise to social behaviour that has serious health implications. The absence of potable water makes the fishing villages susceptible to water-borne diseases such as cholera and dysentery. The fishers use the untreated lake water. Studies need to be carried out to assess the quality of the lake water especially from a bacteriological perspective. Some fishers have been known to form liaisons with female fish traders and the fishers end up providing fish to the traders in exchange for sexual favours. This behaviour can fuel the spread of sexually transmitted infections

(STIs), as well as HIV. The prevalence of such behaviour on both sides of Lake Kariba requires further study. The studies should also assess the levels of health awareness (especially with respect to HIV/AIDS) among fishing communities on Lake Kariba.

The artisanal fishers have an impact on woodlands and grasslands. They use fuel-wood as their main energy source for household requirements. The fuel-wood is also used for post-harvest fish processing, to smoke and preserve the fish. Most of the dwellings in the fishing villages are pole and dagga (mud) houses with grass thatch. It is important to study the extraction rates, especially for fuel-wood, to assess whether they are ecologically sustainable.

In the kapenta fishery, the fishing boats (rigs) use diesel generators and hence are a potential pollution source. The pollution can be in form of noise pollution, water pollution (e.g. diesel leakages, especially in harbours) or air pollution (e.g. exhaust smoke). Quantitative data on the pollution levels are not readily available. The noise from rigs is a source of conflict with other users, such as the tourism industry (hotels, lodges and camp sites), boat-owners (especially house-boat owners) and safari hunting industry (hunting camps).

Conflicts sometimes arise between the kapenta fishing operations and cage culture operations. The kapenta boats are sometimes perceived as a risk in terms of both theft of fish from the cages, as well as physical damage to the cages in the case of the kapenta boats drifting to the cages in a storm. The cage culture operations are also sometimes seen as detrimental to kapenta operations as they may be sited in prime kapenta fishing grounds (i.e. competition for space).

Human–wildlife conflicts occur in the fishery on Lake Kariba. Artisanal fishers and subsistence anglers are sometimes attacked by elephants (*Loxodonta africana*) and buffalo (*Syncerus caffer*). These attacks usually occur in wildlife-protected areas, such as National Parks and Safari Areas. In some instances, the rogue buffalo or elephant would have previously broken through wire snares (*pers. obs.*). Although the frequency of these attacks is low, a study should be conducted to document them.

Artisanal gill-net fishers and subsistence anglers have also reported attacks by crocodiles and hippopotami. The subsistence anglers are usually attacked while fishing in the shallow waters of the lake (bank fishing). The crocodiles also damage the artisanal fishers' gill-nets and hippos sometimes damage both the gill-nets and the boats.

Crocodile attacks on pleasure boats have also been reported. Most boat owners view the crocodiles as a safety threat, and following some fatalities, an increased number of people are now lobbying for a reduction in crocodile numbers (*Ibid*). However, there is need to study the crocodile population on Lake Kariba.

Conflict also occurs between the gill-net fishers and the hotel and lodge owners for several reasons. On one hand, the boats (especially speed boats) from the lodges are motorised and their propellers sometimes damage the fishers' gill-nets. On the other hand, the fishing grounds are sometimes close to the hotels and lodges and the hoteliers/lodge owners view the presence of gill-net fishers as compromising the aesthetic beauty (wilderness experience) that their clients desire. Incidences have been reported of lodge owners removing gill-nets, in contravention of the law (*pers. obs.*).

Apart from the boats from hotels, conflicts often arise between the fishers and the house-boat and speed-boat owners. The boat owners sometimes damage the fishers' gill-nets. The house-boats are usually moored in remote sections of the shoreline, especially along the shoreline of wildlife-protected areas. Their owners view the presence of artisanal fishers as a disruption of their holidays as they will be seeking that quiet, wilderness experience.

Disputes sometimes arise between the fishers and the authorities in charge of the wildlife protected areas. They are usually more pronounced in those fishing villages adjacent to protected areas and arise from the fact that in some instances wildlife poachers have either used the fishing villages as spring-boards into the protected areas, or the poachers would have colluded with some residents in the fishing villages in carrying out their clandestine poaching activities.

4.6. Conclusion

Interactions between the fishery resource and other sectors are varied and may be considered in ecological, socio-economic and political dimensions. Most of these interactions have either not been studied in detail, or were studied more than a decade ago. In view of the serious lack of research data, there is need to conduct in-depth studies of these interactions. Given that there are so many interactions to be studied, prioritisation of the studies will be necessary. Criteria for prioritisation could include the availability of financial resources (i.e. budgetary requirements of these studies) as well as the availability of researchers (including undergraduate and post-graduate students).

References

Anonymous 1997. *Working Group on Bioeconomic Assessment of Kapenta (Limnothrissa miodon) in Lake Kariba (Zambia/Zimbabwe).* Zambia/Zimbabwe SADC Fisheries Project. Project Report No. 50.

Balon E.K. & Coche A.G. 1974. *Lake Kariba: A Man-made Ecosystem in Central Africa.* W. Junk. The Hague.

Bell-Cross G. & Bell-Cross B. 1971. 'Introduction of *Limnothrissa miodon* and *Limnothrissa tanganicae* from Lake Tanganyika into Lake Kariba', *Fisheries Research Bulletin of Zambia* **5**: 207-214.

Bourdillon M.F.C., Cheater A.F. & Murphree M.W. 1985. *Studies of Fishing on Lake Kariba*. Mambo Occasional Papers – Socioeconomic Series. No. 20. Mambo Press. Gweru, Zimbabwe.

Chifamba P.C. 1998. 'Status of *Oreochromis niloticus* in Lake Kariba, Zimbabwe.' In: Cowx I.G. (ed) *Stocking and Introduction of Fish*. Fishing News Books. Oxford.

Chifamba P.C. 2000. 'The relationship of temperature and hydrological factors to catch per unit effort, condition and size of the freshwater sardine, *Limnothrissa miodon* (Boulenger) in Lake Kariba', *Fisheries Research* **22**: 205–226.

Chitembure R.M., Mungomba J., Karenge L., Ncube L.D. & Mugwagwa M. 1995. *Joint Fisheries Statistical Report. Lake Kariba*. Zambia/Zimbabwe SADC Fisheries Project Report No. 43.

Chitembure R.M., Karenge L. & Mugwagwa M. 1997. *1996 Joint Fisheries Statistical Report. Lake Kariba*. Zambia/Zimbabwe SADC Fisheries Project. Project Report No. 51.

Department of Fisheries. 2006. *National Aquaculture Strategy*. Ministry of Agriculture and Co-operatives. Republic of Zambia.

Department of Fisheries. 2008. *National Fisheries Policy (2010–2020)*. Ministry of Agriculture and Co-operatives. Republic of Zambia.

Douthwaite R.J. 1992. 'Effects of DDT on the fish eagle (*Haliaeetus vocifer*) population of Lake Kariba in Zimbabwe', *Ibis* **134**: 250–258.

Food and Agricultural Organisation (FAO). 2011. *Lake Kariba Fishery Frame Survey Report. Zimbabwe*. FAO, Harare.

Government of Zambia. 2011. *Fisheries Act. No. 22 of 2011*. Republic of Zambia.

Hutton J.M. 1991. *Lake Kariba, Zimbabwe. A Background to Planning. Paper II. Current Resource Utilisation and Associated Land Use with Financial Assessments of Potential for Expansion*. Zambia/Zimbabwe SADC Fisheries Project. Document 10.

Karenge L. & Kolding J. 1995. 'On the relationship between hydrology and fisheries in man-made Lake Kariba, central Africa', *Fisheries Research* **22**: 205–226.

Kenmuir D. 1983. *Fishes of Kariba*. Mardon Printers. Harare. Zimbabwe.

Kibria M.G., Klingelhoefer E., Hitula A., Currie B.,Wall B.C.W. & Endjala J. 2009. *Epizootic Ulcerative Syndrome (EUS). An On-site Survey Report*. Directorate of Aquaculture (DOA). Ministry of Fisheries and Marine Resources (MFMR). Windhoek, Namibia.

Lindem T. 1988. *Results from the Hydro Acoustic Survey in Lake Kariba, September 1988*. Report prepared for the Zambia/Zimbabwe SADCC Fisheries Project. Kariba, Zimbabwe.

Mabaye A.B.E. 1994. 'The behaviour and ecology of three major cichlids in Lake Kariba, Zimbabwe.' *PhD thesis*. University of Maryland. USA.

Magadza C.H.D. 2011. 'Indications of the effects of climate change on the pelagic fishery of Lake Kariba, Zambia–Zimbabwe', *Lakes & Reservoirs: Research and Management* **16**: 15–22.

Malasha I. 2003. 'Colonial and post-colonial fisheries regulations: The case of Zambia and Zimbabwe.' In: Jul-Larsen E., Kolding J., Overa R., Raakjaer Nielsen J., Zwieten P.A.M. van (eds) *Management, Co-management or No Management? Major Dilemmas in Southern African Freshwater Fisheries. Two Case Studies*. FAO Fisheries Technical Paper. No. 426/2. Rome, FAO.

Marshall B.E. 1988. 'Seasonal and annual variations in the abundance of pelagic sardines in Lake Kariba, with special reference to the effects of drought', *Archiv für Hydrobiologie* **112**: 399–409.

Marshall B.E. 2006. 'A checklist of the fishes of Lake Kariba (Zimbabwe–Zambia)', *Arnoldia Zimbabwe* **10**: 257-274.

Marshall B.E. 2012. 'Does climate change really explain changes in the fisheries productivity of Lake Kariba (Zambia-Zimbabwe)?' *Transactions of the Royal Society of South Africa* **67(1)**: 45–51.

Marshall B.E., Junor F.J.R. & Langerman J.D. 1982. *Fisheries and Fish Production on the Zimbabwean Side of Lake Kariba*. Kariba Studies No. 10. Lake Kariba Fisheries Research Institute. Kariba, Zimbabwe.

Masundire H. 1989. 'Zooplankton composition and abundance in relation to water transparency and production', *Archic für Hydrobiologie* **33**: 513–520.

Mbewe M., Mweemba C., Habulembe I., Silwimba E. 2011. *Lake Kariba Fishery Frame Survey Report*. Chilanga, Zambia.

McCarton B. & Mhlanga W. 1994. 'Fish.' In: Douthwaite R.J., Tingle C.C. (eds) *DDT in the Tropics: The Impact on Wildlife in Zimbabwe of Ground Spraying for Tsetse- fly Control*. Natural Resources Institute, Chatham, UK.

Mhlanga W. 2000a. 'An assessment of the fish population of the lower reaches of the Sanyati River, Zimbabwe', *African Journal of Aquatic Science* **25**: 84–88.

Mhlanga W. 2000b. 'Mercury in tigerfish (*Hydrocynus vittatus*), green happy (*Serranochromis codringtonii*) and kapenta (*Limnothrissa miodon*) from Lake Kariba. Zimbabwe', *African Journal of Ecology* **38**: 224–229.

Mhlanga W., Mbulawa R.E. & Gurure R. 1998. *Assessment of 2,4D (Dichlorophenoxy Acetic Acid) in Lake Kariba following the 1998 Water Hyacinth (Eichhornia Crassipes) Control Exercise*. Lake Kariba Fisheries Research Institute. Kariba, Zimbabwe.

Mhlanga W., Ngalande P. & Songore N. 1995. *Hydroacoustic Assessment of Kapenta (Limnothrissa Miodon) Abundance in Lake Kariba*. Paper presented at the First Pan-African Fisheries Congress. (Fisheries Society of Africa). Nairobi. Kenya. 31st July–4th August 1995.

Minshull J.L. 1973. *The Establishment of a Fishery among the Resettled Batonka People at Lake Kariba, Rhodesia*. In the collected papers of the Symposium held by the Commission Internationale des Grands Barrages. Madrid.

Moreau J., Cronberg G., Games I., Hustler K., Kautsky N., Kiibus M., Machena C. & Marshall B. 1997. Biomass Flows in Lake Kariba, towards an ecosystem approach. In Moreau J. (ed) *Advances in the Ecology of Lake Kariba*. University of Zimbabwe Publications, Harare. Zimbabwe. pp 219–237.

Mtsambiwa M.Z. 1996. 'Some management aspects of pre-recruitment ecology of the freshwater sardine *Limnothrissa miodon* in Lake Kariba.' *PhD thesis*. Faculty of Graduate Studies. University of British Columbia.

Mwamoto B.A.S., Rushoke K, Kahwa F. & Mhlanga W. 1993. 'Preliminary report on the study of the Lake Kariba kapenta fishery for possible adoption into Tanzanian waters.' *Unpublished report* (FAO/UNDP Project URT/90/005). Kariba, Zimbabwe.

Mwera P. 2012. 'Importance of the relationship between government and private sector to support fish exports.' Available from www.rr-africa.oie.int/docspdf/en/2012/AAH/10_Lake_Harvest_P_Mwera.pdf. [Accessed 22 October 2012].

Ndebele-Murisa M.R., Mashonjowa E. & Hill T. 2011. 'The implications of a changing climate on the kapenta fish stocks of Lake Kariba, Zimbabwe', *Transactions of the Royal Society of South Africa* **66(2)**: 105–119.

Nyikahadzoi K. & Raakjaer J. 2009. 'Policy evolution and dynamics of governance at the Lake Kariba kapenta fishery', *Development Southern Africa* **26(4)**: 639-648.

Sanyanga R.A., Lupikisha J. & Muchabaiwa L. 1992. *Lake Kariba 1991. Joint Statistical Report.* Zambia/Zimbabwe SADCC Fisheries Project Report No. 12. Kariba, Zimbabwe.

Sanyanga R.A., Machena C. & Kautsky N. 1995. 'Abundance and distribution of inshore fish in fished and protected areas in Lake Kariba, Zimbabwe', *Hydrobiologia* **306**: 67–68.

Scudder T. 1965. 'The Kariba case: Man-made lakes and reservoir development in Africa', *Bulletin of Atomic Scientists***21(10)**:6–11.

Skelton P.H. 2001. *A Complete Guide to the Freshwater Fishes of Southern Africa.* Struik Publishers. Cape Town, South Africa.

Songore N., Moyo A. & Mugwagwa M. 1999. *Fisheries Statistics.* Lake Kariba Fisheries Research Institute. Project Report No. 95. Kariba, Zimbabwe.

Scudder T. 1967. 'Lake Kariba fishermen: Preliminary report.' *Unpublished manuscript.* Food and Agricultural Organisation, Rome.

Tendaupenyu I.H. 2012. 'A comparative analysis of surplus production and analytical models for assessing kapenta (*Limnothrissa miodon)* stock in Lake Kariba.' *Master's thesis.* Pukyong National University. Korea.

Zengeya T.A. & Marshall B.E. 2008. 'The inshore fish community of Lake Kariba half a century after its creation: What happened to the Upper Zambezi species invasion?' *African Journal of Aquatic Science* **33(1)**: 99–102.

Hippos. Photo: Kathleen Garrigan

5. Cross-commons interactions among other aquatic resources in Lake Kariba

Crispen PHIRI and Lindah MHLANGA

5.1. Introduction

The sustainable exploitation of ecosystems requires an understanding of ecosystem processes and function (Reynolds 1998). A common goal in freshwater ecology, conservation and management is to understand how communities are structured in space and time, and how biotic and abiotic factors affect their distribution and abundance. The main challenge in attaining this goal is that aquatic ecosystems are complex and the unravelling of biotic and abiotic interactions within these systems can be a bewildering task. This chapter examines the available body of knowledge on the aquatic organisms of Lake Kariba, with the exception of fish assemblages. Aspects of the algal (i.e., phytoplankton and periphyton), macrophyte (aquatic vegetation), invertebrates (zooplankton and macroinvertebrates) and vertebrate assemblages of Lake Kariba are discussed. Also considered is the ecological, social and economic importance of these assemblages, as well as the effect of some human activities on aquatic organisms in the lake and their possible impacts on the health and functioning of the ecosystem.

5.2. Phytoplankton

Although Lake Kariba is now over 50 years old there have been few studies on its algal community. There have been even fewer studies done on the algal communities that grow attached to organic and inorganic substrates (i.e. periphyton). The studies by Ramberg (1984 & 1987) and Cronberg (1997) are the only ones that have so far quantitatively assessed the composition of phytoplankton species in Lake Kariba. Ramberg (1984) found no significant differences in phytoplankton composition and biomass in three of the five basins of Lake Kariba, namely basins III, IV and V. Overall, 82 phytoplankton species were recorded in basin V (Sanyati Basin), with taxa richness dominated by the Chlorophyceae (30 species), Cyanophyceae (15), Bacillariophyceae (12) and Dinophyceae (11) (Ramberg 1987). The biomass composition, though, was dominated by the Cyanophyceae, which comprised an overall mean of 60%, followed by Bacillariophyceae (18%) and Dinophyceae (13%). In the rainy season Cyanophyceae made up between 70% and 90% of the total biomass. Three species, *Cylindrospermopsis raciborskii*,

Anabaena sp. and *Lyngbya* sp., made up 94% of the Cyanophyceae biomass. The Bacillariophyceae dominated the phytoplankton biomass composition between May and August. Two species, *Synedra acus* and *Melosira granulata*, made up 71% of Bacillariophyceae biomass (*Ibid*). There are estimated to be about 150 algal taxa, the dominant taxa being green algae, blue-green algae, chrysophytes and diatoms (Cronberg 1997). The most common phytoplankton species in the lake are the blue-green algae *Cylindrospermopsis raciborskii* and two diatoms *Aulacoseira* and *Synedra* (Cronberg 1997).

Moyo (1993), who studied nitrogen fixation and phytoplankton production in Lake Kariba, also noted a successional pattern, with the Cyanophyceae dominating in the hot-wet season (October–April) and the Bacillariophyceae dominating in the cool–dry season (May–September). Moyo (1993) also found that biological nitrogen fixation contributed about 46.4% to the total nitrogen budget of the lake and was correlated with the occurrence of *C. raciborskii*, with levels being highest during the hot–wet season. According to Moyo (1993), Lake Kariba is oligotrophic–mesotrophic with low phytoplankton productivity. The nitrogen/phosphorus ratio is an important determinant of phytoplankton species composition and biomass in Lake Kariba, with phosphorus being the primary limiting nutrient during most of the year and nitrogen co-limiting at other times (*Ibid*).

5.3. Periphyton

Aquatic macrophytes and submerged trees are important substrates for periphyton in Lake Kariba. According to Ramberg *et al.* (1987) the periphyton mainly grow on two submerged macrophytes, *Lagarosiphon* and *Najas*, while *Vallisneria* and some other species seem to be avoided. However, Phiri *et al.* (2007) recorded 40 diatom genera attached to *Vallisneria* from shallow marginal waters of Sanyati Basin. The most abundant genera were *Achnanthidium* and *Gomphonema*, which made up 23.4% and 42.9% of the total diatom count, respectively. Ramberg *et al.* (1987) found that the same algal species occurred on the different macrophytes and largely consisted of blue-green algae, with the most important being heterocyst-forming *Gloeotrichia* sp., followed by a number of *Oscillatoria* and *Lyngbya* species. In an earlier study, Burne (1971) found that the periphyton associated with submerged macrophytes largely consisted of diatoms and desmids. Thus, only a few studies have been done and little is known about periphytic algal assemblages in Lake Kariba.

5.4. Algal community structure and ecosystem function in Lake Kariba

Algae are at the bottom of the food chain in all aquatic ecosystems. They are the main food source for most invertebrates and the larval and juvenile stages of most fish species (Cardozo *et al.* 2007). They are therefore essential to the overall production in aquatic environments. Changes in the quantity (Hill *et al.* 2010) and quality of algae have been shown to affect invertebrate and fish assemblages. According to Ramberg (1987) the variation in the catches of *Limnothrissa miodon*, the basis of the pelagic fishery in Lake Kariba, are likely due to factors that control the dynamics of phytoplankton. Zooplankton, which are the main food item of *L. miodon* (Mandima 2000), have been shown to be unable to consume and fully utilise blue-green algae such as *C. raciborskii* and *Lyngbya* (Padisák 1997). Thus, the dominance of blue-green algae in Lake Kariba may result in some disruption of energy transfer through the food chain from phytoplankton through zooplankton then to *L. miodon*. Together with the comparatively low phytoplankton primary production, this probably limits the productivity of *L. miodon* in Lake Kariba.

The dominance of blue-green algae in the phytoplankton community of Lake Kariba is also of great importance since it has recently been shown that some species produce toxins. In both freshwater and marine environments about 75 algal species are known to produce toxins (Hallegraeff *et al.* 2003) that can bioaccumulate in the food chain to very high concentrations in fish and other aquatic organisms (Cazenave *et al.* 2005, Cardozo *et al.* 2007). The toxins pose a health hazard for humans, domestic animals and wildlife with toxicological effects including neurotoxity, hepatotoxicity, cytotoxicity and dermatotoxicity (Kujbida *et al.* 2006, Cardozo *et al.* 2007). Among the most common freshwater algae toxins is cylindrospermopsin produced by certain strains of *Cylindrospermopsis raciborskii* and other blue-green algal species (Valerio *et al.* 2005). The production of cyanotoxins and its effect on other aquatic organisms in Lake Kariba has not been investigated but the dominance of blue-green algal species such as *C. raciborskii* is of concern and needs further investigation, especially with respect to the productivity of the pelagic fishery. It is now acknowledged that harmful algal blooms (HABs) of cyanobacteria have serious implications for human health and the economy (Jonsson *et al.* 2009). A number of developed countries have initiated monitoring programmes to determine the effects of HABs on aquatic organisms and their bioaccumulation in fish and seafood (Cardozo *et al.* 2007).

Most fish species in Lake Kariba primarily reside in the littoral zone, within which periphyton are probably the main component at the bottom of the food chain. Generally, periphyton plays an important role in primary productivity (Liboriussen & Jeppesen 2009), nutrient dynamics (Vander Zanden & Vadeboncoeur

2002) and food web interactions in aquatic systems (Vadeboncoeur *et al.* 2005). Through the photosynthetic process periphyton producers release oxygen into the aquatic environment and are an important food source for grazing invertebrates and fish (Bronmark 2005). There is still very little that is known about the ecology of phytoplankton and periphyton communities in Lake Kariba and further studies are needed especially considering the great impact these communities probably do have on overall production of the lake and so have a significant socio-economic impact.

5.5. Aquatic macrophytes of Lake Kariba: A historical account

When Kariba's dam wall was closed in 1958, the inundation of large amounts of vegetation, as well as other organic and inorganic matter, resulted in high productivity in the first five to seven years of Lake Kariba's life (Balinsky & James 1960, Harding 1966, Petr 1975). The early, eutrophic years of the lake were characterised by widespread occurrence of a free-floating fern, *Salvinia molesta* (Mitchell 1972, 1973a, b), and high fish yields (Balon 1974). Productivity gradually decreased as nutrients largely from decaying vegetation were lost through outflow (Harding 1964, 1966) and by the 1970s the lake had become oligotrophic (Mitchell 1973a, Coche 1974).

About forty species of vascular aquatic plants have been recorded in Lake Kariba since its creation. In the initial phases of the lake, high nutrient concentrations and rising water levels favoured the growth and establishment of free-floating macrophytes. The most abundant aquatic plants recorded at the time were *Utricularia inflexa* var. *inflexa*, *Pistia stratiotes*, *S. molesta* and *Lemna* sp. (Balinsky & James 1960, Schelpe 1961). An explosive growth of *Utricularia* spp. in the first few months stopped in October 1959, and by 1961 the plant had become uncommon (Mitchell 1969). The water fern, *S. molesta*, an exotic plant native to south America, then became the dominant aquatic macrophyte, with *P. stratiotes* comprising appreciable though lesser numbers (Balinsky & James 1960, Mitchell 1969). *Salvinia* was initially recorded from the Zambezi River system above the Victoria Falls in 1948 (Mitchell 1969). At its maximum occurrence in May 1962, it covered about 21.5% of the lake's surface (Mitchell 1969). As nutrient levels in the lake decreased, the area covered by *Salvinia* also decreased, and fluctuated between about 10% and 15% from the mid-1960s to the early 1970s (Mitchell 1973b). By 1980, it covered only about 1% of the lake's surface (Marshall & Junor 1981). *Salvinia* now occurs in small quantities on Lake Kariba, and the most dominant and widespread, floating aquatic macrophyte is the water hyacinth, *Eichhornia crassipes*. Although it is now a common feature on the lake's surface, the coverage of *E. crassipes* has not been as extensive as that achieved by

Salvinia in the early years of the lake, most probably due to lower nutrient levels (Mhlanga 2001).

Two emergent aquatic plants with floating leaves, *Nymphoides indica*, and *Nymphaea* sp., occurred in pools that became part of the lake as water levels rose, but these plants did not survive long after inundation (McLachlan 1968) and have generally failed to establish in the lake, likely due to lake level fluctuations. Eighteen emergent macrophyte species have been recorded since the lake was created, including *Phragmites mauritianus*, *Typha latifolia*, *Scirpus cubensis*, *Ludwigia stolonifera*, *Polygonum senegalense* and *Panicum repens*. The establishment of these species during the initial stages of the lake's development was adversely affected by the *Salvinia* mats. The mats not only made conditions unsuitable for emergent plants to establish themselves within the water column but, according to Magadza (1970), the drying *Salvinia* mats left behind on the shoreline by falling lake levels inhibited the germination of other plants. The decrease in the coverage of the lake surface by *Salvinia* did not result in establishment of permanent stands of the many emergent macrophytes on the shores of the lake due to annual lake level fluctuations which favour species that are able to survive a near-annual cycle of submergence in water as levels rise followed by drying as levels fall. *Panicum repens*, a grass that grows in water and on emergent soils, is widespread and prominent along the lakeshore, because its subsurface stolons enable it to survive periodic desiccation (Magadza 1970). Other common emergent plant species include *L. stolonifera* and *P. senegalense*.

The widespread occurrence of *Salvinia* mats in the early years of Lake Kariba, prevented light from reaching much of the lower layers of water and used most of the available nutrients, which resulted in low occurrence of submerged aquatic vegetation (Mitchell 1969). *Ceratophyllum demersum* in 1960 (Schelpe 1961), which occurred up to depths of about 10 metres (McLachlan 1968, Donnelly 1968) and *Potamogeton pusillus* in 1964 (McLachlan 1968), which grew in water up to a depth of four metres, were the first submerged plant species recorded in the lake. *Lagarosiphon ilicifolius* was first recorded in reasonably deep sheltered areas in 1966 (Donnelly 1968). *Vallisneria aethiopica* and *Najas pectinata* were first recorded in 1969 and 1971 respectively (Bowmaker 1973). Machena & Kautsky (1988), in a lake-wide survey, recorded seven submerged macrophyte species, *L. ilicifolius*, *N. pectinata*, *C. demersum*, *V. aethiopica*, *Potamogeton octandrus*, *Potamogeton schweinfurthii* and *Potamogeton thunbergii*, with the biomass dominated by *L. ilicifolius* (52%), *N. pectinata* (33%) and *V. aethiopica* (11%). *Lagarosiphon* occurred between 0 and 5 m depth and was present throughout the lake; *Vallisneria* was found to dominate in the western part, basins 1 and 2, largely occurring between 0 and 2 m depth, and was present in small amounts in the other three basins, while *Najas* was largely found in basins 4 and 5, between 0 and 6 m.

Machena & Kautsky (1988) also noted that the peak biomasses of *Lagarosiphon*, *Vallisneria* and *Najas* occurred at 1–2 m, 1 m and 3 m depth respectively.

5.6. Aquatic macrophytes: Ecosystem effects on Lake Kariba

The aquatic macrophytes of Lake Kariba are dominated by submerged macrophytes, although floating macrophytes, *E. crassipes*, *Lemna*, *P. stratiotes* and *S. molesta* are quite common. Earlier work on Lake Kariba showed the dominance of Chironomidae in mud (McLachlan 1968, Bowmaker 1973), macrophytes (McLachlan 1969, Bowmaker 1973) and submerged trees (McLachlan 1970). Bowmaker (1973) also showed the numerical dominance of chironomids on three submerged macrophytes, *Ceratophyllum* (45.9% of total number of organisms), *Potamogeton* (70.1%) and *Lagarosiphon* (37.9%). The early work by McLachlan in the late 1960s, which largely focused on mud and submerged trees, recorded a comparatively small number of macroinvertebrate species, a total of only 25 species, comprising 15 species of Chironomidae, four of Trichoptera, three of Oligochaeta, two of Ephemeroptera and one of Gastropoda. Bowmaker (1973) recorded a total 26 species from *Ceratophyllum*, *Potamogeton* and *Lagarosiphon*, and 98 species from the floating macrophyte, *Salvinia molesta*. In a recent study Phiri (2010) recorded 86 macroinvertebrate taxa on *Lagarosiphon*, which is in sharp contrast to the earlier studies, which found that submerged macrophytes were associated with comparatively low numbers of macroinvertebrate taxa. The relatively low numbers of taxa recorded during the early years of Lake Kariba were probably due to heavy surface coverage by *Salvinia*, which inhibited widespread occurrence of submerged macrophytes (Mitchell 1969) and made physicochemical conditions in the littoral zone unfavourable for the development of many invertebrate organisms (McLachlan 1969). Thus, it seems as if the virtual disappearance of *Salvinia* has resulted in an increase in the macroinvertebrate taxa associated with *Lagarosiphon*, which is now the most widespread and abundant aquatic macrophyte in the lake.

Phiri (2010) compared the epiphytic macroinvertebrates associated with *Lagarosiphon* and *Vallisneria* in the shallow inshore waters of Sanyati Basin. The two macrophytes are structurally or morphologically different. *Lagarosiphon* is morphologically more complex than *Vallisneria*. Generally, there were no significant differences in macroinvertebrate assemblage composition, richness and diversity between the two macrophytes. However, the abundances of most taxa and overall macroinvertebrate abundance were significantly greater on *Lagarosiphon* than on *Vallisneria*. The differences in macroinvertebrate community were attributed to differences in the physical morphology of the two plants. The small but numerous leaves on the stems of *Lagarosiphon* create a more complex habitat, which harbours larger quantities of particulate organic matter as well as providing more attachment surfaces for invertebrates than the long strips of leaves of *Vallisneria*. The surfaces of macrophytes with complex morphologies have been shown not only to trap greater amounts of fine and coarse particulate organic matter (Rooke 1986), but also to have greater amounts of periphyton (Warfe & Barmuta 2006), which are an important food source for many epiphytic invertebrates. Complex morphology also provides better refuge for invertebrates from fish predation (Cheruvelil *et al.* 2002). Thus the greater morphological complexity of *Lagarosiphon* possibly increased food availability and protection from predation for macroinvertebrates.

Studies done in other water systems have shown that both *Lagarosiphon* and *Vallisneria* are important habitats and sources of food for a number of organisms. *Lagarosiphon* spp. offers a substrate for a great variety of invertebrates and are eaten by some water birds (Symoens & Triest 1983). Several species of water birds (Zhang & Lu 1999), and freshwater crabs, herbivorous fish and turtles (Armstrong & Booth 2005) are known to feed on *Vallisneria* spp. In an experimental study, Chifamba (1990) showed that when offered a selection of four submerged plants (*Ceratophyllum demersum*, *L. ilicifolius*, *Najas pectinata* and *V. aethiopica*) juveniles of the red breasted cichlid, *Tilapia rendalli*, primarily fed on *Vallisneria*. According to Feldman (2001) the leaves of *Vallisneria* may support large numbers of invertebrates. Thus, although the ecological impacts of aquatic macrophytes on Lake Kariba have of late received little attention, these communities probably play a vital role in the health, function and productivity of the lake.

5.7. Zooplankton

In Lake Kariba some zooplankton studies have been done on the pelagial assemblage but few studies have been done on the littoral assemblage. Masundire (1989a) recorded 57 zooplankton species from the pelagic zone of Lake Kariba, consisting of 40 species of rotifers, nine cladocerans and eight copepods. In another study done between 1986 and 1988, Masundire (1997) recorded 21 zooplankton species in the pelagial of the five basins of Lake Kariba, with very little differences in crustacean species composition among the basins. The zooplankton of Lake Kariba is dominated by small species or small individuals possibly due to predation by *L. miodon* (Green 1985, Masundire 1989a, b, c, 1991). The assemblage is largely dominated by two species, *Bosmina longirostris* and *Mesocyclops leuckarti* (Ramberg *et al.* 1987, Masundire 1989a, b, c, 1997).

The biomass of the zooplankton assemblage is characterised by two periods of high density, which coincide with periods of high nutrient fluxes (Masundire 1994). The first density peak in January–February, which is associated with the rainy season, is dominated by *Mesocyclops leuckarti* and the second one in June–August, associated with turnover and mixing, is dominated by *Bosmina iongirostris*. Cochrane (1984) showed that the growth and survival of *L. miodon* is primarily dependent on availability of its major food item, the zooplankton. The highest catches of *Limnothrissa* are generally obtained two to three months after the phytoplankton and zooplankton maxima and the decline in catches occurs in November–December following the low plankton biomasses in October–November (Cochrane 1984, Ramberg *et al.* 1987). Thus, in Lake Kariba pelagial zooplankton are vital to the productivity of *Limnothrissa*, which in turn forms the base of an important commercial fishery. According to Ramberg *et al.* (1987) the pelagic system of Lake Kariba has a structurally simple, linearly arranged food chain, consisting of phytoplankton, zooplankton, *Limnothrissa* and *Hydrocynus vittatus* (tigerfish).

5.8. Littoral zone macroinvertebrates

In Lake Kariba, the early studies that were done on littoral macroinvertebrates largely focused on assemblages within the mud and submerged trees. The macroinvertebrate assemblages in mud and macrophytes were largely dominated by chironomids (McLachlan 1968, 1969, 1970, Bowmaker 1973). McLachlan, who focused on mud and submerged trees, recorded a total of 25 species, while Bowmaker (1973) recorded 26 species from three submerged macrophytes species, that is, *Ceratophyllum*, *Potamogeton* and *Lagarosiphon*. Bowmaker (1973) though, collected 98 species from the floating macrophyte, *Salvinia molesta*, which was then the most dominant aquatic macrophyte in Lake Kariba. In sharp contrast to the earlier studies, Phiri (2010) collected a greater number of macroinvertebrate taxa – 86 – on *Lagarosiphon*, the most dominant macrophyte in Lake Kariba. The relatively low numbers of taxa collected from submerged macrophytes during the early years of Lake Kariba were probably due to heavy surface coverage by *Salvinia*, which inhibited widespread occurrence of submerged macrophytes (Mitchell 1969) and made physicochemical conditions in the littoral zone unfavourable for the development of many invertebrate organisms (Bowmaker 1968, McLachlan 1969).

In a lake-wide survey on benthic vegetation and fauna of Lake Kariba, Machena & Kautsky (1988) found that the benthic fauna biomass was dominated by three mussels *Caelatura mossambicensis*, *Corbicula africa* and *Mutela dubia*, and the snails *Melanoides tuberculata*, *Cleopatra* spp. and *Bellamya capillata*. The molluscs made up nearly the entire biomass of the benthic animals (prosobranchs 4.1% and bivalves 95.8%) (Machena & Kautsky 1988). The dominance of molluscs though was probably due to the fact that few fish species in Lake Kariba prey on them. The Australian red claw crayfish, *Cherax quadricarinatus* (von Martens), a decapod crustacean was introduced into Lake Kariba in 2009/2010 and is rapidly spreading in the Sanyati Basin. The red claw crayfish is endemic to freshwater river systems and lakes of northern Australia and parts of Papua New Guinea (Pavasovic 2008). Over the next few years, it will likely become one of the dominant macroinvertebrates in Lake Kariba.

5.9. Invertebrate assemblages and ecosystem function processes in Lake Kariba

Although it is widely acknowledged that the littoral invertebrate fauna in lakes and reservoirs are an important component of food web dynamics and ecosystem function, few studies have been conducted on the utilisation of invertebrate fauna by fish in Lake Kariba. Sanyanga (1998) assessed the food composition and selectivity of the catfish *Synodontis zambezensis* in the lake, and found that although it fed on a range of food items, it was primarily molluscivorous, actively selecting the pulmonate *Lymnaea natalensis*. In another study, Moyo & Fernando (1999) identified a size-related shift in the diet of the cichlid, *Sargochromis codringtonii*, with juveniles feeding primarily on zooplankton and chironomid larvae, subadults on soft-shelled pulmonates and adults on the prosobranchs, *Melanoides tuberculata* and *Bellamya capillata*.

Forty-five fish species have been recorded from Lake Kariba (Marshall 2006) and all are found within the littoral zone at some stage in their life cycle, usually among the submerged macrophytes. Most African freshwater fishes depend on invertebrates as their link to the photosynthetic food base and only a few feed directly on living plant matter or detritus (Bowen 1988). All of the fish species in Lake Kariba are also believed to utilise the invertebrate fauna as a primary food source at some stage during their life cycle. The inshore artisanal fishery of Lake Kariba is based on a range of species, which include cichlids (mainly *Sargochromis codringtonii*, *Tilapia rendalli*, *Tilapia sparrmanii* and *Oreochromis niloticus*), the tigerfish, *Hydrocynus vittatus*, and momyrids. Apart from *H. vittatus*, which uses both littoral and pelagic zones, all the other species are generally confined to the littoral zone and probably use littoral macroinvertebrates as a key food source.

Freshwater crayfish are an economically and ecologically important crustacean group (Austin 1998). Therefore, the introduction and spread of *C. quadricaritanus* will have important ecological as well as economic consequences for Lake Kariba. The introduction of crayfish into new environments may have adverse impacts on indigenous species assemblages through predation on and competition with indigenous species (Vorburger & Ribi 1999), the introduction of diseases (Horwitz 1990) and the alteration of food webs, leading to changes in nutrient and energy flows (Nyström *et al.* 1999). Red claw crayfish has been shown to disrupt the feeding and spawning behaviour of tilapia (Brummett & Alon 1994), so it may negatively affect the productivity of tilapia and other cichlid-based fisheries in African water bodies (de Moor 2002). The inshore fishery of Lake Kariba, which supports many poor communities in Zambia and Zimbabwe, is based on a variety of fish species largely dominated by cichlids. The introduction of *C. quadricarinatus* may therefore have a negative impact on the livelihoods of communities dependent on the fishery. On the other hand, *C. quadricarinatus* has a fast growth rate, is tolerant of a wide range of water temperatures and crowded conditions, and can achieve high (600 g) maximum weights (Webster*et al.* 2004). Over the last few decades, it has become an important aquaculture species and is now cultured in many countries (Muzinic *et al.* 2004). Consequently, it has a high commercial potential, for both aquaculture and wild stocks harvesting, and may develop into another important livelihood resource for communities around Lake Kariba.

The littoral invertebrate assemblage of Lake Kariba has a number of species that are of great importance with respect to human health. *Bulinus globosus* and *Biomphalaria pfeifferi*, two snail vectors for bilharzias, are common in Lake Kariba. Preliminary work has shown that bilharzia is quite common on both the Zambian (Chimbari *et al.* 2003) and Zimbabwean shores of Lake Kariba (Chimbari & Chirundu 2003, Chimbari *et al.* 2003). A wide range of species of *Bulinus* and *Biomphalaria* have also been reported to act as intermediate hosts for amphistomes that affect wildlife and livestock in Africa (Chingwena *et al.* 2001). Chingwena *et al.* (2002) showed that *B. globosus*, *B. pfeifferi* and *Melanoides tuberculata* can serve as snail hosts for *Calicophoron microbothrium*, a disease-causing fluke in ruminants. It appears that the littoral invertebrate assemblage of Lake Kariba is not only a significant part of the food web dynamics of the lake but some of its taxa are important intermediaries for disease-causing agents in humans, wildlife and livestock.

5.10. Vertebrates

Apart from fish, the main vertebrate organisms in Lake Kariba are the Nile crocodile, *Crocodylus niloticus*, the hippopotamus, *Hippopotamus amphibious*, and a variety of water birds.

Crocodilians exist throughout the tropics and are considered 'keystone' species that maintain ecosystem structure and function (Bourquin 2007) by selectively predating on fish species (Pooley 1982), recycling nutrients and maintaining wet refugia in droughts (Thorbjarnarson 1992). Many crocodilian species worldwide are exploited for their skins. The crocodile skin trade generates an international income of about US$ 500 million annually (Ross 1998). In Zimbabwe, farming of the Nile crocodile is an important and lucrative activity, which provides employment, meat for human consumption and skins for the leather industry. Crocodile farming depends on regular harvesting of eggs or live animals from the wild for incubation or breeding in a controlled environment. The crocodile hide is the most valuable product, most of which is exported. On Lake Kariba there are now seven farms, which produce more than 90% of the crocodile skins exported from Zimbabwe. Games & Moreau (1997) assessed the impact of crocodiles on fish populations in Lake Kariba. They established that there is no major competition between crocodiles and fishermen for the fish resources of Lake Kariba. The importance of fish in a crocodile's diet increases while crocodiles are between 1.4 and 2.6 m long, when fish account for an estimated 98% of their diet, but this declines to around 33% in adult crocodiles (Games & Moreau 1997).

The hippopotamus is a herbivore that lives in water by day and emerges to feed on grass by night. Like African elephants (*Loxodonta africana*), hippopotami are megaherbivores that influence natural systems at large temporal and spatial scales, creating a mosaic of habitat for smaller organisms and altering habitat structure (Owen-Smith 1988). Hippopotami have strong temporal and spatial constraints on their foraging behaviour. They are temporally constrained in that they forage primarily at night (Lewison & Carter 2004) and are spatially constrained by their aquatic habitat requirements; a foraging bout typically begins at a water source and ends at the same or a nearby water source (Field 1970). The foraging activities and other activities of hippos probably have an impact on nutrient cycling in Lake Kariba, especially in the littoral zone. Although hippos are common and abundant on Lake Kariba no studies have been done on them and little is known about how they affect ecosystem processes in and around the lake.

About 50 aquatic bird species have been recorded on Lake Kariba. The only studies on aquatic birds on Lake Kariba are by Hustler (1991, 1997), who studied the ecology and impact of fish-eating birds on the commercial fishery of Lake Kariba. He found that the abundance of most birds had a distinctly seasonal variation and the most numerous fish-eating birds were the Reed cormorant (*Phalacrocorax africanus*) and the Darter (*Anhinga melanogaster*). Hustler (1991,1997) further estimated the amount of fish eaten by birds in Lake Kariba per year to be about 300 tons. However, most of the fish species eaten by the birds were not commercially exploited and equated to only about 1.3% of the total ecological fish production of the inshore fish community (about 16% of the commercial inshore fisheries catch); therefore the birds had an insignificant impact on the fish community and inshore fisheries of Lake Kariba.

Generally, very little is known about water birds on Lake Kariba, although over the last few decades there has been a realisation that birds associated with aquatic systems are important in the spread of some human diseases, such as influenza and microsporidiosis. Thus, studies on wild aquatic birds, which have largely been ignored on the lake, are essential since wild birds may have some bearing on public health.

5.11. Anthropogenic impacts on aquatic organisms in Lake Kariba

Anthropogenic activities that are likely to have significant impact on the physicochemical and biological attributes of Lake Kariba over the next few decades include agriculture, aquaculture, water abstraction, mining and global climate change. Land clearing for agriculture in the catchment areas of Lake Kariba is likely to increase over the next few decades, resulting in increased loads of nutrients and sediments into Lake Kariba. Globally, phosphorus and nitrogen fertiliser use have increased by two- and seven-fold respectively during the last 40 years (Tilman *et al.* 2001). With this in mind, the possibility of eutrophication in some portions of Lake Kariba is likely to increase, with algal blooms becoming more frequent as more land within its catchment areas is converted to agricultural use.

High nutrient levels in aquatic environments tend to favour the blue-green algae (or cyanobacteria), especially harmful toxic genera such as *Anabaena*, *Aphanizomenon*, *Nodularia*, *Microcystis*, *Cylindrospermopsis* and *Oscillatoria*, which are adept at exploiting nutrient-enriched conditions. The algal blooms can cause deoxygenation of bottom waters (hypoxia and anoxia) of lakes and reservoirs and are generally associated with high levels of toxins, fish kills and food web alterations. High levels of inorganic nutrients also have adverse effects on less tolerant organisms. Sediments can greatly affect the composition, structure and dynamics of organisms, and increased sediment loads as a result of anthropogenic activities can be a threat to the diversity and functioning of aquatic ecosystems.

The existing and potential contribution of aquaculture to economic growth and food security has received increasing recognition in recent years (FAO 2002, 2004). Although in comparison to the rest of the world, aquaculture production in Africa is still insignificant and accounted for a paltry 0.9% of total global production in 2000 (FAO 2003), aquaculture production has generally been on an upward trend over the last three decades. On Lake Kariba, plans are underway to increase aquaculture production and it is envisaged that in the near future, demand for aquaculture production units will increase. Currently, annual aquaculture production of *O. niloticus* does not exceed 10 000 tons but production may be as high as 30 000 tons annually over the next decade. This will result in increased aquaculture impacts on the physicochemical and biological environment in the lake through the release of increased loads of aquaculture effluent.

On a global scale there has been over the last two decades an increase in water use from domestic, industrial and agricultural production so as to meet the demands of a growing population and to enhance human wellbeing (WWAP 2006). This has generally resulted in major adverse impacts on aquatic ecosystems. By 2025 water withdrawals are predicted to increase by 50% in developing countries (WWAP 2006), which will obviously drastically increase pressures on freshwater ecosystems. There are plans for possible large-scale abstraction of water from the Zambezi River for industrial, domestic and agricultural use in a number of countries in the region, which will have an impact on aquatic biodiversity in the Zambezi River and Lake Kariba.

Both Zambia and Zimbabwe have a number of mining activities within the catchment areas of Lake Kariba and exploration for more mineral deposits is ongoing in both countries. Pollution of Lake Kariba from mining activities will potentially increase in the near future.

Climate change is predicted to increase air temperature and extreme weather events as well as alter spatial patterns in precipitation and runoff (Milly *et al.* 2005). The Earth's mean surface temperature is projected to warm between 1.4 and 5.8^{O}C by the end of the 21st century, with land areas warming more than oceans, and the high latitudes warming more than the tropics (Gitay *et al.* 2002). It has been predicted that at mid-latitudes and in the dry tropics there will be a decrease of between 10 and 30% of average river runoff by 2050 (Kundzewicz *et al.* 2008). On the Zambezi River, the mean monthly flow will be reduced by an estimated 36% (Harrison & Whittington 2002), which will have an impact on water levels in Lake Kariba, thus affecting the biological assemblages in the lake.

Temperature has a profound impact on a variety of biological processes from the cellular to the organismal level of organisation (Rome *et al.* 1992). In general, temperature increases the metabolic rates of ectotherms (Kruhoffer *et al.* 1987) and directly affects the growth and development of aquatic organisms (Moore & Townsend 1998). The higher water temperatures, together with changes in extremes of floods and droughts, are also projected to affect water quality and exacerbate many forms of water pollution (Bates *et al.* 2008). Thus, global warming will possibly have adverse impacts on the biodiversity of aquatic organisms in Lake Kariba. It is likely that the production will decrease in plankton-eating pelagic fisheries in southern Africa (Gitay *et al.* 2002), probably due to the effect of climate change on algal communities.

5.12. Conservation and management of Lake Kariba freshwater biological resources

In Zambia, the conservation and management of natural resources falls under the Ministry of Land, Natural Resources and Environmental Protection (MLNREP). Within the MLNREP, the Environment and Natural Resources Management Department (ENRMD) is responsible for overall policy formulation on environment, natural resources and pollution control, and also monitors and evaluates the operation of the agencies that have been created to implement policies on environment and natural resources management. These agencies include the Zambia Wildlife Authority (ZAWA) and Environmental Council of Zambia (ECZ). ZAWA is governed by the Zambia Wildlife Act 12 of 1998, and its primary objectives include improving the quality of life of communities in wildlife estates, maintaining sustainable biodiversity in national parks and game management areas, and reversing the decline in wildlife resources. The ECZ is mandated to protect Zambia's environment and control pollution levels so as to provide for the health and welfare of the public and the environment, through the Environmental Protection and Pollution Control Act of 1990. Its core functions include: enforcing regulations related to water, air and noise pollution, pesticides and toxic substances, waste management and natural resources management; conducting studies and making recommendations on standards related to improvement and maintenance of sound ecological systems; and monitoring trends in the use of natural resources and their impact on the environment. The conservation and management of freshwater orgasnism such as the crocodile and hippopotamus on the Zambian side of Lake Kariba is under ZAWA, whilst the Department of Fisheries (DoF), which is under the Ministry of Agriculture and Cooperatives, implements fisheries management and conservation policies.

In Zimbabwe the Environmental Management Act (Chapter 20:27), administered by the Ministry of Environment and Natural Resources Management (MENRM), deals with the sustainable management of natural resources and protection of the environment. The implementation agency of the Act is the Environmental Management Agency (EMA). The agency's mandate includes: formulating quality standards on air, water, soil, noise, vibration, radiation and waste management; monitoring and regulating the discharge or emission of pollutants or hazardous substances into the environment; monitoring and regulating the control of invasive alien species; and regulating and monitoring the management and utilisation of ecologically fragile ecosystems. In Zimbabwe, the conservation and management of freshwater biological resources on Lake Kariba including fisheries, falls under the Parks and Wildlife Management Act (Chapter 20:14), which is administered by the MENRM through the Parks and Wild Life Management Authority (PWLMA). As can be seen, there are areas of overlap between Environmental Management Act and the Parks and Wildlife Management Act. However, in cases where inconsistencies exist between the two, the Environmental Management Act takes precedence.

Zambia and Zimbabwe are members of the 14-member Southern African Development Community (SADC). The SADC Treaty encourages member countries to co-operate in all areas so as to foster regional development and integration. Both countries are therefore signatories to the SADC Protocol on Fisheries, which defines fish as any aquatic plant and animal, and aims to promote responsible and sustainable use of the region's living aquatic resources and aquatic ecosystems. The two countries are also party to the SADC Protocol on Shared Watercourse Systems, which seeks sustainable utilisation of shared watercourse systems. There have also signed bilateral agreements with respect to the Zambezi River and Lake

Kariba, the Zambezi River Authority Act (Chapter 20:23) and an addendum to the Protocol on Economic and Technical Co-operation between the two countries. The Zambezi River Act led to the formation of the Zambezi River Authority, whose functions include the operation, monitoring and maintenance of the dam, and the collection and processing of hydrological and environmental data from the river and dam for the better performance of its functions and any other purpose beneficial to the two countries. The first addendum to the Protocol on Economic and Technical Co-operation between Zambia and Zimbabwe deals with the management and development of fisheries on Lake Kariba and transboundary waters of the Zambezi River, and led to the establishment of the Joint Fisheries Management Committee. Although the main function of the Joint Fisheries Management Committee is to ensure management, conservation and regulation of the exploitation of the fisheries resources on Lake Kariba and the Zambezi River, it is also tasked with monitoring the aquatic environment, controlling the introduction of exotic species, and undertaking research and exchange of biological data and statistical information.

In addition to the already mentioned regional and bilateral agreements, Lake Kariba now falls within Kavango-Zambezi Transfrontier Conservation Area (KAZA TFCA), which was established 2010 in recognition of the area's rich and diverse natural resources. The KAZA TFCA consists of parts of Angola, Botswana, Namibia, Zambia and Zimbabwe, and contains a number of protected conservation areas under varied management regimes, with largely poor rural communities living in and around these areas. It is therefore is a conservation and development initiative with its primary aims to improve the management and conservation of natural resources as well as enhancing their sustainable utilisation for the development of the region.

It can be argued that there are adequate national and regional legislative and institutional frameworks for conservation and management of aquatic biological resources in Lake Kariba. At the same time, the need for comprehensive conservation management of freshwater resources grows ever more urgent, an approach which involves the wider public and all stakeholders to ensure environmental benefits and protect biodiversity for future generations. Unfortunately, the planning and enacting of conservation and management programmes for freshwater resources in southern Africa is still largely dominated by government agencies with low participation of the wider public and, in many remote areas, little involvement of local communities. This trend has tended to alienate local communities, resulting in reduced effectiveness of the conservation and management programmes. Furthermore, initiatives and institutions involved in natural resource management and conservation suffer from limited and unsustainable funding, and research is inadequate, with few development initiatives. The conservation and management of freshwater resources on Lake Kariba generally mirrors these regional trends in resource conservation and management.

In this chapter we have illustrated that there is a paucity of information on the distributions, population status and trends, habitats and ecology of most aquatic organisms in Lake Kariba. Thus, conservation and management plans on the lake are currently based on a severely limited information base. Coupled with inadequately funded natural resources management agencies and low public awareness of conservation issues, the effectiveness of conservation and management plans may be quite limited, especially with the continued increase in human population and demand for natural resources. If conservation and management programmes are to be successful there is an immediate need to carry out research on the basic ecology of species, including habitat preferences and environmental tolerances, as well as historical and contemporary evolutionary processes (Cowx & Collares-Pereira 2002).

5.13. Summary and suggestions for future research on Lake Kariba

Freshwater ecosystems have over the last century been heavily affected by intense human exploitation, resulting in habitat loss and degradation (Dudgeon *et al.* 2006), and as a result, many aquatic species have become extinct or are highly endangered. According to the IUCN (2010) 21% of freshwater species in continental Africa are threatened with extinction, putting the livelihoods of millions of people at risk. The biggest threats come from agriculture, water abstraction, dams and invasive alien species. On Lake Kariba, there a serious lack of information on distributions, population status and trends, habitats and ecology of plankton, macrophytes, macroinvertebrates and aquatic vertebrates such as the Nile crocodile, hippopotamus and birds. In order to enact effective management and conservation plans for freshwater resources on Lake Kariba it will be essential to develop capacity in the generation of information on the ecology and use of aquatic organisms in the lake.

References

Armstrong G. & Booth D.T. 2005. 'Dietary ecology of the Australian freshwater turtle (*Elseya* sp.: Chelonia: Chelidae) in the Burnett River, Queensland', *Wildlife Research* **32**: 349–353.

Austin C.M. 1998. 'Comparison of clutch and brood size in the red claw, *Cherax quadricarinatus* (von Martens) and the yabby, *C. destructor* Clark (Decapoda: Parastacidae)', *Aquaculture* **167**: 135–145.

Balinsky B.I. & James G.V. 1960. 'Explosive reproduction of organisms in the Kariba Lake', *South African Journal of Science* **56**: 101–104.

Balon E.K. 1974. 'Fish production of a tropical ecosystem.' In: Balon E.K. & Coche A.G. (eds) *Lake Kariba: A Man-made Tropical Ecosystem in Central Africa*. Monographiae Biologicae 24, Dr. W. Junk Publishers, The Hague. pp 249–573.

Bates B.C., Kundzewicz Z.W., Wu S. & Palutikof J.P. (eds) 2008. *Climate Change and Water*. Technical Paper of the Intergovernmental Panel on Climate Change, IPCC Secretariat, Geneva.

Bourquin S.L. 2007. 'The populations ecology of the Nile crocodile (*Crocodylus niloticus*) in the panhandle regions of the Okavango Delta, Botswana.' *PhD thesis*. Department of Conservation Ecology and Entomology, Faculty of Agrisciences, University of Stellenbosch.

Bowen S.H. 1988. 'Detritivory and herbivory.' In: Leveque C., Bruton M.N. & Ssentongo G.W. (eds) *Biology and Ecology of African Freshwater Fishes*. ORSTROM, Paris. pp. 243–247.

Bowmaker A.P. 1968. 'Preliminary observations on some aspects of the biology of Sinamwenda estuary, Lake Kariba', *Proceedings & Transactions of the Rhodesia Scientific Association* **53**: 3–8.

Bowmaker A.P. 1973. 'A hydrobiological study of the Mwenda River and its mouth, Lake Kariba.' *PhD thesis*. University of Witwatersrand, Johannesburg.

Bronmark A.L. 2005. *The Biology of Lakes and Ponds*. Oxford University Press, Oxford.

Brummett R.E. & Alon N.C. 1994. 'Polyculture of Nile tilapia (*Oreochromis niloticus*) and Australian red claw crayfish (*Cherax quadricarinatus*) in earthern ponds', *Aquculture* **122**: 47–54.

Burne R.H. 1971. *A Preliminary Comparative Study of Epiphytes Associated with: Najas pectinata; Potamogeton schweinfurtii; Potamogeton pusillus; Lagarosiphon ilicifolius; Ceratophyllum demersum in Basin 5 of Lake Kariba, Summer 1970-71*. Mimeographed report, Lake Kariba Fisheries Research Institute, Kariba, Zimbabwe.

Cardozo K.H.M., Guaratini T., Barros M.P., Falcão V.R., Tonon A.P., Lopes N.P., Campos S., Torres M.A., Souza A.O., Colepicolo P., & Pinto E. 2007. 'Metabolites from algae with economical impact', *Comparative Biochemistry and Physiology* **146**: 60–78.

Cazenave J., Wunderlin D.A., Bistoni M.D.L., Ame M.V., Krause E., Pflugmacher S. & Wiegand C. 2005. 'Uptake, tissue distribution and accumulation of microcystin-RR in *Corydoras paleatus*, *Jenynsia multidentata* and *Odontesthes bonariensis*—a field and laboratory study', *Aquatic Toxicology* **75**: 178–190.

Cheruvelil K.S., Soranno P.A., Madsen J.D. & Roberson M.J. 2002. 'Plant architecture and epiphytic macroinvertebrate communities: The role of an exotic dissected macrophyte', *Journal of the North American Benthological Society* **21**: 261–277.

Chifamba P.C. 1990. 'Preference of *Tilapia rendalli* (Boulenger) for some species of aquatic plants', *Journal of Fish Biology***36**: 701–705.

Chimbari M.J. & Chirundu D. 2003. 'Prevalence and intensity of the schistosomiasis situation along the Zimbabwean urban and peri-urban shoreline of Lake Kariba', *Central African Journal of Medicine* **49**: 8–12.

Chimbari M.J., Dhlomo E., Mwadiwa E. & Mubila L. 2003. 'Transmission of schistosomiasis in Kariba, Zimbabwe, and a cross-sectional comparison of schistosomiasis prevalences and intensities in the town with those in Siavonga in Zambia', *Annals of Tropical Medicine and Parasitology***97**: 605–616.

Chingwena G., Mukaratirwa S., Kristensen T.K. & Chimbari M. 2001. 'Larval trematodes infecting freshwater gastropods from the highveld and lowveld areas of Zimbabwe.' In: Madsen H., Appleton C.C. & Chimbari M. (eds) *Proceedings of Workshop on Medical Malacology in Africa*. Danish Bilharziasis Laboratory. Copenhagen, Denmark.

Chingwena G., Mukaratirwa S., Kristensen T.K. & Chimbari M. 2002. 'Susceptibility of freshwater snails to the amphistome *Calicophoron microbothrium* and the influence of the species on susceptibility of *Bulinus tropicus* to *Schistosoma haematobium* and *Schistosoma mattheei* infections', *Journal of Parasitology* **88**: 880–883.

Coche A.G. 1974. 'Limnological study of a tropical reservoir.' In: Balon E.K. & Coche A.G. (eds) *Lake Kariba: A Tropical Man-made Ecosystem in Central Africa*. Monographiae Biologicae 24, Dr. W. Junk Publishers, The Hague. pp 1–247.

Cochrane K.L. 1984. 'The influence of food availability, breeding seasons and growth rate on commercial catches of *Limnothrissa miodon* (Boulenger) in Lake Kariba', *Journal of Fish Biology* **24**: 623–635.

Cowx I.G. & Collares-Pereira M.J. 2002. 'Freshwater fish conservation: Options for the future.' In: Collares-Pereira M.J., Cowx I.G. & Coelho M.M. (eds) *Conservation of Freshwater Fishes: Options for the Future*. Fishing News Books, Blackwell Science. Oxford. pp 443–452.

Cronberg G. 1997. 'Phytoplankton in Lake Kariba 1986-1990.' In: Moreau J. (ed) *Advances in the Ecology of Lake Kariba*. University of Zimbabwe Publications, Harare.

De Moor I. 2002. 'Potential impacts of alien freshwater crayfish in South Africa', *African Journal of Aquatic Science* **27**: 125–139.

Donnelly B.G. 1968. 'Preliminary survey of the tilapia nurseries in Kariba during 1967', *Hydrobiologia* **34**: 195–206.

Dudgeon D., Arthington A.H., Gessner M.O., Kawabata Z.I, Knowler D.J., Lévêque C., Naiman R.J., Prieur-Richard A.H., Soto D., Stiassny M.L.J. & Sullivan C.A. 2006. 'Freshwater biodiversity: importance, threats, status and conservation challenges', *Biological Reviews* **81**: 163–182.

Food and Agricultural Organisation (FAO) 2002. *The State of World Fisheries and Aquaculture (SOFIA 2002)*. FAO. Rome.

FAO 2003. Fisheries statistics. http://www.fao.org

FAO 2004. *The State of World Fisheries and Aquaculture (SOFIA 2004)*. FAO. Rome.

Feldman R.S. 2001. 'Taxonomic and size structures of phytophilous macroinvertebrate communities in *Vallisneria* and *Trapa* beds of the Hudson River, New York', *Hydrobiologia* **452**: 233–245.

Field C.R. 1970. 'A study of the feeding habits of the hippopotamus in the Queen Elizabeth National Park, Uganda, with some management implications', *African Zoology* **5**: 71–86.

Games I. & Moreau J. 1997. 'The feeding ecology of two Nile crocodile population in the Zambezi Valley.' In: Moreau J. (ed)*Advances in the Ecology of Lake Kariba*. University of Zimbabwe Publications, Harare.

Gitay H., Suárez A., Watson R.T. & Dokken D.J. 2002. *Climate Change and Biodiversity*. Intergovernmental Panel on Climate Change, Technical Paper V. Geneva, Switzerland.

Green J. 1985. 'Horizontal distribution of zooplankton in Lake Kariba', *Journal of Zoology* (London)**206**: 225–239.

Hallegraeff G.M., Anderson D.M. & Cembella A.D. 2003. *Harmful Algal Blooms. A*

Global Review. Manual on Harmful Marine Microalgae. IOC Manuals and Guides Vol. 33. UNESCO. Paris.

Harding D. 1964. 'Hydrology and fisheries in Lake Kariba', *Verhandlungen der Internationale Vereiningung für Limnologie* **15**: 139–149.

Harding D. 1966. 'Lake Kariba. The hydrology and development of fisheries.' In: McConnell R.H. (ed) *Man-made Lakes.* Symposia of the Institute of Biology No. 15. Academic Press, London. pp 7–20.

Harrison G.P. & Whittington H.W. 2002. 'Susceptibility of the Batoka Gorge hydroelectric scheme to climate change', *Journal of Hydrology* **264**: 230–241.

Hill W.R., Ryon M.G., Smith J.G., Adams S.H. & Boston H.L. 2010. 'The role of periphyton in mediating the effects of pollution in a stream ecosystem', *Environmental Management* **45**: 563–576.

Horwitz P. 1990. 'The translocation of freshwater crayfish in Australia: Potential impact, the need for control and global relevance', *Biological Conservation* **54**: 291–305.

Hustler K. 1991. 'The ecology of fish-eating birds on Lake Kariba with special reference to the diving pelecaniformes.' *PhD thesis.* Department of Biological Sciences, University of Zimbabwe, Harare.

Hustler K. 1997. 'The ecology of fish eating birds and their impact on the inshore fisheries of Lake Kariba.' In: Moreau J (ed) *Advances in the Ecology of Lake Kariba.* University of Zimbabwe Publications. pp 196–218.

IUCN (2010) African freshwater species threatened livelihoods at stake. Cambridge, UK. http://www.iucnredlist.org/news/african-freshwater-species-threatened-livelihoods-at-stake

Jonsson P.R., Pavia H. & Toth G. 2009. Formation of harmful algal blooms cannot be explained by allelopathic interactions. *Proceedings of the National Academeny of Sciences* **106 (27)**: 11177–11182.

Kruhoffer M., Glass M.L., Abe A.S. & Johansen K. 1987. 'Control of breathing in an amphibian *Bufo paracnemis*: effects of temperature and hypoxia', *Respiratory Physiology* **69**: 267–275.

Kujbida P., Hatanaka E., Campa A., Colepicolo P. & Pinto E., 2006. 'Effects of microcystins on human polymorphonuclear leukocytes', *Biochemical Biophysical Reseach Communications***341**: 273–277.

Kundzewicz Z.W., Mata L.J., Arnell N.W., Döll P., Jimenez B., Miller K., Oki T., Sen Z. & Shiklomanov I. 2008. 'The implications of projected climate change for freshwater resources and their management', *Hydrological Sciences* **53**: 3–10.

Lewison R.L. & Carter J. 2004. 'Exploring behaviour of an unusual megaherbivore: A spatially explicit foraging model of the hippopotamus', *Ecological Modelling* **171**: 127–138.

Liboriussen L. & Jeppesen E. 2009. 'Periphyton biomass, potential production and respiration in a shallow lake during winter and spring', *Hydrobiologia***632**: 201–210.

Machena C. & Kautsky N. 1988. 'A quantitative diving survey of benthic vegetation and fauna in Lake Kariba – a tropical man-made lake', *Freshwater Biology* **19**: 1–14.

Magadza C.H.D. 1970. 'A preliminary survey of the vegetation of the shore of Lake Kariba', *Kirkia* **7**: 253–267.

Mandima J.J. 2000. 'Spatial and temporal variations in the food of the sardine *Lim-*

nothrissa miodon (Boulenger, 1906) in Lake Kariba, Zimbabwe', *Fisheries Research* **48**: 197–203.

Marshall B.E. & Junor F.J.R. 1981. 'The decline of *Salvinia molesta* on Lake Kariba', *Hydrobiologia* **83**: 477–484.

Marshall B.E. 2006. 'A checklist of the fishes of Lake Kariba (Zimbabwe–Zambia)', *Arnoldia Zimbabwe* **10**: 257–274.

Masundire H. 1989a. 'Zooplankton composition and abundance in relation to water transparency and predation in Lake Kariba, Zimbabwe', *Ergebnisse der Limnologie* **33**: 513–520.

Masundire H. 1989b. 'Zooplankton population dynamics in the Sanyati Basin, Lake Kariba, Zimbabwe', *Ergebnisse der Limnologie***33**: 469–473.

Masundire H. 1989c. 'Bionomics and production of zooplankton in relation to *Limnothrissa miodon* Boulenger in Lake Kariba, Zimbabwe.' In: Magadza C.H.D. (ed) *Ecology of Lake Kariba*. ULKRS Bulletin 1/90. Zimbabwe. pp 36–49.

Masundire H. 1991. 'Seasonal variation in size of *Bosmina longirostris* O. F. Muller in tropical Lake Kariba, Zimbabwe', *Internationale Vereinigung fuer Theoretische und Angewandte Limnologie* **24**: 1455–1459.

Masundire H. 1994. 'Seasonal trends in zooplankton densities in Sanyati Basin: multivariate analysis', *Hydrobiologia* **272**: 211–230.

Masundire H. 1997. 'Spatial and temporal variations in the composition and density of crustacean plankton in the five basins of Lake Kariba, Zambia–Zimbabwe', *Journal of Plankton Research* **19**: 43–62.

McLachlan A.J. 1968. 'A study of the bottom fauna of Lake Kariba, Rhodesia.' *PhD thesis*. University of London. U.K.

McLachlan A.J. 1969. 'The effect of aquatic macrophytes on the variety and abundance of benthic fauna in a newly created lake in the tropics (Lake Kariba)', *Archiv für Hydrobiologie***66**: 212–231.

McLachlan A.J. 1970. 'Submerged tress as a substrate for benthic fauna in the recently created Lake Kariba (Central Africa)', *Journal of Applied Ecology* **7**: 253–266.

Mhlanga L. 2001. 'Water quality of the eastern basin of Lake Kariba, Zimbabwe in relation to the encroachment of *Eichhornia crassipes*', *Verhandlungen der Internationale Vereiningung für Limnologie* **27**: 1–4.

Milly P.C.D., Dunne K.A. & Vecchia A.V. 2005. 'Global pattern of trends in stream flow and water availability in a changing climate', *Nature* **438**: 347–350.

Mitchell D.S. 1969. 'The ecology of vascular hydrophytes on Lake Kariba', *Hydrobiologia* **34**: 448–464.

Mitchell D.S. 1972. 'The Kariba weed: *Salvinia molesta*', *British Fern Gazette* **10**: 251–252.

Mitchell D.S. 1973a. 'Supply of plant nutrient chemicals in Lake Kariba.' In: Ackermann W. C., White G.F. & Worthington E.B. (eds) *Man-made Lakes: Their Problems and Environmental Effects*. Geophysical Monograph Series Vol. 17. American Geophysical Union. Washington, D.C. pp 165–169.

Mitchell D.S. 1973b. 'Aquatic weeds in man-made lakes.' In: Ackermann W.C., White G.F. & Worthington E.B. (eds) *Man-made Lakes: Their Problems and Environmental Effects*. Geophysical Monograph Series Vol. 17. American Geophysical Union. Washington, D.C. pp 606–611.

Moore M.K. & Townsend V.R. 1998. 'The interaction of temperature, dissolved oxygen and predation pressure in an aquatic predator-prey system', *Oikos***81**: 329–336.

Moyo N. & Fernando C.H. 1999. 'The food of *Sargochromis codringtonii* (Boulenger, 1908) in Lake Kariba, Zimbabwe', *Hydrobiologia* **411**: 129–137.

Moyo S.M. 1993. 'Cyanobacterial nitrogen fixation and phytoplankton primary production in Lake Kariba, Zimbabwe.' *PhD thesis*. University of Zimbabwe. Harare.

Muzinic L.A., Thompson K.R., Morris A., Webster C.D., Rouse D.B., Manomaitis L. 2004. P'artial and total replacement of fish meal with soybean meal and brewer's grains with yeast in practical diets for Australian redclaw crayfish *Cherax quadricarinatus*',*Aquaculture* **230**: 359–376.

Nyström P.C., Brönmark C. & Granéli W. 1999. 'Influence of an exotic and a native crayfish species on a littoral benthic community',*Oikos* **85**: 545–553.

Owen-Smith R.N. 1988. *Megaherbivores: The Influence of Very Large Body Size on Ecology*. Cambridge University Press. Cambridge.

Padisák J. 1997. '*Cylindrospermopsis raciborskii* (Woloszynska) Seenayya et Subba Raju, an expanding, highly adaptive cyanobacterium: Worldwide distribution and review of its ecology', *Archiv für Hydrobiologie***107 (4)**: 563–593.

Pavasovic, A. 2008. 'Evaluation of the nutritional requirements of redclaw crayfish, *Cherax quadricarinatus*.' *PhD thesis*. School of Natural Resource Sciences, Queensland University of Technology. Australia.

Petr T. 1975. 'On some factors associated with the initial high fish catches in new African man-made lakes', *Archiv für Hydrobiologie* **75**: 32–49.

Phiri C., Day J., Chimbari M. & Dhlomo E. 2007. 'Epiphytic diatoms associated with a submerged macrophyte, *Vallisneria aethiopica*, in the shallow marginal areas of Sanyati Basin (Lake Kariba): A preliminary assessment of their use as biomonitoring tools', *Aquatic Ecology* **41**: 169–181.

Phiri C. 2010. 'Ecological aspects of the macroinvertebrates associated with two submersed macrophytes in Lake Kariba.' *PhD thesis*. University of Cape Town. South Africa.

Pooley T. 1982. *Discoveries of a Crocodile Man*. 1st Edition. William Collins & Co Ltd, Johannesburg.

Ramberg L. 1984. 'Phytoplankton gradients during the rainy season in Lake Kariba', *Verhandlungen der Internationale Vereiningung für Limnologie* **22**: 1590–1593.

Ramberg L. 1987. Phytoplankton succession in the Sanyati Basin, Lake Kariba. *Hydrobiologia* **153**: 193–202.

Ramberg L., Bjork-Ramberg S., Kautsky N. & Machena C. 1987. 'Development and biological status of Lake Kariba – a man-made tropical lake', *Ambio***6**: 314–321.

Reynolds C.S. 1998. 'The state of freshwater ecology', *Freshwater Biology* **39**: 741–753.

Rome L.C., Stevens E.D. & John-Alder H.B. 1992. 'The influence of temperature and thermal acclimation on physiological function.' In: Feder M.E. & Burggren W.W. (eds) *Environmental Physiology of the Amphibians*. University of Chicago Press. Chicago. pp 183–205.

Rooke J.B. 1986. 'Macroinvertebrates associated with macrophytes and plastic imitations in the Eramosa River, Ontario, Canada', *Archiv für Hydrobiologie* **106**: 307–325.

Ross J.P. 1998. *Crocodiles: Status Survey and Conservation Plan*. IUCN. Gland, Switzerland.

Sanyanga R.A. 1998. 'Food composition and selectivity of *Synodontis zambezensis* (Pisces: Mochokidae) in Lake Kariba, and the ecological implications', *Hydrobiologia* **361**: 89–99.

Schelpe E.A. 1961. 'The ecology of *Salvinia auriculata* and associated vegetation on Kariba Lake', *Journal of South African Botany* **27**: 181–187.

Thorbjarnarson J.B. 1992. *Crocodiles: An Action Plan for their Conservation*. IUCN–The World Conservation Union. Gland, Switzerland.

Tilman D., Fargione J., Wolff B., D'Antonio C., Dobson A., Howarth R., Schindler D., Schlesinger W.H., Simberloff D. & Swackhamer D. 2001. 'Forecasting agriculturally driven global environmental change', *Science* **292**: 281–284.

Vadeboncoeur Y., McCann K.S., Vander Zanden M.J. & Rasmussen J.B. 2005. 'Effects of multi-chain omnivory on the strength of trophic control in lakes', *Ecosystems***8**: 682–693.

Valerio E, Pereira P., Saker M.L., Franca S. & Tenreiro R. 2005. 'Molecular characterisation of *Cylindrospermopsis raciborskii* strains isolated from Portuguese freshwaters', *Harmful Algae* **4**: 1044–1052.

Van der Zanden M.J. & Vadeboncoeur Y. 2002. 'Fishes as integrators of benthic and pelagic food webs in lakes', *Ecology* **83**: 2152–2161.

Vorburger C. & Ribi G. 1999. 'Aggression and competition for shelter between a native and an introduced crayfish in Europe', *Freshwater Biology* **42**: 111–119.

Warfe D.M. & Barmuta L.A. 2006. 'Habitat structural complexity mediates food web dynamics in a freshwater macrophyte community', *Oecologia* **150**: 141–154.

Webster C.D., Thompson K.R., Muzinic L.A., Yancey D.H., Dasgupta S., Xiong Y.L., Rouse D.B. & Manomaitis L. 2004. 'A preliminary assessment of growth, survival, yield, and economic return of Australian red claw Crayfish,*Cherax quadricarinatus*, stocked at three densities in earthen ponds in a cool, temperate climate', *Journal of Applied Aquaculture* **15**: 37–50.

World Water Assessment Programme (WWAP) 2006.*The State of the Resource. World Water Development Report 2, Chapter 4*. WWAP, United Nations Educational, Scientific and Cultural Organisation (UNESCO). Paris. [Available at: http://www.unesco.org/water/wwap/wwdr2/pdf/wwdr2_ch_4.pdf. Accessed on 10 November 2012]

Zhang J.X. & Lu J.J. 1999. 'Feeding ecology of two wintering geese species at Poyang Lake, China', *Journal of Freshwater Ecology* **14**: 439–446.

Impact of elephants on woodlands. Photo: Craig R. Sholley

6. Fragmentation of woodland and grassland commons management around Lake Kariba

Lindah MHLANGA and Wilson MHLANGA

6.1. Introduction

Habitat fragmentation creates a landscape different from that shaped by natural disturbances to which species have adapted over evolutionary time (Groom *et al.* 2006). According to Groom *et al.* (2006) fragmentation results in both a reduction in the area covered by a natural habitat type in a landscape and a change in the habitat configuration, with the remaining habitat apportioned into smaller and more isolated patches. Human settlement, agriculture, road network development or any form of development converts a natural landscape into a patchwork of small, isolated islands in a sea of development. Since these will be managed by different authorities it also results in fragmented management. A typical example is the impoundment of Lake Kariba on the Zambezi River in 1959 and the ensuing developments that resulted in the fragmentation of a previously intact wilderness within the Gwembe Valley. Prior to the damming of the river, the large expanse of the Gwembe Valley wilderness was utilised by the Valley Tonga for floodplain farming and fishing; however the creation of the dam disrupted these activities and reduced connectivity between the Zambian and Zimbabwean sides of the valley. The previous wilderness landscape was fragmented into two national regions – the Zambian side and the Zimbabwean side, with approximately 5 400 km^2 inundated by the lake. Today Lake Kariba occupies most of the former Gwembe valley.

The woodlands surrounding this vast water body, especially on the Zimbabwean side, form part of an important wildlife conservation area within the Zambezi Valley. Along the Zimbabwean lakeshore, they have been preserved for biodiversity conservation, tourism and as habitat for wildlife. They have significant ecological and socio-economic importance because they occur in an ecologically fragile, semi-arid, climatically harsh environment where agriculture potential is limited. Except for the valley floor, the area has a rugged terrain, steep slopes and soils that are highly prone to erosion if vegetation cover is disrupted. As elsewhere in the Zambezi Valley, communities are consequently heavily dependent on natural resources harvested from the woodlands (Cumming & Lynam 1997). Household survival strategies rely on extracting woodland resources. Agriculture in the area is hampered by inadequate rainfall, infertile soils and poor access to inputs. So any loss of vegetation cover with the consequent soil erosion, loss of habitat for wildlife and disruption of livelihood sources and tourism activities, will reduce the long-term sustainability of the area.

The existing management and governance system of the resources around Lake Kariba is fragmented due to independent focus on separate sectors, which include agriculture, fishing, wildlife, tourism, settlement and forestry by different governance entities. This is in contrast to the ecosystem approach to natural resource management, which emphasises the interrelatedness of the ecological and economic dynamics of natural resources and therefore the need to integrate sectoral interconnections in common pool resources management.

6.2. Nature of the woodland resource

Woodlands found around the Lake Kariba area are part of the Zambezian biome. They are sub-tropical, marked by a dry season, and mostly moist or dry woodland interspersed with grassland (Timberlake 2000). Timberlake postulates that prior to the damming of the mid-Zambezi the vegetation communities would have been typified by narrow floodplains, rapids and large fluctuations in seasonal flow, with a wide range of vegetation types from evergreen forests on the flanks of the high peaks through mesic woodlands on the watershed and higher ground to drought-adapted deciduous woodlands in the low lying broad valley. The construction of Lake Kariba modified this biological character. The landscape is now dissected, ranging from mountains and other high land down to broad, dry valleys typically covered in *Colophospermum mopane* and other forms of drought-adapted deciduous woodlands (Timberlake 2000).

Vegetation types

White (1983) described the vegetation within the Zambezian biome as wetter or drier miombo woodland. Miombo woodland is dominated by trees of the genera *Brachystegia*, *Julbernardia* or *Isoberlinia*, with a well-developed grass layer. Other vegetation types found within the Zambezian biome are mopane woodland (dominated by *Colophospermum mopane*), and mosaics of various types of woodlands, dry forest with grassland and open woodland dominated by various species of *Acacia*.

The vegetation of the mid-Zambezi Valley where Lake Kariba occurs is predominantly savanna woodland dominated by *Colophospermum mopane* interspersed with thicket vegetation (Wild & Barbosa 1967, Child 1969, Balon & Coche 1974). The vegetation in the Lake Kariba area has two broad communities, namely mopane woodland in the valley plain, and miombo woodland on the Zambezi escarpment. Mopane woodland occur on shallow, poorly drained sodic soils and is dominated by *Colophospermum mopane* present as pure stands or in association with *Terminalia* spp., *Acacia* spp., *Adansonia digitata*, *Acacia nigrescens*, *Combretum* spp. and *Kirkia accuminata*. Although the dominant vegetation type in the valley floor is *Colophospermum mopane*, ten micro-community types were distinguished by Schramm (1978) according to species dominance. Dyer (1985) also found several communities determined by underlying geology. *Acacia* woodlands are found on deep fertile alluvial soils along tributaries flowing into Lake Kariba where soils are good for crop cultivation and support good pastures. Species within this woodland include *Acacia* spp., *Combretum* spp. and *Terminalia* spp. The vegetation type occur in woodlands in parks and wildlife estates, communal areas and forest reserves and there is usually good grass cover.

Shoreline vegetation has been studied over time at various stages in the development of the lake (Magadza 1970, Skarpe 1997). A study by Mhlanga & Mapaure (1999) describes in detail the vegetation communities that have colonised the immediate mainland and islands on the Zimbabwean shoreline (see summary in Table 13). They distinguished ten woodland types, namely *Colophospermum mopane* woodland, *Colophospermum mopane –Combretum apiculatum* woodland, *Colophospermum mopane* mixed woodland, *Combretum apiculatum* mixed woodland, Mixed *Combretum* woodland, *Combretum elaegnoides* mixed woodland, *Julbernardia globiflora* woodland, *Ficus sycamorous* woodland, *Acacia nilotica* woodland and *Acacia nigrescens –Afzelia quanzensis* woodland. They also distinguished four types of woodland thickets and thickets namely *Karomia tettensis* thicket, *Diospyros quiloensis* thicket, *Combretum celastroides* woodland thicket and *Guibourtia conjugata* woodland thicket. Mhlanga & Mapaure (1999) also described four shrublands. These include *Colophospermum mopane* shrubland, which is dominated by shrubs of *Colophospermum mopane* of less than 3 m in height, *Mundulea cerecea* shrubland, *Croton menyhartii* shrubland, *Pteliopsis myrtifolia* shrubland and *Indigofera tinctoria* shrubland.

Although *Panicun repens* grassland is the dominant grassland within the lakeshore, in a detailed floristic study of the Zimbabwean shoreline, Mhlanga & Mapaure (2000a) defined six grassland types. They noted a gradation of grass species down the shoreline slope. *Panicum repens* grassland is dominant in the gentle sloping lower shoreline on sandy soils near the water's edge; it is constantly inundated and shifts downwards as the lake recedes. It occurs with *Polygonum senegalensis* and *Ludwigia stolonifera*. *Panicum repens* thrives on moist sandy soils (Surrel 1978) and can withstand prolonged periods under water (McLachlan & McLachlan 1971). It is restricted more or less to the inundation zone where it is constantly subjected to drought and inundation when the lake rises and falls (Surrel 1978). *Eragrostis viscosa* grassland and *Urochloa trichopus* grassland dominate in the middle shoreline where soils are drier while *Melinis repens* grassland, *Aristida adscensionis* grassland and *Heteropogon contortus* grassland with species tolerant to mesic conditions occur on steeper rocky terrain in the upper shoreline, which has not been inundated for a long time (see summary in Table 14).

Table 13 below summarises the different woodland micro-ecosystems while Table 14 summaries the grassland types found within the Lake Kariba area. Detailed descriptions of the vegetation types may be found in Mhlanga & Mapaure (1999, 2000a).

Table 13: Woodland micro-ecosystems in the Lake Kariba area

Vegetation type	Dominant/co-dominant species	Habitat type
Woodlands		
Colophospermum mopane woodland	*Colophospermum mopane* with cover abundance over 50%. Common shrub *Combretum elaeagnoides.*	Coarse, loamy sands and medium to coarse sandy loams.
Colophospermum mopane- Combretum apiculatum woodland	Co-dominance of *Colophospermum mopane* and *Combretum apiculatum.*	Wide range of shallow soils ranging from fine to coarse sand clay loams, clay soils, sandy clay and loamy sands.
Colophospermum mopane mixed woodland	Typical tree species include *Colophospermum mopane, Combretum elaeagnoides, Combretum apiculatum, Commiphora mossambicensis* and *Afzelia quanzensis.*	Coarse sand, sandy loams and loamy sands.
Combretum apiculatum mixed woodland	*Combretum apiculatum* with cover abundance up to 50%. Typical species are *Colophospermum mopane, Diospyros quiloensis, Pteliopsis myrtifolia, Afzelia quanzensis* and *Commiphora mossambicensis.*	Medium sandy soils and deep fine sandy soils.

Vegetation type	Dominant/co-dominant species	Habitat type
Mixed *Combretum* woodland	*Combretum zeyheri*, *Combretum elaeagnoides* and *Combretum apiculatum*.	Deep coarse sands and sandy clay loams.
Combretum elaegnoides mixed woodland	*Combretum elaegnoides*, *Commiphora africana*, *Afzelia quanzensis* and *Triplochiton zambesiacus*.	Sandy loams and medium to coarse loamy sands.
Julbernardia globiflora woodland	*Julbernardia globiflora* with *Combretum apiculatum* and *Combretum zeyheri*.	Deep sandy soils.
Ficus sycomorus woodland	*Ficus sycomorus.*	Rocks and boulders.
Acacia nilotica woodland	*Acacia nilotica* with *Dichrostachys cinerea.*	Medium sandy loams.
Acacia nigrescens-Afzelia quanzensis woodland	*Acacia nigrescens*, *Afzelia quanzensis*, *Combretum mossambicensis*, *Terminalia sericea* and *Markhamia zanzibarica.*	Coarse to medium sandy loams.
Thickets and woodland thickets		
Karomia tettensis thicket	*Karomia tettensis* with cover abundance ranging from 50-75%. *Combretum elaegnoides* and *Combretum apiculatum.*	Coarse loamy sands and medium sandy loams.
Diospyros quiloensis thicket	*Diospyros quiloensis* with 100% cover abundance. Can occur with *Combretum elaegnoides*, *Karomia tettensis* and *Combretum apiculatum.*	Coarse sands.
Combretum celastroides woodland thicket	*Combretum celastroides* with cover abundance ranging from 60 to 75%. *Karomia tettensis* sometimes co-dominating.	Coarse sands, loamy sands and sandy loams.

Vegetation type	**Dominant/co-dominant species**	**Habitat type**
Guibourtia conjugata woodland thicket	*Guibourtia conjugata* with *Meiostemon tetrandrus*, *Combretum celastroides* and *Karomia tettensis* in the shrub layer.	Deep sandy loams.
Shrublands		
Colophospermum mopane shrubland	*Colophospermum mopane* associated with *Terminalia stulhmanii*, *Erythroxylum zambesiacum*, *Markhamia zanzibarica* and *Combretum elaegnoides*.	Coarse loamy sands and medium to coarse sandy loams.
Mundulea sericea shrubland	*Mundulea sericeae* with cover abundance of over 50%. Associated shrubs include *Lonchocarpus eriocalyx*, *Combretum apiculatum*, *Pteliopsis myrtifolia* and *Sclerocarya birrea*.	Shallow soils covered with rocks and boulders.
Croton menyhartii shrubland	*Croton menyhartii* associated with *Gardenia resiniflua* and *Acacia taxacantha*.	Coarse sandy clay loams.
Pteliopsis myrtifolia shrubland	*Pteliopsis myrtifolia* with *Meiostemon tetrandrus* and *Karomia tettensis*.	Coarse sands and coarse loamy sands.
Indigofera tinctoria shrubland	*Indigofera tinctoria* assuming 100% dominance. Occasional shrubs of *Colophospermum mopane*, *Kirkia acuminata* and *Lonchocarpus eriocalyx*.	Coarse sandy soils loamy sands and sandy loams.

Table 14: Grassland micro-ecosytems in the Lake Kariba area

Vegetation type	Dominant/co-dominant species	Habitat type
Aristida adscensionis grassland	*Aristida adscensionis* with cover abundance of up to 25%. *Heteropogon contortus*, *Aristida congesta* and *Melinis repens*.	Clay soils, fine to medium sandy clay loams, medium sands and fine loamy sands on the lower shoreline.
Heteropogon contortus grassland	*Heteropogon contortus* with cover abundance ranging from 25 to 75%, *Aristida rhiniochloa, Schmidtia pappophoroides* and *Melinis repens.*	Shallow fine sandy loams and coarse sands on steeper slopes on the lower shoreline, with boulders and pebbles on the surface.
Eragrostis viscosa grassland	*Eragrostis viscosa* with cover abundance up to 75%. *Cynodon dactylon, Setaria sphacelata, Melinis repens* and *Panicum maximum.*	Lower shoreline on fine sandy loams.
Urochloa trichopus grassland	*Urochloa trichopus* with a cover abundance of up to 100%. Other grass species include *Heterepogon contortus*, *Bothriochloa bladhii*, *Pogonarthria squarrosa* and *Echinochloa colona.*	Gently sloping shoreline on sandy loam soils mainly in the middle shoreline where soils are drier.
Panicum repens grassland	*Panicum repens* with cover abundance of 50 to 100%. *Andropogon eucomus*, *Eragrostis viscosa*, *Melinis repens*, *Pogonarthria squarrosa* and sedges.	Lower shoreline on gentle slopes on coarse to fine sandy soils.
Melinis repens grassland	*Melinis repens* with a cover abundance of up to 75%. Occasional shrubs of *Colophospermum mopane.*	Steep rocky slopes.

The major environmental variables influencing shoreline vegetation dynamics are lake level fluctuation and shoreline topography. During the early years after lake formation in 1958 the shoreline was an ecotone characterised by annual submersion and exposure as the level was lowered in February–March in anticipation of floods (Magadza 1970). Later, from 1985 there was a persistent fall in lake level that led to the establishment of a broad drawdown zone distinguishable into lower, middle and upper shoreline where pioneer species, mixed species composition and woody species from the adjacent woodland have developed respectively (Mhlanga & Mapaure 2000). In the middle and upper shore, which have not been inundated for over 20 years, leguminous woody species have encroached. Timberlake *et al.* (1993) observed that dry forests and thickets occur on elevated areas of unconsolidated sand while miombo woodlands occur on sandy soils or gravely soils in flatter areas. Mopane woodlands occurred on heavier soils. Mhlanga & Mapaure (2000) also found a relationship between vegetation type and soil. *Colophospermum mopane* and *Combretum apiculatum* dominated on basaltic soil. Sandy karoo soil favoured *Combretum celastroides* woodland thicket and *Pteliopsis myrtifolia* shrubland.

There are no areas designated as national parks along the Zambian shoreline. Two small islands, Nchete and Sikula (16 km^2 and 5 km^2 respectively), are designated as national parks for bird preservation although wildlife has been recorded on these islands (Ngalande 2000). Since these islands have national parks status and are far away from human habitation the woodlands on them are presumably well preserved. The woodland type, extent of areas preserved, usage and critical interacting issues within the national parks and safari areas along the Zimbabwean shoreline are shown in Table 15. Of particular importance are the critical interacting issues which are primarily a result of fragmented management. Detailed vegetation surveys have not been done in these protected areas. Timberlake *et al.* (1993) described the vegetation within communal areas surrounding Chete Safari Area as alternating between *Julbernardia*/*Mopane* mix and *Combretum*/*Mopane* mix. These vegetation types should be similar to that found within the safari area.

Table 15: Status of the woodlands in protected areas and safari areas on the Zimbabwean side

Area name	**Woodland/grassland types**	**Uses**	**Critical interacting issues**
Charara Safari Area (1 692 km^2)	- *Panicum repens* grassland - Mopane woodland - *Brachystegia boehmii*/*Julbernardia* woodland	Safari hunting	- Elephant/fire/woodland damage - Firewood

Matusadonha National Park (1 407 km^2)	- *Panicum repens* grassland - Mopane woodland - *Brachystegia boehmii/ Julbernardia* woodland	Photographic tourism	Elephant/fire/ woodland damage
Chete Safari Area (1 081 km^2)	- *Panicum repens* grassland - *Julbernardia/Mopane mix* - *Combretum*/Mopane mix	- Safari hunting - Photographic tourism	Elephant/fire/ woodlands damage
Sijarira Forest Area (256 km^2)	—	- Safari hunting - Photographic tourism	- Elephant/fire/ woodlands damage - Grazing, firewood, thatching grass
Kavira Forest Area (282 km^2)	—	—	- Illegal human settlement - Grazing, firewood, thatching grass

6.3. Resource use and value

The most apparent economic value of the woodlands and grasslands along Lake Kariba is their unique and attractive wilderness character, which has resulted in considerable tourism related investments in the area. They constitute a major attraction on the Zimbabwean side and are also valued for game viewing drives along the lakeshore and in game reserves as well as for safari hunting (Magadza 1986).

Woodland tree species like *Brachystegia*, *Julbernardia*, Mopane and Zambezi teak have important use in construction. Important non-timber forest products and services include honey production, grazing and the provision of wildlife habitat. Important timber species include *Pericopsis angolensis*, *Afzelia quanzensis*, *Dalbergia melanoxylon*, *Millettia stuhlmanii* and *Combretum imberbe* (Timberlake 2000). According to Timberlake species that have been exploited heavily for commercial timber to produce furniture, parquet flooring blocks and railway sleepers are Zambezi teak, false mopane or mchibi (*Guibourtia coleosperma*) and bloodwood, mukwa or kiaat (*Pterocarpus angolensis*).

Historically the woodlands within the Gwembe valley were used for the extraction of woody and non-woody resources by the Valley Tonga. According to Colson (1960) these people, like all ancient societies, had a close relationship with their natural environment and made full use of the surrounding vegetation to support their livelihoods. Colson describes in detail the enthography and social changes of the Gwembe Tonga. They practised traditional slash-and-burn strategies that required relatively frequent opening up of new fields and relocation of settlements. Agriculture focused on yearly replenished floodplain fields, which they cultivated as far back as 1860. They established 'temwa gardens' on fertile soils, which supported mixed woodland of *Colophospermum mopane*, *Triplochiton zambesiacus*, *Pterocarpus antunesii*, *Combretum* spp. and *Commiphora* spp. The Valley Tonga used grasses/tree species as indicators of soil fertility and suitability for cultivation. They also understood the diversity of woodlands with respect to agricultural productivity. For example, 'luwani woodlands', where *Colophospermum mopane* dominated on heavier clay soils of either alluvial or colluvial origin, were less cultivated. Instead, farmers preferred 'lusaka woodlands', where *Colophospermum mopane* occurred with other species on deep sandy and clay loams of Karoo derivation.

Today on the Zimbabwean side, there are five wildlife areas and three forest areas. The national park (Matusadona) and three safari areas (Charara, Sibilobilo, Chete) cover 40% of the lakeshore frontage (M.E. Associates 1996). Their vegetation is protected by national statutes, and the areas may only be used for tourism and are therefore not available for local communities to use. Local settlements along the lakeshore are restricted to 42 designated fishing villages spread along the lakeshore (Sanyanga 1995) and the intervening forest areas are designated for biodiversity preservation. The protected areas are preserved as wildlife sanctuaries that support intact woodlands. Adjacent to the protected areas are communal areas previously set aside as native reserves and purchase land. Woodlands in communal areas are under open access management while those in national parks are protected. However, some woodlands in the communal areas along the lakeshore are part of safari hunting concessions that span across human settlements and agricultural land. This is a feature that is reproduced across many parts of Southern Africa where protected nature conservation areas and functions are prominent islands in broad landscapes.

6.4. Institutional arrangements and management

Institutional arrangements for managing woodlands in the Lake Kariba area have evolved over time. According to Reynolds & Cousins (1993) prior to the colonial period the basic land-tenure system for the Valley Tonga was the right of a farmer over any land which he or she had brought into cultivation; in that way no land was regarded as private property. Rights over pioneer land were acquired through clearing the bush while that of previously cultivated land was acquired through inheritance (Scudder 1962). The community did not own land but managed it

(Reynolds & Cousins 1993) and used set rules of access and use of natural resources. Land disputes over boundaries or over use of an entire garden or portions thereof were settled within the village or neighbourhood (Scudder 1962).

According to Colson (1960) the Valley Tonga practised an egalitarian social order that encouraged individual freedom to decide and act with minimum external control. The household head was dependent on his immediate family and cultivated other links through kinship. The Valley Tonga lived clustered into neighbourhoods (*cisi*) consisting of two to seven villages. The *cisi* was the largest political unit with members belonging to a number of dispersed exogamous matrilineal clans (Scudder 1962). Clans had the same inheritance rights to land and property through ancestral spirits. One lineage that was first to cultivate the land took ritual precedence over others through a ritual leader whose function was to initiate and co-ordinate agricultural and gathering activities (Scudder 1962).

Chiefs and headmen within the Gwembe Valley (Zambian side) were later appointed by the colonial governments who created a new political structure at the beginning of the 20th century (Colson 1960). These today on both sides are locally based institutions whose positions are inherited through lineage and kinship ties. Their appointment shifted power of woodland management from ritual leaders and *cisi* to the chiefs.

During the colonial period, after the construction of Lake Kariba and forced relocation, physical fragmentation of the landscape ensued especially on the Zimbabwean side where large tracks of land were excised from the landscape and designated as protected areas for wildlife. Traditional management systems were consequently replaced with European models whereby legislative controls on woodland use were established through provisions of the Natural Resources Forest Produce Act (1928), Natural Resources Act (1942) and the Forest Act (1948). It became the responsibility of formal state institutions and structures to enforce rules and regulations of woodland management and use. According to Mandondo (2000) colonial resource governance systems resulted in over-centralisation because they were crafted in the context of conquest and subjugation. In Zimbabwe the Natural Resources Act of 1941 provided for the establishment of the Natural Resources Board, which acted as the national conservation watchdog comprising state-appointed members (Mandondo 2000). The Natural Resources Act (1941) vested the board with broad and sweeping powers of intervention in the area of environmental conservation by imposing restrictions e.g. on cutting trees (Scoones & Matose 1993).

According to Scoones & Matose (1993) the Natural Resources Act provided for a command and control approach to conservation among peasant communities. During the colonial period informal traditional institutions (kraal heads and chiefs) also had a role in woodland management. They used traditional regulations to protect territorial sacred woodlands and shrines. Woodland resources were governed largely by informal rules and norms falling within the traditional ambient. Traditional leaders then wielded significant power in woodland management but after independence in Zimbabwe this power was shifted from traditional authorities to the state under the District Councils Act (1988) and the Communal Lands Act (1982). The District Councils Act (1980) removed power to allocate land from traditional chiefs and headmen to District Councils. The District Councils Act (1988) under the Ministry of Local Government and National Housing gave Rural District Councils power to enact legally binding land use and conservation by-laws that apply to areas under their jurisdiction (Mandondo 2000). The Act basically recentralised power at district level (Mandondo 2000).The major challenge is that the land use plans do not factor in the peasant communities' livelihood coping strategies (Scoones *et al.* 1996) resulting in illegal procurement of woodland resources.

Through the provisions of the Communal Lands Act (1982) chiefs lost the power to allocate land, which was vested in them in the 1960s. The Act vested control over land in the president and devolved its administration to rural district councils and district administrators under the then Ministry of Local Government and Urban Development (Mandondo 2000). Further structural changes occurred through the Prime Minister's directive on decentralisation of local government in 1984 whereby local institutions known as Village Development Committees (VIDCOs) and Ward Development Committees (WADCOs) were established in each district as a form of decentralisation of local government. The Village Development Committee is presently the lowest government planning unit in Zimbabwe. Since these committees were involved in natural resources management they further assumed the role played by traditional leaders at community level. They essentially became a parallel institution to traditional authority at village level, stripping them of land allocation powers. Authority of chiefs was restored in 2000 through the enactment of the Traditional Leaders Act (1998), which empowered traditional leaders to manage the commons within their jurisdiction. Chiefs can prohibit over-cultivation, overgrazing and deforestation of woodlands. Presently there are two statutes supporting two parallel power structures at local level resulting in a fragmented tenure system and a sectoral approach to the management of natural resources. Village and ward development committees exist side by side with traditional institutions and in practice the two systems do not have clearly defined mandates and communication processes, making conflict between them inevitable (Mandondo 2000).

We found both physical fragmentation of the landscape along Lake Kariba and fragmented governance. Woodlands in communal areas belong to the state and are administered by the rural district council and at village level by the traditional authority structures and local central government structures.

After realising the weaknesses of the fragmented/sectoral approach in natural resources management, the Environmental Management Agency (previously the Department of Natural Resources) was instituted under the Environmental Management Act (2002) to co-ordinate the management of different resources by various ministries. The EMA Act sought to rationalise the country's fragmented environmental laws by integrating them to ensure consistency with each other (Mandondo 2000). As such, the Environmental Management Agency manages forest resources within communal areas. Other stakeholders with interest in woodlands include the tourism industry whose clients require aesthetic wilderness setting devoid of people.

Mandondo identified three formal hierarchical systems spanning from the state to the grassroots that are involved in woodlands management, namely the customary chieftaincy system, the multi-sectoral hierarchy of government ministries and the local government's rural district council system. According to Sithole (1997) these three hierarchies fan out, at the local level, into several administrative, developmental, social, political and other bodies, adding to the number of those that already exist. The major challenge, however, is the lack of resources and capacity by the state to effectively enforce control over woodland management.

The principal legislation on the Zimbabwean side to date is the Parks and Wildlife Act (1975 amended 1982 and 2001), which is used to manage all woodlands within protected areas by Zimbabwe Parks and Wildlife Management Authority (ZPWMA), whose main interest is conservation and sustainable use of forest resources under its jurisdiction. A summary of formal agencies directly or indirectly involved in woodlands management on the Zimbabwean lakeshore area is given in Table 16.

It is apparent that prior to the colonial period traditional indigenous systems were used to manage woodland resources within the Gwembe valley. After the colonial period, authorities used centrally directed legislative controls – founded upon the expropriation of land, resources and power from indigenous communities – to manage woodlands. Although some of the colonial rules were amended after independence, there is still recentralisation at district level (Mandondo 2000).

Table 16: Formal agencies directly or indirectly involved in woodland management on the Zimbabwean side

Formal agency	Responsibilities	Relevant legislation
Environmental Management Agency	- Enforcement of regulations on environmental damage - Preservation of natural resources including prevention and control of erosion (bush fires etc)	Environmental Management Act (2002)
Department of Physical Planning	- Overall responsibility for physical or land use planning - Preparation and approval of land use plans in rural district council areas	Regional Town Country Planning Act (1976)
Ministry of Local Government Rural and Urban Development	- Supervision of local authorities - Lease of General State Land	Rural District Councils Act (1988) Urban Councils Act (1975)
Ministry of Environment and Natural Resources Management	Tourism development in the area	Environmental Management Act (2002)
Rural district councils (Binga, Nyaminyami and Hwange)	- General administration and development of the Communal land and general state land - Allocation of rights to use communal land for traditional agricultural purposes - Preparation of general development plans	Rural District Councils Act (1988)

Formal agency	Responsibilities	Relevant legislation
Zimbabwe Parks and Wildlife Management Authority	- Administration and development of all parks and wildlife estates - Overseeing the welfare of vegetation with regards to protection, utilisation and conservation	Parks and Wildlife Act (1975, amended 1982 and 2001)
Forestry Commission	- Jurisdiction over designated forest land (Sijarira and Kavira)	Forest Act (1948, amended 1982) Forest Products Act (1928)
Municipality of Kariba	- General administration and development of land within its area of jurisdiction	Urban Councils Act (1975)

In Zambia, similar sectoral legislation has been developed that has implications for the management of woodlands along the lakeshore area (see Table 17). Conservation of forests in Zambia is governed by the Forest Act 7 (1999) but there is no law that regulates the cutting down of trees in open forests (Nyambe 2000). The Forestry Department manages and controls forestry areas. Three district councils – Gwembe, Sinazongwe and Siavonga – administer the lakeshore on the Zambian side.

Table 17: Formal agencies directly or indirectly involved in woodland management on the Zambian side

Formal agency	Responsibilities	Relevant legislation
Environmental Council of Zambia	- Protection of the environment	Environmental Protection and Pollution Control Act (1990, Chapter 204)
Ministry of Tourism, Environment and Natural Resources	- Protection of plant life and vegetation (environment and natural resources management) - Ensuring sustainable use of forest resources and ecosystem management	Natural Resources Conservation Act (1970)

Formal agency	**Responsibilities**	**Relevant legislation**
Forestry Department	- Managing forest resources	Forest Act (1973, Chapter 1999)
Ministry of Lands, Natural Resources and Environmental Protection	- Land ownership	Lands Act 29 (1995, Chapter 184)
Local authorities (Gwembe, Sinazongwe, Siavonga)	- Natural resources within local areas - Preparation and implementation of development plans	Local Government Act 22 (1991)
Ministry of Agriculture and Cooperatives	- Natural vegetation, agricultural land	Agricultural Lands Act (1960, Chapter 187) Pests and Plants Act (1959)
Ministry of Energy and Water Development	- Procurement of firewood and charcoal	Energy Regulation Act 16 (1995, Chapter 436)

As can be seen from Tables 15 and 16, different authorities administer protected areas, agriculture land and forestry areas on different sides of the lake. Institutions involved in woodland management range from national to local, informal to formal operating either independently or alongside each other. Managing the dynamics of this multiplicity of institutions will be a key challenge in addressing fragmentation of resources.

As with other resources in the area, the major challenge with regard to woodland preservation and management is that legislation has been developed on sectoral lines and in many cases there are overlaps. This is causing a decline in the general efficiency and effectiveness of the various central and local government agencies involved in woodland management therein, posing challenges to sustainable development. The discussion below on ecosystem interactions illustrates how fragmented management is threatening woodland resources.

6.5. Ecosystem interactions

Within a large ecosystem like Lake Kariba and its environs, which is rich and diverse in resources, there are complex, interacting ecosystem processes. Sustainable future development and management of the area requires the recognition of both positive and negative connections among the main sectors (agriculture, wildlife, fishing and tourism) and between different types of activities within each sector. In the section below the critical ecosystem interactions that relate to the exploitation of woodland and grassland commons are discussed.

Interactions with agriculture

Agriculture is the main source of livelihood for two thirds of the population living in communal areas within the Zimbabwean lakeshore, while on the Zambian side 62.7% of the respondents in lakeshore communities indicated farming as their main source of income (Anon 1993). In Siavonga, Gwembe and Sinazongwe Districts in Zambia cultivation is carried out both on the escarpment and on the valley floor. Despite poor productivity agriculture is a major driver of deforestation, as farmers open up woodlands for small-scale cultivation. Deforestation is especially problematic for riparian forests and alluvial woodlands that occur in river valleys on fertile soils. Increasing demand for agricultural land due to the natural rate of population increase as well as in-migration is putting pressure on the fragile ecosystem. Tree clearance exposes the soil to agents of erosion. The challenge here is how to promote smallholder agriculture expansion, which is the basic means of livelihood for most of the rural population, and also preserve the fragile environment by maintaining natural vegetation cover.

Communities on either side of Lake Kariba keep livestock, mainly cattle, goats, donkeys and sheep. Livestock are important for supporting the livelihoods of the local communities and the cattle population has increased following tsetse eradication. Cattle are important in this agro-based community for provision of draught power, transport and manure and to act as surety in times of drought. Cattle also play an important role in lineage social organisations, for payments of lobola (bride price), for ceremonies and for compensatory payments (Cousins *et. al.* 1989). In the three districts on the Zambian side the estimated cattle population in 1999 was 111 188 (Ngalande 2000) while in Binga District on the Zimbabwean side an estimated population of 60 000 cattle was recorded in 1999 (BRDC 1999).

Although pastures are now an important resource following tsetse fly eradication, the Valley Tonga previously did not own cattle (Magadza 1986). Livestock production is now of significant importance to the lakeshore communities. Cattle especially within the whole lakeshore on the Zambian side graze on natural pasture. The most commonly used and thus most important system is grazing in the drawdown zone throughout the year and on the escarpment during the rainy season. Grassland communities along the lakeshore are consequently an important resource for the survival of livestock and the community's livelihood. Prior to the creation of Lake Kariba and tsetse fly (*Glossina* spp.) eradication, keeping livestock in the Gwembe valley was constrained by animal trypanosomiasis (Scudder 2005). The land surrounding Lake Kariba was infested with *Glossina morsitans* and *G. palidepes* and thus unsuitable for animal husbandry (Magadza 1986).

On the Zimbabwean side a 5 km buffer zone along the shoreline is excluded from grazing but cattle graze in woodlands and grasslands within the communal areas. Livestock production within the lakeshore districts on the Zambian side and in communal areas on the Zimbabwean side is associated with land degradation and soil erosion due to overgrazing. With the social and economic importance of cattle for smallholder farmers the challenge is how to limit the number of cattle and other livestock within the lakeshore to an environmentally sustainable carrying capacity.

Interactions with wildlife

The Lake Kariba environs, especially on the Zimbabwean side, support rich wildlife resources. Large numbers of wildlife occur mainly in wildlife areas, forest areas and to a varying extent in communal areas. On the Zambian side the wildlife population is very low. Due to endowment with wildlife the Kariba area is therefore of significant national and international interest for tourism. The animals include elephant (*Loxodonta africana*), buffalo (*Syncerus caffer*), lion (*Panthera leo*), leopard (*Panthera pardus*) and zebra (*Equus burchelli*). Elephants are the main problem animals, posing a greater threat to woodlands when occurring in large numbers. The increased concentration of elephant populations in designated wildlife areas and in communal areas is leading to woodland destruction. Elephants also move from the Zimbabwean side to the Zambian side, where they destroy woodlands.

Elephants occurring in large numbers can modify vegetation structure, converting woodland to shrubland (Timberlake 1995) and modifying species composition. This has been observed on a study carried out on the islands in Lake Kariba where *Colophospermum mopane* is the predominant vegetation type (Mapaure & Mhlanga 2000). About 77.6% of the trees on the studied islands had been damaged. Due to heavy elephant damage the vegetation had been transformed to shrubland with *Colophospermum mopane* of height < 1m, which was prevented by browsing from recruitment to higher size classes. All plants forked below 2 m, an indication of damage to the terminal part of the plant while still young (Caughley 1976). The mopane trees are heavily and extensively damaged, multi-stemmed and stunted. Undisturbed *Colophospermum mopane* is usually single-boled (Mapaure & Mhlanga 2000). Thus continuous browsing effectively maintained a *Colophospermum mopane* shrubland of 1.5–2 m. Within the immediate Zimbabwean lakeshore and on the islands increasing populations of elephants have changed vegetation structure from being predominantly *Colophospermum mopane* woodland or *Colophospermum mopane –Combretum apiculatum* woodland to thickets, woodland thickets and shrubland, as observed in the Serengeti – Mara ecosystem in East Africa (Dublin *et al.* 1990). A detailed study on vegetation utilisation and damage, elephant density and seasonal migration should be carried out.

Elephants constitute a large proportion of the large herbivores on the Zimbabwean shoreline, with consequent effect on woodland. Heavy utilisation by elephants and buffaloes has led to the development of *Karomia tettensis* thickets, *Combretum celastroides* woodland thickets, *Diospyros quiloensis* thickets and *Pteleopsis myrtifolia* shrublands. When undisturbed, *Combretum celastroides* and *Pteliopsis myrtifolia* form dry layered forests (Jesse bush) and are scattered across the Zambezi Valley on karroo sediments (Timberlake *et al.* 1993). Thus elephants changed the vegetation structure from an original dry layered thicket to dense shrubland thickets with few emergents. This has been observed in Eastern Gokwe (Timberlake *et. al.* 1993), Busi Sengwa (Muller & Timberlake 1982) and Mana Pools National Park (Muller & Pope 1982). Disturbed woodland types within communal areas, national parks and safari areas consist of shrublands, thickets and woodland thickets.

Grasslands that are a predominant vegetation type along the shoreline are a source of highly nutritious fodder to large herds of wildlife on the Zimbabwean side, especially hippopotamus (*Hippopotamus amphibious*), elephant (*Loxodonta africana*), buffalo (*Syncerus caffer*) and impala (*Aepyceros melampus*). Buffaloes are especially dependent on *Panicum repens* lakeshore grasslands (Taylor 1985). Grasslands thus provide fodder for wildlife. However there are indications of overgrazing. The indicator of overgrazing by wildlife within grassland communities along the Zimbabwean lakeshore is the encroachment of *Dichrostachys cinerea*, *Acacia nilotica*, *Indigofera tinctoria* and *Calotropis procera* in grassland communities. *Dichrostachys cinerea* is a persistent invader in overgrazed areas (Simpson 1975).

Elephants usually occur in large numbers in an area unless connections exist to allow them to move to available habitat in the broader landscape, including transboundary connections. The key management challenge therefore is to ensure the appropriate wildlife carrying capacity that will not result in woodland destruction.

Interactions with veld burning

Veld fires caused by humans are a common phenomenon in the Zambezi valley in general. These fires are a major ecological factor affecting vegetation structure and are a seasonal phenomenon associated with the dry season. Burning is usually done just before the wet season to provide livestock with early pastures soon after the first rains. These frequent fires can permanently trap the woodlands in the regeneration phase that may slowly regress to a fire-climax grassland (Mapaure & Mhlanga 2000b). Bush fires usually occur from June to November when plants are developing new leaves, flowering and fruiting, and so the fires are very destructive to woodlands. Annual fires destroy and weaken the vulnerable small plants and coppicing shoots thereby converting woodland to shrubland or grassland savannah (Boughey 1963). The combined effect of human caused fires and elephant damage can have profound effects on woodlands. Elephants and fire were observed to hinder recruitment of trees to height classes greater than 2 m in *Brachystegia* woodlands in Matusadona National Park (M.E. Associates 1996). Although fire has been traditionally used to stimulate early sprouting of fodder, to minimise the effect of wild fires by early burning and to manipulate the proportionate cover of woody species in relation to grassland, the major challenge in the area now is uncontrolled fires. Frequent uncontrolled fires can kill off the woody component and reduce grass cover which can consequently result in desertification.

The interaction of elephants and fire and their relative contribution to loss of woodlands in the area is poorly understood. Detailed studies are required to elucidate the interactive effects of elephants and fire on woodlands and grasslands within the Lake Kariba area. There is also need to obtain data on fire regime, seasonality, intensity and their effect on the physiological effect on the developmental state of the vegetation.

Interactions with human settlements

Human settlements along the Zimbabwean shoreline include two urban centres, namely Kariba and Binga, and 42 fishing villages spread along the shoreline. On the Zambian side the main urban centre is Siavonga while the three districts within the lakeshore are Sinazongwe, Gwembe and Siavonga and 69 fishing villages (Ngalande 2000). These areas of human settlement are associated with excessive utilisation of open woodland and protected forest area resources.

On the Zambian side only 34,875 ha is covered by protected local forests (Ngalande 2000) compared to a larger portion on the Zimbabwean side (refer to Table 14). Due to ineffective law enforcement on the Zambian side woodlands in designated forest areas and open forests are threatened by deforestation from commercial extraction for timber and charcoal production. Charcoal burning occurs on a large commercial scale along the Zambian lakeshore, with forests in Siavonga and Sinazongwe Districts being extensively exploited for charcoal (Ngalande 2000). Locals derive significant income from selling charcoal at a price of US$1 per 25 kg. There is a high demand for charcoal within the lakeshore districts and in urban areas that has increased the demand and consequently pressure on woodlands. Trees are cut without licences, and charcoal burning is a significant contributor of deforestation on the Zambian side.

Cutting of trees for timber is widespread and intensive. Indiscriminate cutting of trees was observed in Siavonga and Sinazongwe district and this has led to extensive deforestation (Anon 1993). For timber, selective harvesting of hardwoods occurs, mainly *Pterocarpus angolensis*, *Afzelia quanzensis*, *Sterculia quinqueloba*, *Afrormosia angolensis*, *Colophospermum mopane* and *Parinari curatellifolia*. These are used to make beams and planks for sale to both locals and people from outside the lakeshore area (Losse 1998). While people usually extract timber with a permit, due to demand unlicensed and unregulated extraction of trees is creating considerable loss of woodlands, resulting in ecological problems and likely depletion of forest areas (Ngalande 2000). Increasing pressure on woodland resources linked to population growth means more deforestation within the lakeshore area and consequently destruction of forests (BRDC 1999). Due to high land pressure re-growth of vegetation is hindered.

Trees and shrubs are also indiscriminately cut down for firewood for cooking and smoking fish, for construction of garden and livestock kraals, and homesteads and woodwork. Deforestation has been observed around fishing villages where trees are harvested for fish processing and cooking but there is no data available on extent of deforestation and its impact on species composition and diversity within the woodlands.

Demand for firewood is high in urban settlements. In the case of Kariba town approximately 36% of the population use firewood in combination with electricity and paraffin for cooking (Hawkes & Magadza 1988, Minton 1993). Woodlands around Kariba town are harvested illegally or with permits. The impact of overharvesting has been observed in the form of low tree density near Kariba town and smaller trees compared to areas further inland (Chifamba 2000). Notable also is deforestation around fishing camps, where wood is used as fuel (Magadza 1986). The major threat is the increasing loss of woodlands for firewood as communal area residents respond to demands from dealers serving urban areas. Deforestation is significant in Chipepo and Sinazongwe areas on the Zambian side where in the shoreline area of these districts, tracts of land are now devoid of trees suitable for firewood (Ngalande 2000).

People harvest highly utilised fruit species of masawu (*Ziziphus mauritiana*) and the tamarind (*Tamarindus indica*) from *Acacia –Combretum* woodlands. Miombo woodlands are an important woodland type that provides fruit trees, medicinal plants, grazing, fuelwood, construction wood and forest products like mushrooms. The grass and herb understory in miombo woodlands supports livestock. Generally the use of woodlands and products associated with woodlands are varied, including organic fertiliser, fibre, honey production, thatching grass, gums, silks and dyes (Campbell *et al.* 1991, 1993).

On the Zimbabwean side there are two protected forest areas along the shoreline, namely Sijarira and Kavira, falling under Binga district. Due to increasing pressure in designated communal areas, incursions of local people have occurred into Kavira with unsuccessful evictions by the Forestry Commission (BRDC 1999). Local communities residing in Communal areas adjacent to Kavira and

Sijarira Forest Areas use these forests for grazing, collecting firewood and thatching grass. An increase in demand for extraction of forest resources and land for settlement is threatening the preservation of the woodlands within designated forest areas. Murombedzi (1990) predicted that settlement in the marginal Zambezi valley ecosystem would continue until communal areas exceeded their capacity, after which invasion into national parks and forest areas will occur. This critical interaction between livelihood requirements and woodland preservation highlights the need for a balance between the preservation of designated forest areas for biodiversity preservation, conservation and soil protection, and the livelihood requirements of local people. As the lakeshore populations grow, so the threat to trees and bushes will also increase.

Interactions with tourism

Tourism is an important economic activity within the lakeshore area. On the Zimbabwean side, with respect to conservation, this has resulted in the protection of large tracts of woodlands in five designated wildlife areas along the shoreline. These parks and wildlife estates account for approximately 40% of the lakeshore frontage (LKFRI 1995) and are not available for use by local communities, as tourism is the only form of land use allowed. Although people illegally extract resources from these areas the woodlands are still relatively intact except for damage from wildlife.

Hunting and photographic tourism utilise the wilderness aspect of the area, an activity that enhances the protection of woodlands (refer to Table 14). In order to support tourism, culling of elephants is prohibited through the Convention on International Trade of Endangered Species (CITES). This has resulted in an increasing elephant population with a consequent negative impact on woodland health.

Softwood trees are also selectively harvested for woodcraft production and sale to tourists. While this is a very common activity there is currently no data on quantities harvested and its impact.

6.6. Conclusion

Fragmentation of a previously integrated large landscape in the Gwembe valley is presenting management challenges that threaten resource sustainability and livelihoods. We argue that there is need to re-establish the interactions and interdependencies among the different resources, different sectors and livelihood requirements within the Lake Kariba environs (Mhlanga 2009) and then manage the entire resource base in an integrated way. Such a cross-sectoral ecosystem approach to natural resources management will ensure integration rather than fragmentation thereby enhancing the conservation of the resource base upon which community livelihoods are dependent.

The socio-economic value of woodlands for human livelihoods is very significant. This dependence, however, is linked to ecosystem protection and sustainable management of the resource base. A holistic management of the landscape that focuses on ecosystem interactions as well as integrating all human activities and stakeholders can ensure sustainability. In 2010 UNESCO designated the middle Zambezi biosphere reserve covering 40 000km^2 of riverine and terrestrial ecosystem, including Lake Kariba on the Zimbabwean side. This model, if implemented, will be a step towards defragmentation, since it is a concept and tool that can be used to achieve a sustainable balance among conservation of biological diversity, promoting human development and maintaining associated cultural values.

With regards to woodland resources issues that need to be addressed include:

- poaching and encroachment into protected area, which is threatening the woodlands;
- deforestation and biodiversity loss;
- adjustment of power relations to make governance more effective;
- linking the roles of woodland in catchment protection, tourism, animal habitat and provision of livelihoods to lakeshore communities; and
- overgrazing of grasslands by livestock and wildlife.

To effectively address the above issues, the following quantitative data will need to be gathered for decision making:

- assessing the extent of deforestation, soil erosion and siltation of rivers flowing into Lake Kariba;
- quantifying the impact that tree harvesting for timber and charcoal is having on the woodlands and the ecosystem;
- assessing the extent of woodland damage by elephants, impact on biodiversity conservation, extent of habitat destruction, estimates of elephant density, seasonal movement of elephants in relation to vegetation utilisation;
- assessing the impact of elephants on woodlands as they cross over into Zambia from the Zimbabwean side;
- assessing the interactive effects of elephants and fire on woodlands;
- assessing the impact of human-caused fires; and
- assessing the wildlife populations around Lake Kariba especially buffaloes that are dependent on the *Panicum repens* grasslands so that the appropriate density for the lakeshore grasslands can be determined.

Due to inadequate quantitative data, in our study, we were unable to indicate how the different resources are interrelated within one ecosystem and the major dynamics that link the different resources. For example there is scant data to clearly illustrate the impact of woodland disturbance on both the environment and livelihoods. As such, research should generate data on extent of deforestation, viable wildlife and livestock population sizes, extent and interactive impact of veld burning with elephant damage, in-migration (new settlements) and land clearing and the extent of soil erosion and its impact on rivers and the dam. Future conceptualisation of the required relevant research to feed policy should consider the critical interactions in other sectors including fish, water, wildlife and land. Such research would then inform policy with regards to addressing, among other resources, woodland preservation versus need for agricultural production, firewood, grazing land, settlement and other livelihood necessities. Any future plans should acknowledge first and foremost that lakeshore communities rely on woodland commons for their household sustenance strategies; however, the resource base is threatened by loss of biodiversity, deforestation and overgrazing.

References

Anon. 1993. *Lakeshore Development Planning. Lake Kariba–Zambia: Part I: Current Socio-economic Activities, Resources and Infrastructure.* Agrindco International (Z). Ltd. (MS).

Balon E.K. & Coche A.G. (eds) 1974. *Lake Kariba: A Man-made Tropical Ecosystem in Central Africa.* W. Junk. The Hague.

Binga Rural District Council (BRDC) 1999. *Land Use and Wildlife Management Plan.* BRDC. Binga, Zimbabwe.

Boughey A.S. 1963. 'Early shoreline vegetation on Lake Kariba.' Record of a research symposium held at Fisheries Research Institute June 1965. Lake Kariba Fisheries Research Institute, Kariba.

Campbell B.M., Grundy I., & Matose F. 1993. 'Tree and woodland resources; The technical practice of small-scale farmers.' In P.N. Bradley & McNamara, K. (eds) *Living with Trees: Policies for Forestry Management in Zimbabwe.* World Bank Technical Paper, 210: 29-62.

Campbell B.M., Vermeulen S.J. & Lynam T. 1991. *Value of Trees in the Small-scale Farming Sector of Zimbabwe.* IDRC-MR302e. IDRC. Ottawa, Canada.

Caughley G. 1976. 'The elephant problem: An alternative hypothesis', *East African Wildlife Journal* **14**: 265-284.

Chifamba P. 2000. 'Environmental problems and issues along Lake Kariba coastal zone.' In:University Lake Kariba Research Station. *Lake Kariba. A Case for Integrated Coastal Zone Management.* Southern Africa Network for Training and Research on the Environment. Institute of Environmental Studies, University of Zimbabwe. Harare.

Child G. 1969. *Behaviour of Large Mammals during the Formation of Lake Kariba.* Trustees of the National Museums of Rhodesia. Harare.

Colson E. 1960. *The Social Organisation of the Gwembe Tonga.* Manchester University Press. U.K.

Cousins B., Jackson C & Scoones I.C. 1989. *People, Land and Livestock.* Proceedings of a workshop on the socio-economic dimensions of livestock production in the Communal Lands of Zimbabwe. 12-14 September 1998. Centre for Applied Social Studies, University of Zimbabwe. Harare.

Cumming D.H.M. & Lynam T. 1997. *Land Use Changes, Wildlife Conservation and Utilisation and the Sustainability of Agro-ecosystems in the Zambezi Valley.* World Wildlife Fund. Harare.

Dublin H.T., Sinclair A.R.E. & McGlade J. 1990. 'Elephants and fire as causes of multiple stable states in the Serengeti-Mara woodlands', *Journal of Animal Ecology* **59**: 1147-1164.

Dyer C. 1985. 'A preliminary survey of vegetation and soils of the Dinosaur Island, Lake Kariba.' *BSc thesis*. University of Witwatersrand. South Africa.

Groom M.J., Gary K.M. & Carroll C.R. 2006. *Principles of Conservation Biology*. 3rd Edition. Sinauer Associates. Sunderland Massachusetts.

Hawkes R. & Magadza C.H.D. 1988. 'Report on energy usage preferences in Kariba, Zimbabwe', *ULKRS Bulletin* No. 2/88.

Lake Kariba Fisheries Research Institute (LKFRI). 1995. *Tourism and the National Parks and Wildlife Estates on Lake Kariba.* Zambia/Zimbabwe SADC Fisheries Project.

Losse G.F. 1998. *The Small-scale Fishery on Lake Kariba in Zambia*. Schriftenreihe der GTZ No. 265 Wiesbaden Universum Verlagsantalt, Germany.

M.E. Associates Private Limited. 1996. *Tourism and the National Parks and Wildlife Estate on Lake Kariba. A Contribution to the Combination Lake Kariba Master Plan.* Zambia-Zimbabwe SADC Fisheries Project (Lake Kariba).

Magadza C.H.D. 1970. 'A preliminary survey of the vegetation of the shore of Lake Kariba', *Kirkia* **7(2)**: 253–268.

Magadza C.H.D. 1986. 'Conflicts of resource use on the Lake Kariba environs', *Nature and Resources* **22(4)**: 2–12.

Mandondo A. 2000. *Situating Zimbabwe's Natural Resource Governance Systems in History*. Occasional Paper No. 32. Center for International Forestry Research, Indonesia.

Mhlanga L. & Mapaure I. 1999. *Vegetation Studies of Selected Islands and Adjacent Mainland on Lake Kariba, Zimbabwe*. Institute of Environmental Studies (IES) Working Paper 9. University of Zimbabwe. Harare.

Mhlanga L. & Mapaure I. 2000. 'A floristic classification of shoreline vegetation around Lake Kariba, Zimbabwe', *Kirkia* **17(2)**: 153–169.

Mapaure I. & Mhlanga L. 2000. 'Patterns of elephant damage to *Colophospermum mopane* on selected islands in Lake Kariba, Zimbabwe', *Kirkia* **17(2)**: 189–198.

Mhlanga L. 2009. 'Fragmentation of resource governance along the shoreline of Lake Kariba, Zimbabwe', *Development Southern Africa* **26(4)**: 585–596.

McLachlan A.J. & McLachlan S.M. 1971. 'Benthic fauna and sediments in a newly created Lake Kariba (Central Africa)', *Ecology* **52**: 800–809.

Minton R. 1993. 'Wood fuel survey.' University Lake Kariba Research Station (mimeo).

Muller T. & Pope G. 1982. 'Vegetation report for the impact assessment of the proposed Mupata gorge and Batoka dams on the Zambezi River.' In: du Toit R.F. (ed) *A Preliminary Assessment of the Environmental Implications of the Proposed Mupata and Batoka Hydroelectric Scheme (Zambezi River, Zimbabwe):* 53-67. Natural Resources Board. Harare.

Muller T. & Timberlake J. 1982. 'Areas for plant conservation in Zimbabwe', *Zimbabwe Science News* **26(10/12)**: 88–95.

Murombedzi J. 1990. *Communal Land Tenure and Common Property Resource Management: An Evaluation of the Potential for Sustainable Common Property Resource Management in Zimbabwe's Communal Areas.* Centre for Applied Social Sciences, University of Zimbabwe. Harare.

Ngalande P. 2000. 'Socio-economic assessment and resource utilisation along the coastal zone of Lake Kariba.' In: University Lake Kariba Research Station. *Lake Kariba. A Case for Integrated Coastal Zone Management.* Southern Africa Network for Training and Research on the Environment. University Lake Kariba Research Station. Kariba, Zimbabwe.

Nyambe I. 2000. 'Legal framework and institutional arrangements in coastal zone management: Lake Kariba.' In: University Lake Kariba Research Station. *Lake Kariba. A Case for Integrated Coastal Zone Management.* Southern Africa Network for Training and Research on the Environment. University Lake Kariba Research Station. Kariba, Zimbabwe.

Reynolds P. & Cousins C.C. 1993. *Lwaamo lwanyika. Tonga Book of the Earth (Books from the South).* Baobab Books. Harare, Zimbabwe.

Sanyanga R. 1995. 'Management of Lake Kariba inshore fishery and some thoughts on biodiversity and conservation issues, Zimbabwe', *Environmental Conservation* **22(2)**: 111–116.

Schramm E. 1978. 'A preliminary survey of the vegetation and distribution of the Loranthaceae of Dinosaur Island (Island 126/127), Lake Kariba, Rhodesia.' *BSc dissertation.* University of the Witwatersrand. South Africa.

Scoones I. & Matose F. 1993. 'Local woodland management: Constraints and opportunities for sustainable resource use.' In: Bradley P.N. & McNamara K. (eds) *Living with Trees: Policies for Woodland Management in Zimbabwe.* World Bank. Washington. D.C.

Scoones I., Chibudu C., Chikura S., Jeranyama P., Machaka D., Machaya W., Mavedzenge B., Mombeshora B., Mudhara M., Mudziwo C., Murimbarimba F. & Zirereza A. 1996. *Hazards and Opportunities: Farming Livelihoods in Dryland Africa: Lessons from Africa.* ZED Books. New Jersey.

Scudder T. 1962. *The Ecology of the Gwembe Tonga.* Kariba Studies II. Manchester University Press. U.K.

Scudder T. 2005. *The Kariba Case Study.* Social Science Working Paper 1227. Division of the Humanities and Social Science, California Institute of Technology. Pasadena, California.

Simpson C.D. 1975. 'A detailed vegetation study on the Chobe River in northeast Botswana', *Kirkia* **10(1)**: 185–217.

Sithole B. 1997. *The Institutional Framework for the Management and Use of Natural Resources in the Communal Area of Zimbabwe: Village Cases of Access to and Use of Dambos from Mutoko and Chiduku.* Centre for Applied Social Sciences, University of Zimbabwe. Harare.

Skarpe C. 1997. 'Ecology of the vegetation in the drawdown zone of Lake Kariba.' In: Moreau J. (ed) *Advances in the Ecology of Lake Kariba*: 120–138. University of Zimbabwe. Harare.

Surrel K. 1978. *The Shore Types of Lake Kariba, Zimbabwe: a Case Study Using LANDSAT MSS.* Working Paper 47. Swedish University of Agricultural Sciences. Uppsala.

Taylor R.D. 1985. 'The response of buffalo, *Syncerus caffer* (Sparrman) to the Lake Kariba lakeshore grassland (*Panicum repens* L.) in Matusadonha National Park.' *PhD thesis*. University of Zimbabwe. Harare.

Timberlake J.R. 1995. '*Colophospermum mopane*: annotated bibliography and review', *Zimbabwe Bulletin of Forest Research No. 11*. Forestry Commission. Harare.

Timberlake J.R., Nobanda N. & Mapaure I. 1993. 'Vegetation survey of the communal lands-north and west Zimbabwe', *Kirkia* **14(2)**: 171–241.

Timberlake J. 2000. *Biodiversity of the Zambezi Basin*. Occasional Publications in Biodiversity No. 9. Biodiversity Foundation for Africa. Bulawayo, Zimbabwe.

White F. 1983. *The Vegetation of Africa: A Descriptive Memoir to Accompany the UNESCO/AEFAT/UNSO Vegetation Map*. Natural Resources Research 20. UNESCO. Paris.

Wild H. & Barbosa L.A.G. 1967. *Vegetation Map of the Flora Zambesiaca Area*. Collins. Harare.

A herd of buffalo along the shoreline of Lake Kariba. Photo: Mark Boulton

7. Challenges surrounding wildlife management within the Lake Kariba environs and in the Zambezi Valley

Vupenyu DZINGIRAI, Lindah MHLANGA and Gift MUSINAKE

7.1. Introduction

Wildlife is a key resource within the woodlands along Lake Kariba and in the Zambezi Valley. The magnificent wildlife that exists within the Lake Kariba environs is also of international interest (Magadza 1986). Prior to the formation of Lake Kariba the area was one consolidated wildlife sanctuary with unrestricted movement of animals. At the creation the lake, the project dubbed "Operation Noah" was instituted to rescue stranded animals, a process that exposed the magnificent wildlife that existed in the area to the international community (Magadza 1986). The process of fragmentation began when the then Southern Rhodesia government designated five wildlife areas and two forest areas along the shoreline as wildlife sanctuaries. Today on the Zimbabwean side Parks and wildlife estates account for approximately 40% of the lakeshore frontage (LKFRI 1995).

The creation of Lake Kariba, for a single purpose of power generation transformed a previously vast interlinked ecosystem to a multiple resource that became available for exploitation to a wider-community locally, nationally and regionally. Today land use designation on the Zimbabwean side focuses on the preservation of wildlife and the development of wildlife interest. Large areas of land excised from common land and dedicated entirely to conservation is under state ownership. These wildlife sanctuaries are in juxtaposition with human settlements and other land uses that are incompatible with free ranging wildlife. The major challenge with wildlife management in the area hinges on a set-up where incompatible resource use activities are in juxtaposition presenting a challenge to wildlife, which are mobile resources. This has resulted in major conflicts over resource use and management.

On Lake Kariba and in the Zambezi Valley wildlife remains the focus of a fragmented management approach. Its management remains devoid of co-ordination between organisations and various legislation instruments governing wildlife utilisation and management. Wildlife, however, is one of the elements that constitute the environment and are central to livelihood and wealth accumulation strategies of most marginalised communities. Wildlife management and wildlife-related development initiatives have tended to operate in a fragmented way that is not cognisant of the intertwined and complex relationship between wildlife and other components of the environment. In this chapter we illustrate how multiple institutions, legislation and policies governing wildlife resources and its utilisation have led to fragmented and compartmentalised control and management of the resource.

7.2. State of the resource

The Zambezi Valley is generally rich in wildlife. Prior to construction of the dam there were large mammal populations in the valley. Jarman (1972) recorded twenty-six species of large mammals in the middle Zambezi Valley. These included buffalo (*Syncerus caffer* Sparrman), eland (*Taurotragus oryx*), impala (*Aepyceros melampus*), zebra (*Equus burchelli*), black rhinocerous (*Diceros bicornis*) elephant (*Loxodonta africana*), lion (*Panthera leo*) and leopard (*P. pardus*). Flooding of the middle Zambezi Valley moved the animals out of the range they had formally occupied. As the valley was being flooded, animals were rescued and moved into areas designated as National Parks and Safari Areas. Some of the animals ended up being trapped on islands. Early studies on species that survived and adapted to island conditions were carried out by Choate (1973) and Child (1968). The two groups that survived island conditions were mobile animals that swim freely from island to island or to the mainland (e.g. elephants, waterbuck and lion), and those that are reluctant to leave their home area or would not readily enter water and thus easily become isolated (e.g. impala, bushbuck) (Choate 1973).

There is limited data on wildlife populations on both the mainland and islands on Lake Kariba. A study by Choate (1973) recorded eight large mammal species on Christmas island comprising 15 elephants, 10 kudu, 10 waterbuck, 20–30 impala, 5–10 bushbuck, 3–7 duiker and 3–7 grysbok. Generally both the mainland and the islands support large herds of elephants and buffaloes. Although quantifiable data are not available, there has been a decline in wildlife populations due to poaching. Prior to the economic challenges experienced in Zimbabwe, one herd would comprise over twenty buffaloes. Daily movements whereby elephants and buffaloes move from the hinterland to the shore were a common phenomenon. Animals would concentrate along the shoreline in the late afternoons to drink and graze. The predominant vegetation within the foreshore is *Panicum repens* grassland and this is heavily utilised by buffaloes (Taylor 1985).

Other animals reported to occur within the Lake Kariba shoreline include kudu, impala, waterbuck and baboons and a wide variety of antelope and smaller mammals and in the lake, hippotami (*Hippopotamus amphibius*) and crocodiles (*Crocodylus niloticus*). There are large populations of hippos and crocodiles in the lake.

The Lake Kariba area supports a lot of birds. Common species include crowned guinea fowl, black-eyed bulbul, golden-breasted bunting, common waxbill, cardinal woodpecker, African grey hornbill, laughing dove, Cape turtle dove and African jacana. There are several fish-eating birds within the lake that include the black egret, lesser black-backed gull, grey-headed gull and white eating tern. Fish-eating birds include surface plungers (kingfishers, terns, fish eagle and osprey), waders (herons, egrets and stocks) and divers (cormorants and darters).

Information on animal density is limited. However, large populations occur in the mainland and shoreline close to Chizarira National Park and Chete Safari Area. The greatest species diversity and number per species occurs in protected areas. Studies by Jarman (1972) and Hughes (1970) identified fifteen and thirteen species respectively along the Sinamwenda mainland. Elephants, buffalo, kudu, impala, klipspringer and baboons had densities of 15, 9.1, 80, 10.7, and 20 animals per square mile respectively (Jarman 1972). Hughes (1970) counted 75, 83, 25, 46 and 632 elephant, zebra, buffalo, kudu and impala respectively along the Sinamwenda mainland.

Wildlife also occurs in Kariba town. The town is bordered by Hurungwe Safari Area in the North and Charara Safari Area the east. Since it is situated within a national park it is generally rich in wildlife. The common large species that occur in Kariba town include buffalo, zebra, elephant and baboons. Since the Safari Area is not fenced, animals move freely in the Kariba town area. Due to poaching animal populations have declined in Kariba town. As the town has expanded game corridors have been built negatively impacting on animals.

There is very little wildlife on the Zambian shore except in the game reserves on islands and in the privately owned Kotakota game range (Losse 1998). The large animals were eliminated during and after the Zimbabwean liberation war. Over exploitation of the animals that cross the lake from the Zimbabwean side make it impossible for animal populations to be established again.

The biggest threat to the wildlife populations is human encroachment and exploitation. The population of most large game counted in aerial surveys has fluctuated yearly. Table 18 shows trends in some species between 1980 and 1998. The most endangered large game species is the black rhino (*Diceros bicornis*). The number of black rhino declined in the years between 1980 and 1998 due to poaching for horns.

Table 18: Wildlife population trends in the Sebungwe region, 1980–1998

Years	Elephant	Buffalo	Black rhino	Sable *(Hippotragus niger)*	Zebra
1980	11 144	12 521	482	–	–
1981	8 797	6 846	322	800	418

Years	Elephant	Buffalo	Black rhino	Sable *(Hippotragus niger)*	Zebra
1983	9 302	18 980	570	1 460	1 254
1991	13 533	30 682	500	1 778	1 445
1993	10 836	25 500	185	906	1 740
1995	11 797	20 752	–	903	1 060
1996	13 257	17 445	16	552	2 501
1997	13 383	14 956	26	–	–
1998	10 144	11 775	–	283	1 227

Sources: Cumming *et al*. 1997 and Mackie 1999

The rising human population has negatively impacted on wildlife communities such that wildlife populations across the Zambezi valley in general, have fluctuated in both time and space. Visibly there is a link between wildlife population and anthropogenic activities in the Zambezi valley which cannot be complete without proper reference to the colonial era. The colonial government perceived overpopulation on the plateau area bordering the valley as early as the late 1940s (Alexander 2000) but had little options to deal with it. It was not to be until the Native Land Husbandry Act of 1951 was passed that destocking and reducing of populations in the plateau became possible (Lan 1985). The Zambezi valley provided a solution to this problem. With the belief that increased populations and settlement in the valley would reduce the amount of tsetse fly and *trypanosomiasis* at the back of their minds, the colonial Rhodesian government used native farmers to open up the tsetse infested areas in the valley (Ranger 1985). The need to utilise the valley plains for livestock production was threatened by tsetse which was believed to coexist with wildlife. The period from the 1930s saw the unselective killing of an average of 20 000 animals per year until the 1950s when the idea was challenged (Derman 1995). The idea was to eliminate tsetse from spreading into commercial cattle herds.

In-migration into the valley is a major factor that has influenced wildlife population dynamics. Land in the valley has been used as a strategic resource to resettle landless peasants (Braton 1994). Apart from the effect these settlements have of driving away animals (Rihoy 1992), these immigrants' practices are generally unfriendly to wildlife. The Tonga people are traditionally subsistence farmers (Dzingirai 1996) who supplement their protein requirements by hunting using 'primitive' means (Murombedzi 1991). On the other hand, the immigrants use modern methods of farming and clear vast tracts of land for cultivation (Taylor 1991). The introduction of modern agriculture has transformed the landscape through which wildlife and human beings, originally in the valley, interfaced in a variety of ways. This dimension has raised much socio-economic and bio-ecological concern for three reasons:

- Concentration of food has enabled populations to grow larger than could have been supported by hunting and gathering.
- Wildlife populations have declined in the face of habitat destruction and excessive exploitation (Hasler 1993).
- Exclusive land-use has intensified the competition between expanding human populations and diminishing wildlife populations.

Under the given circumstances wildlife became a liability to the agrarian (mainly immigrants) society's livelihoods and security as it was a threat to crop wellbeing and human life. All these developments in the human society were also reflected in the health of the wildlife populations.

While it may not be an easy task to trek and numerically communicate the actual quantities of wildlife in the valley across various time-spans, data on wildlife population in CAMPFIRE communities is showing some trends in wildlife population dynamics. The estimated average number of elephants in the valley has been oscillating around 7 000 since independence, ranging from a minimum 4 181 in 1989 to a maximum 12 707 elephants in 2001 (Blanc 2005). Densities of 0.43 animals per square-kilometer found in CAMPFIRE communities are approximately half or less those found in state protected areas, but consistent with the maintenance of the woodlands and healthy habitats for other wildlife population (Cumming 1997). These results also conform to increasing national and regional elephant herds that have grown at an average of 5 percent annually over the past decade or more (Taylor 2009). Due to sampling difficulties, estimates of buffalo numbers tend to be highly variable (Blanc 2005). The mean number estimated was around 12 000 at an average density of 0.96 animals per square-kilometer (Taylor 2009). These numbers may have been influenced by a regional rainfall deficit coupled with periodic droughts in the Zambezi Valley particularly during the early 1990s (Cumming 1997) resulting in substantial wildlife die-offs. Currently there is a general consensus that elephant numbers have increased in campfire areas and buffalo numbers are either stable or have declined slightly (Taylor 2009).

7.3. Institutional arrangements and management of wildlife resources

Various government departments are involved in the management of wildlife in Zimbabwe. In Zimbabwe more than eight ministries and associated parastatals provide the mechanism for the overall management and co-ordination of environmental elements through 18 pieces of legislation (Moyo 1996). Within these ministries are various departments focusing on different issues with each department seeking autonomy in its operations yet the focus should be on the same resource. According to Savory (1990) government departments with an interest in wildlife act like a 'team of blinkered horses' all pulling in different directions, but one is 'forbidden by the system to remove the blinkers' and get the horses pulling together. These government departments only come to some form of co-ordination in wildlife management when it comes to mechanisms for control of finances and budgets (McNeely 1995) an idea Nelson (2003) condemns as having a tremendous focus on money, a symbol, rather than on productivity of wildlife resources, which is true wealth. Not only do these departments pull in opposite directions, but also seek to mobilise much support and ensure a reasonable following. This observation is as true as it is for other countries of the region.

Most government structures divide every aspect of our lives into portfolios, and nowhere can you discuss the whole as one (Mackenzie 1987). This so-called compartmentalisation of practices within natural resource management institutions is visibly a generic form of what Lindsay (1987) termed 'unco-ordinated division of labour'. While looking at system dynamics, his argument was that each system is made up of various components performing different but interrelated tasks that make the system a whole. The moment each component of the system start to work as if it is the only component constituting the system marks the birth of unco-ordinated division of labour and disaster becomes imminent. The scenario become even more complicated when we consider the numbers of parastatals, global, national, provincial and local level organisations that share environmental management responsibilities in general and, wildlife management in particular. This practice has lately been the norm in wildlife management in the Zimbabwean scenario, where departments related to wildlife as veterinary services, National Parks and Wildlife Management Authority (former Department of National Parks and Wildlife Management) and water resources development have more often than not, been embroiled in natural resource conflict (Child 2009). Operating within the context of wildlife resource communally-based, where one cannot even debate the whole and the interconnectedness of all that governments take upon themselves to do, one wonders how can the problems that are created by compartmentalised thinking and acting ever be solved.

There is no co-ordination between all these various organisations which include government and its parastatals, non governmental organisations (NGOs) and private business enterprises with an interest in, or are directly or indirectly involved in, wildlife management in Zimbabwe.

The management of wildlife in Zimbabwe since the colonial era has shifted from one ministry to the other as paradigms and lobbies for wildlife resource utilisation shifted with the passage of time (Murphree 1990). This has been facilitated through various legislation and policies, creation of institutions and institutional arrangements and programmes.

Fragmented legislation and policies

The Zambezi valley including the Lake Kariba area has been home to some of the region's oldest land-use conflicts related to wildlife (Jansen 1990). Starting in the 1950s with the construction of the Kariba Dam (Dzingirai 1996, Dzingirai & Madzudzo 1999) to the tsetse eradication project (Barrett 1994, Derman 1995, Dimbi 1998) and the subsequent establishment of safari concessions (Wunder 1997, Dzingirai 1996), land use conflicts were evident within the valley between competing options that had perceived economic benefits such as agriculture, livestock, wildlife, mining and tourism. A countervailing force to the threat of wildlife from competing land uses was the Parks and Wildlife Act of 1975. The Act provided that all wildlife belonged to the state, but gave private landholders permission to exploit wildlife to their benefit.

The outcome was an increase in the population of wildlife throughout the country because of the financial incentives for land holders to conserve wildlife. The story was completely different in the communal areas as there were no readily available landholders to whom the financial incentives would accrue. The state assumed the responsibility, ownership and benefit from wildlife resources in the communal areas sidelining the locals who bear the costs of coexisting with the resource. In the communal areas the result was continued degradation of the resource.

Other pieces of legislation that affect wildlife management in Zimbabwe are listed in Table 19.

Table 19: Legislation affecting wildlife management in Zimbabwe

Legislation	Provisions	Implementing ministry
National Parks Act (Chapter 149) of 1965	Introduction of National Parks	Ministry of Lands and Natural Resources
Natural Resources Act (Chapter 150) of 1941	Introduction of conservation areas in the Tribal Trust Lands	Ministry of Lands and Natural Resources
Animal Health Act (Chapter 121) of 1961	Eradication and prevention of animal pests	Ministry of Agriculture

7.3. Institutional arrangements and management of wildlife resources

Legislation	Provisions	Implementing ministry
Bees Act (Chapter 122) of 1974	Conservation of bees in the wild	Ministry of Lands and Natural Resources
Fish Conservation Act (Chapter 124) of 1961	Conservation of Rhodesian fish species	Ministry of Lands and Natural Resources
Quelea Control Act (Chapter 130) of 1972	Conservation of Quelea birds	Ministries of Agriculture and Internal Affairs
Trapping of Animals (Control) Act (Chapter 134) of 1974	Control and regulation of certain traps used for trapping animals	Ministry of Lands and Natural Resources
Wildlife Conservation Act (Chapter 135) of 1961	Furthering and better provision of conservation Giving effect to the International Convention of 1933	Ministry of Lands and Natural Resources
Urban and Rural District Councils Act of 1982	Creation of smaller administrative units to be given authority over wildlife management	Ministry of Local Government
Statutory Instrument 123 of 1991. Parks and Wildlife (Management) Notice 1991 (No. 4)	Establishment of more parks and the resettlement of surrounding communities	Ministry of Natural Resources and Tourism
Statutory Instrument 182 of 1991. Parks and Wildlife (Protected Animals) Notice 1991	Selected some species of animals as protected	Ministry of Environment and Tourism

The Ministry of Local Government became the appropriate authority in the communal areas for wildlife management, contrary to the spirit of the Parks and Wildlife Act of 1975, which stipulated that wildlife was to be managed by and benefit the landholder (Cumming 1989). The Department of Parks and Wildlife Management (DPWLM) set hunting quotas for each district and leased safari concessions to safari operators while the revenue was collected by the District

Development Fund (DDF). At independence in 1980, the responsibility of managing wildlife in the communal areas was assumed by the newly formed Ministry of Natural Resources and Water Development. While in some communal areas provision of schools and clinics provided some enthusiasm for wildlife management, the absence of tangible wildlife benefit in others led to a considerable resistance to proposals for wildlife-based development initiatives (Cumming 1989). Ever since then, no substantive revision of natural resources legislation or defined legal framework for devolved wildlife resource management in communal areas has been undertaken. In that regard Taylor (2009) laments and questions why for so long, wildlife policy and legislation has remained fragmented and largely centrally controlled.

Fragmented institutional arrangements

Apart from government ministries, departments and parastatals, the management of wildlife has aroused a lot of interest in a variety of institutions. The management of wildlife resources traditionally has been the responsibility of traditional institutions such as chiefs, headmen and spiritual leaders (Child 2009). With the emergence of modern conservation practices in Zimbabwe, new institutional arrangements in the governance of wildlife are evident. The Urban and Rural District Councils Act (1982) saw the formation of more democratic units of governance in wildlife resource use such as Village Development Committees (VIDCOs), Ward Development Committees (WADCOs) and Rural Development Councils (RDCs). In some districts, as Nyaminyami, Wildlife Management Trustees were erected to work hand in hand with the RDCs in the management of wildlife resources. The range of activities of such trustees included animal population management, problem animal control, compensation for crop damage to local residents, granting hunting concessions and management of concession fees, and cropping of wildlife. The initial years of operation of such trustees have been termed a financial success (Murindagomo 1988) with a strong ecological performance (NWMT 1987).

Non-governmental organisations (NGOs) as institutions have had a keen interest in the management of wildlife to the effect that they have maintained their active presence in the Zambezi valley for decades. These NGOs such as the United Nations Development Programme (UNDP), Overseas Development Assistance (ODA), the International Development Research Centre (IDRC), the Ford Foundation and the World Wildlife Fund (WWF) have limited their roles to building capacity (Dimbi 1998), providing advisory services (Taylor 1988, Muyambi 1989), funding various projects such as the tsetse eradication (Vincent & Thomas 1961, Barrett 1994, Matzke & Nabane 1994) and research and development (Pangeti 1989).

Fragmented programmes

The Zambezi valley has been subjected to changing human interventions especially those that affect the operations of the natural system. Derman (1995) call the valley 'the largest ecological experimentation zone' as most pilot projects related to wildlife have been conducted in the same basin from as early as the tsetse eradication experiment beginning 1917 until the most recent 1980s CAMPFIRE (Communal Areas Management Programme for Indigenous Resources).

WINDFALL

In 1978 the project WINDFALL (Wildlife Industries Development for All) was initiated with the aim of giving back some benefits of wildlife management to the producer communities. The rational for WINDFALL was underpinned on the basic assumption that human/wildlife conflict would be reduced and attitudes towards conservation improved if neighbouring villages received some benefits from wildlife. Under this arrangement, neighbouring villages would receive meat rations from culling especially of elephants while their respective communities received revenues from safari hunting. In as much as these meat rations supplemented the communities' protein requirements and reduced the need to poach, it failed to generate local participation in decision-making and a sense of local-level proprietorship (Murphree 1990). Due to government bureaucracies, little revenue found its way to the communities after prolonged periods of time to an extent that communities could not link the funds to any wildlife-related activities but could only consider it as government handouts. These fundamental deficiencies within the WINDFALL project were an indication that the project would not achieve any meaningful progress in wildlife management, but it did pave the way for another management initiative, CAMPFIRE.

CAMPFIRE

CAMPFIRE was initiated in 1984 by the Department of National Parks and Wildlife Management (DNPWLM) and aimed to address shortfalls in the WINDFALL project. It also symbolised the new government's ideological and policy commitment to localised planning and implementation in the development process (Murombedzi 1992). CAMPFIRE was an attempt to address the 'tragedy of the commons' in communally owned resources. Its aim was to encourage conservation and sustainable management and utilisation of wildlife, grazing, forestry and water (Martin 1986) in a holistic manner. The whole idea was underpinned on the belief that wildlife utilisation as a form of land use will only be endorsed by rural communities when individuals receive direct benefit (Murphree 1991, Bond 1994).

It was not until 1989 when the rural district councils of Nyaminyami received appropriate authority over wildlife from the Minister of Natural Resources and Tourism that CAMPFIRE was set into motion within the Lake Kariba area (Murombedzi 1992). This resulted in the development of CAMPFIRE in lakeshore Communal Areas in Nyaminyami district. CAMPFIRE was introduced in Binga District in 1990. The major CAMPFIRE activity within the lakeshore Communal Areas is safari hunting. Lakeshore Communal areas under Binga and Nyaminyami District Councils have been dermacated into hunting concessions that are leased to safari operators for hunting. This caused further fragmentation of land within the lakeshore area. The major concensus is that local communities within the Lake Kariba area have not significantly benefited from CAMPFIRE (BRDC 1999). In fact CAMPFIRE especially in Binga, become a major source of conflict with other land uses. Conflicts related to wildlife and land use as discussed by Mhlanga (2009) include (i) conflicts between local people and wildlife (ii) conflicts between cattle and buffalo and (iii) conflicts between natural resource based commercial enterprises and local institutions.

Conflicts between wildlife and people involve direct confrontation between humans and lions, buffaloes and elephants. Also locals are dependent on crop agriculture and animal husbandry yet these activities are incompatible with free ranging wildlife. Conflicts between cattle and buffalo arises because there interaction results in the transmission of foot-and-mouth disease from buffalo to cattle resulting in an increase in the risk of disease among the cattle. Conflicts also arise due to completion for grazing resources between cattle and wildlife. There are also conflicts of interest between commercial operators and local communities. Commercial operators regard wildlife as an asset since they are directly benefiting from it. Local communities regard it as a problem due to the difficulties they experience by living with wildlife.

One of the major challenges of CAMPFIRE has been the distribution of benefits, which is often uneven, leading local stakeholders to conclude that they are not part of the whole game. The problem with the distribution of benefits has been one of the basic issues of CAMPFIRE and other programmes. Initially, the programme seemed to have taken a step in the right direction towards holistic natural resource management. When Allan Savory wrote his book *Holistic Natural Resource Management* in 1990, he praised CAMPFIRE as the first-ever attempt made by humans to manage the environment as a whole because it took a holistic stance towards wildlife resource management. However, the programme had only been rolled out a couple of years earlier and it was only a matter of two or three years later that wildlife resource management became fragmented once more. At the same time various tourism initiatives were being promoted by both the public and the private sector.

7.4. Users impacting on wildlife resources

A range of users impacts on the wildlife resources of Lake Kariba's environs, from tourists to agriculture, livestock keeping and mining.

Impact of tourism initiatives

Tourism, mainly wildlife based, has been Zimbabwe's third foreign exchange earner after mining and agriculture since the 1990s (Mamimine 1998). The Zambezi Valley is endowed with most of the country's major tourist attractions, among them Victoria Falls, Lake Kariba and Mana Pools. Wildlife is arguably the valley's most valuable resource (Jansen 1990, Derman 1995). Seventy percent of the valley supports large numbers of wildlife and if sustainably harvested, has the potential to improve livelihoods of many households and take them out of poverty.

Wildlife harvesting activities in the Zambezi Valley and specifically within the Lake Kariba area can be broken down into four components: commercial safari hunting, cropping, subsistence hunting and poaching. *Commercial safari hunting* is carried out in Safari areas where the Parks and Wildlife Management Authority determines the maximum number of each species that can be harvested while ensuring that animal populations are maintained at sustainable levels (Fitzgerald 2002). Safari harvesting takes place in safari concession areas and within communal lands (Hasler 1993). *Cropping* takes place on communal lands, is largely limited to impala and provides an important source of protein (Olthof 1995). *Subsistence hunting*, although illegal, is carried out by rural people in most parts of the valley and provides protein in areas where the tsetse fly prevents raising livestock (Murindagomo 1988), or where livestock farming is not part of the local culture (Hasler 1993). However, *poaching* in the National Parks and communal lands is a serious problem. In the eastern part of the valley wildlife resources have been depleted to levels that will no longer support a sustainable harvest (Frank 1989). Commercial poaching is primarily for rhinoceros, but now is extending to elephants as rhinoceros become increasingly scarce. Such activities as poaching have been condemned as a threat to biodiversity and subsequently to the tourism sector (DPWLM 1988).

Impact of agriculture

The greater part of the Zambezi Valley falls into Zimbabwe's agro-ecological regions IV and V, which are best suited to extensive livestock production systems either in the form of domestic stock or wildlife (Vincent & Thomas 1961). The rainfall is too low and uncertain for reliable, rainfed cash cropping except in certain very favourable localities or seasons, or else under irrigation. Principle rainfed crops include maize, sorghum, groundnuts, sunflower and cotton, usually with yields that have been argued to be well below national average levels (Derman 1995, Hasler 1993). UNDP (1989) notes that subsistence agriculture, based on drought resistant food crops, has been dominant in the past and is likely to remain the prevalent form of land husbandry in the settled areas of the valley. In the face of an increasing population and lately the opening up a new mining industry, land-use competition and conflicts are likely to take an upward trajectory. This fragile situation calls for holistic approaches to natural resource management of the Zambezi Valley.

Impact of livestock

Data on the cattle populations within the communal area around Lake Kariba is limited. However, what is known is that the population increased following tsetse fly (*Glossina* spp.) eradication. The land surrounding Lake Kariba was infested with *G. morsitans* and *G. palidepes*, and thus was unsuitable for animal husbandry (Magadza 1986). According to Magadza, in their original lifestyle the Tongans owned no cattle as their environment was dominated by the tsetse fly. However, following resettlement they required cattle for draught power in cultivation in order to produce enough food. Significant efforts were consequently made to eradicate tsetse, resulting in an increase in cattle herds.

The concurrent influx of large numbers of immigrants has added another dimension to the livestock factor. Not only have they commercialised livestock production (Dimbi 1998) but also have introduced donkeys to take advantage of the pastures (Reynolds 1991) ironically adding competition for pastures that may have undesired implications for the fragile ecosystem of the valley (Rihoy 1992). Such environments require holistic and efficient land-use controls in the communal farming zones, a requirement which will be objectionable to the farmers. Whether the ecosystem can sustain both a high wildlife population and a high cattle population remains the greatest ecological question in the valley (Mhlanga 2009).

Impact of mining

The mining industry contributes about 45% of Zimbabwe's total export earnings and 8% to gross domestic product (GDP). Most of the country's minerals are found in the great dyke where more that 40 minerals are mined. The scale of operation is still generally small in the valley but there is high potential for both precious and industrial minerals (SADC/IUCN/ZRA/SARDC 2000). This attractive exploration potential is a target for potential investors as the past decade has seen Rio Tinto Zimbabwe developing a six million ton-a-year opencast mine north-west of Gokwe and there is a proposed 1,400 MW power station within the same area (SADC/IUCN/ZRA/SARDC 2000). These developments come with increased road and rail networks, and the establishment of rural centres and power distribution lines, which will intensify land-use competition within the valley.

7.5. Ecosystems interactions and the consequences of fragmented management

Wildlife management cannot be considered in isolation since wildlife interacts with other resources and processes within an ecosystem. The major challenge with regards to wildlife management around Lake Kariba is that a large ecosystem that was previously interlinked, with free-ranging animals, and with a resource base supporting a low population that freely utilised the resources has now been demarcated into enclaves. The area has essentially been dissected into different incompatible land use interests (Magadza 1986) resulting in many conflicts. For example, the impact of the increase of elephant populations on woodlands is discussed in Chapter 6. High elephant populations have significant impact on woodland structure. Studies on selected islands on Lake Kariba have shown that elephants occurring in large numbers can modify vegetation structure (Mapaure & Mhlanga 1998, Mapaure & Mhlanga 2000). Continous browsing by elephants results in small and medium-sized trees. The interactive effects between elephants and fire can also result in the decline of woodlands and their conversion to grassland or savanna ecosystem. Frequent fires can permanently trap the woodlands in the regeneration phase, which may slowly regress to a fire-climax grassland.

Wildlife also interact with agricultural activities (see Chapter 6) with regards to destruction of crops, transmission of tsetse trypanosomes – which cause debility and finally death in vertebrates – and competition for limited grazing resources. Lakeshore communities depend primarily on agriculture supplemented by fishing and a small amount of formal employment in the tourism industry. Agriculture is the main economic activity. Farmers cultivate crops on dry land but rainfall is unreliable therefore yields are low. Damage by wildlife also lowers yields. The presence of wildlife in communal areas creates conflict between wildlife and people because there are no physical barriers separating cultivation and grazing areas from wildlife. Animals encroach into settlements and grazing areas and in the process damage crops, and sometimes kill domestic animals and people. Since livestock are important to the locals their populations have increased and these large livestock herds compete with wildlife for limited grazing resources.

Of particular concern in the area is the interaction of wildlife with human settlements. A study done in Kariba town by Mhlanga (2001) revealed conflicts between wildlife and people in the town. The area, which was devoid of human settlement not long ago, is now heavily developed. Owing to the increasing need for land here, some of the game corridors have been closed by urban development, while the shoreline area around the town has been developed into residential and commercial properties. This development restricts access of animals to the lakeshore and consequently leads to increased conflict between animals and people, with people generally feeling hostile towards wildlife and wildlife conservation authorities, since they feel that preference is being given to wildlife conservation (Mhlanga 2001). Conflicts also occur in communal areas along the lake shore. For example, Dzingirai (1995) reports a case in Kabuba (Binga) where the community objected to the construction of an electric fence, preferring that marauding elephants be killed instead.

The interventions that have so far been instituted in wildlife management (e.g. CAMPFIRE) were intended to ensure a harmonious co-existence between the human and the wildlife communities. On the contrary, year after year, programme after programme, regime after regime, the outcomes of these activities have usually been antagonistic to their intitial aims. Fragmented system of governance in wildlife resource management has, more often than not, yielded poor results:

- *Weak monitoring and lack of co-ordination in the management of wildlife resources*: As a result of a fragmented approach to wildlife management, funding has decreased significantly to the wildlife sector. This has tended to further marginalise the chances of any meaningful co-ordination between interested stakeholders. In-migration into the area and poaching continue unabated.
- *Conflict between institutions at both planning and implementing levels:* Various ministries and associated parastatals remain the chief mechanism for the overall management and co-ordination of environmental elements. In contrast, the Ministry of Lands and Rural Resettlement scrambles for land designated as Parks.
- *Increased pressure on local communities as migration escalates:* Formerly beneficial projects like CAMPFIRE have become increasingly compromised by different livelihood strategies practiced by in-migrants who are moving into the valley for a variety of reasons.
- *Limited capacity for further monitoring, management and control of wildlife resources*: We argue that, in the light of a multiplicity of institutions governing the resource with jurisdictions more often overlapping than complementing, co-ordination of efforts is most unlikely. These processes have led to the build-up of a considerable resistance to proposals for wildlife-based development initiatives, making the development and implementation of new initiatives nearly impossible. For example, since the failure of CAMPFIRE, government has not undertaken any new substantive revision of natural resources legislation or defined legal framework for devolved wildlife resource management in communal areas.
- *Duplication of duties and inefficient use of the resource:* When one compares

wildlife resource endowments against the level of development in the area, it is clear that the resource continues to dwindle without much transformation of the landscape.

7.6. Conclusion

The case of the Lake Kariba area and the Zambezi valley in general is a true testimony to Savory (1990)'s idea that '*no whole, be it family, tribe, farm, nation or any other set of resources, can be managed without looking inward to the lesser wholes that contribute to form it, and outward to the greater wholes of which it is a member*'. The fragmentation in part derives from the multiple uses and functions associated with the wildlife resource. Wildlife resource management has been moved and wrestled from one authority to the other since the beginning of the colonial era. In other times and eras, it was divided between authorities with which wildlife has an interface. The sector has continued to be torn between various interested parties as new sovereignties continue to emerge. National interests for power generation, tourism development, livestock production, land resettlement and food security have taken priority as land-use options over wildlife, a resource full of potential that is currently being undermined due to a fragmented system of governance.

Wildlife and other natural resources management regimes have never been in anyway near holistic management. Management of wildlife remains fragmented. This explains the failure of the management initiatives that have been undertaken whose outcomes have taken much longer to be realised, albeit in an incomplete way. In the face of such a fragmented management regime, it takes a lot of political will for the system to be integrated. It calls for dissolution and integration of some ministries and some departments will have to relinquish authority. This is challenging. Why? Because departments are used to working sectorally and enjoying the benefits of selective mandates; consequently they will oppose any move towards holism.

Another key challenge now is to explore how to integrate the natural and social science knowledge and package it in a practical way usable by policy-makers involved with wildlife conservation and sustainable development. Areas of sectoral interconnections have to be identified and articulated and the required research implemented, after which findings can then be translated into advice for policy-makers.

On the practical side, organisations should work together for the good of wildlife and people. The hegemonic wildlife resource management superstructure that currently operates through dysfunctional assemblages of fragmented systems need to be superseded by a limited number of integrated individual units for wildlife conversation, management and use. In this proposed model, in essence we are invoking Darwin's principles of evolution to guide the way in which new institutional mechanisms will develop in conservation management. This we believe is the right way forward.

References

Alexander J., McGregor J. & Ranger, T. 2000. *Violence and Memory. One Hundred Years in the 'Dark Forests' of Matabeleland*. Weaver Press. Harare.

Barrett J. 1994. 'Economic issues in trypanosomiasis control: Case studies from southern Africa.' *PhD thesis*. University of Reading. United Kingdom.

Blanc J., Branes R. F., Craig G. C., Dublin H. T., Hart J. A. & Thouless C.R. 2005. 'Changes in wildlife numbers in major savanna populations in Eastern and Southern Africa', *Pachyderm* **38**: 19-28.

Bond I. 1994. 'The importance of sport-hunted African elephants to CAMPFIRE in Zimbabwe.' Short Communications. *TRAFFIC Bulletin* **14**: 117–119.

Braton M. 1994. 'Land redistribution 1980–1990.' In: Eicher C. & Rukuni M. (eds) *Zimbabwe's Agricultural Revolution*. University of Zimbabwe Publications. Harare.

Binga Rural District Council (BRDC). 1999. *Land Use and Wildlife Management Plan*. BRDC. Binga, Zimbabwe.

Child B. 2009. 'Conservation in transition.' In: Suich H., Child B. & Spenceley A. (eds) *Evolution and Innovation in Wildlife Conservation*. Earthscan. London.

Child G. 1968. *Behaviour of Large Mammals during the Formation of Lake Kariba*. Trustees of the National Museums of Rhodesia. Harare.

Choate T.S. 1973. 'Island populations and their role in wildlife conservation', *Journal of South African Wildlife Management Association* **5(1)**: 53–61.

Cumming D.H.M. 1989. 'Wildlife and land use in Zimbabwe', *Zimbabwe Quarterly* **3(1)**: 11–19.

Cumming D.H.M., Chafota J., Haward M. & Maguchu C. 1997. *Aerial Census Data: Summary for Sebungwe and Dande/Chiswiti Areas from 1980 to 1996.* WWF-SARPO Project Paper No. 60. World Wildlife Fund. Geneva.

Derman B. 1995. *Changing Land Use in the Zambezi valley: Socio-economic Considerations.* CASS/WWF Joint Paper. Harare, Zimbabwe.

Dimbi L.R. 1998. 'The role of leadership in the structure and function of community-based natural resources management organisations: A Zimbabwean case study.' *Master's thesis*. University of KwaZulu-Natal. South Africa.

Dzingirai V. & Madzudzo E. 1999. 'Big men and CAMPFIRE. A comparative study for the role of external actors in conflicts over local resources', *Zambezia* **26(1)**: 77–92.

Dzingirai V. 1996. *Every Man Must Resettle Where He Wants: The Politics Of Settlement In The Context of CAMPFIRE.* Centre for Applied Social Sciences, University of Zimbabwe. Harare.

Dzingirai V. 1995. *Take Back your CAMPFIRE. A Study of Local Level Perceptions to Electric Fencing in the Framework of Binga's CAMPFIRE Programme.* Centre for Applied Social Sciences, University of Zimbabwe. Harare.

Fitzgerald F. 2002. 'A comparative analysis of gender and training in CAMPFIRE micro-projects: A case study of the Tannery and Leathercraft micro-projects in Binga and Nyaminyami Districts, Zimbabwe.' *Master's thesis*. University of Zimbabwe. Harare.

Frank P. 1989. 'An analysis of land use and resource development planning in the Zambezi Valley, Zimbabwe.' *Master's thesis*. Simon Fraser University, Cananda.

Hasler R. 1993. 'The cultural and political dynamics of study of Zimbabwean wildlife resource use in the Zambezi Valley: A case of Chapoto Ward.' *PhD thesis*. Michigan State University. Michigan.

Hughes B.G. 1970. 'Observations on dispersion, activity and feeding patterns of elephant at Sinamwenda.' Certificate in Field Ecology. University of Zimbabwe. Harare.

Jansen D.J. 1990. *Sustainable Wildlife Utilisation in the Zambezi Valley of Zimbabwe: Economic, Ecological and Political Tradeoffs*. World Wildlife Fund. Harare.

Jarman P.J. 1972. 'Seasonal distribution of large mammal populations in the unflooded middle Zambezi Valley',*Journal of Applied Ecology* **9**: 283–299.

Lan D. 1985. *Guns and Rain: Guerillas and Spirit Mediums in Zimbabwe*. ZPH, Harare.

Lindsay W.K. 1987. 'Integrating parks and pastoralists: Some lessons from Amboseli.' In: Anderson D.M. & Grove R.H. (eds)*Conservation in Africa: People, Policies and Practice*: 149–167. Cambridge University Press. U.K.

Lake Kariba Fisheries Research Institute (LKFRI). 1995. *Tourism and the National Parks*. Kariba. Zambia/Zimbabwe SADC Fisheries Project. Kariba, Zimbabwe.

Losse G.F. 1998. *The Small-scale Fishery on Lake Kariba in Zambia*. Schriftenreihe der GTZ No. 265 Wiesbaden Universum Verlagsantalt Germany.

Mackenzie J.M. 1987. 'Chilvary, social darwinism and ritualised killing: The hunting ethos in Central Africa up to 1914.' In: Anderson D. & Grove R. (eds) *Conservation in Africa, People, Policies and Practice*: 41–62. Cambridge University Press. U.K.

Mackie C. 1999. *Aerial Survey of Elephants and Other Large Herbivores in the Sebungwe Region and Gonarezhou National Park, Zimbabwe.* WWF-SARPO Project Paper No. 71. World Wildlife Fund. Harare.

Magadza C.H.D. 1986. 'Conflicts of resource use on the Lake Kariba environs', *Nature and Resources* **22(4)**: 2–12.

Mamimine P.W. 1998. 'Tourism and culture: A case study of Chapungu Sculpture Park.' *PhD thesis*. University of Zimbabwe. Harare.

Mapaure I. & Mhlanga L. 1998. 'Elephants and woodlands: The impact of elephant damage to *Colophospermum mopane* on Namembere Island, Lake Kariba, Zimbabwe', *Zimbabwe Science News* **32(1)**: 15–19.

Mapaure I. & Mhlanga L. 2000. 'Patterns of elephant damage to *Colophospermum mopane* on selected islands in Lake Kariba, Zimbabwe', *Kirkia* **17(2)**: 189–198.

Martin R. 1986. *Communal Areas Management Programme for Indigenous Resources. (CAMPFIRE).* Government of Zimbabwe, Department of National Parks and Wildlife Management, Branch of Terrestrial Ecology. Harare, Zimbabwe.

Matzke G.E. & Nabane N. 1994. *Outcomes of a Community-controlled Wildlife Programme in a Zambezi Valley Community.* Centre for Applied Social Sciences, University of Zimbabwe. Harare.

McNeely J.A. 1995. 'Partnerships for conservation. An introduction.' In: McNeely J.A. (ed) *Expanding Partnerships in Conversation*. Island Press. Washington.

Mhlanga L. 2001. 'Conflict between wildlife and people in Kariba Town, Zimbabwe', *Zambezia* **XXVIII(i)**: 39–51.

Mhlanga L. 2009. 'Fragmentation of resource governance along the shoreline of Lake Kariba, Zimbabwe', *Development Southern Africa* **26(4)**: 585–596.

Moyo S. 1996. *Decision Making and Institutions in Zimbabwe.* A paper presented at the workshop on environmental law reforms. Harare, Zimbabwe.

Murindagomo F. 1988. 'Preliminary investigations into wildlife utilisation and land use in Angwa, Mid-Zambezi Valley, Zimbabwe.' *PhD thesis*. University of Zimbabwe. Harare.

Murombedzi J.C. 1991. *Decentralising Common Property Resource Management: A Case Study of the Nyaminyami Districty Council of Zimbabwe's Wildlife Management Programme.* IED Drylands Network Programme Paper No. 30. IED. London.

Murombedzi J.C. 1992. *Decentralisation or Recentralisation: Implementing CAMPFIRE in the Omay Communal Lands of the Nyaminyami District.* CASS Working Paper. Centre for Applied Social Studies, University of Zimbabwe. Harare.

Murphree M. 1991. *Communities as Resource Management Institutions.* Centre for Applied Social Sciences, University of Zimbabwe. Harare.

Murphree M.W. 1990. *Decentralising the Proprietorship of Wildlife Resources in Zimbabwe's Communal Lands.* Centre for Applied Social Studies, University of Zimbabwe. Harare.

Nelson J. 2003. 'Introduction and overview.' In: Nelson J & Lindsay H. (eds) *Indigenous Peoples and Protected Areas in Africa*: 1–15. FPP. Netherlands.

Nyaminyami Wildlife Management Trust (NWMT). 1987. *The Wildlife of Nyaminyami.* NWMT. Binga, Zimbabwe.

Olthof W. 1995. 'Wildlife resources and local development: Experiences from Zimbabwe's CAMPFIRE Programme.' In Breemer J.P. & Venema L.B. (eds) *Local Resources Management in Africa*: 111–128. Wiley. Toronto.

Pangeti G. N. 1989. *Administration and Interagency Co-ordination of Wildlife Management and the Effects of Legislation in Implementation.* Paper presented at a workshop on wildlife resource management with local participation. Hwange Safari Lodges. Victoria Falls, Zimbabwe.

Ranger T.O. 1985. *Consciousness and Guerrilla war in Zimbabwe.* James Currey. London.

Reynolds P. 1991. *Dance Civet Cat.* Zed Books Limited. London.

Rihoy E.C. 1992. *Community Institutions, Population Movement and the CAMPFIRE Programme in Zimbabwe.* Paper presented to the Fourth World Congress on National Parks and Protected Areas, Carcas, Venezuela.

SADC/IUCN/ZRA/SARDC 2000. *State of the Environment: Zambezi Basin.* SADC. Harare.

Savory A. (ed) 1990. *Holistic Natural Resource Management.* Gilmour Publishing, Albuquerque, USA.

Taylor R. 1991. *Ecologist's Report for 1990.* Nyaminyami Wildlife Management Trust. WWF. Harare, Zimbabwe.

Taylor R. 2009. 'The performance of CAMPFIRE in Zimbabwe: 1986-2006.' In: Suich H., Child B. & Spenceley A. (eds) *Evolution and Innovation in Wildlife Conservation*: 201–221. Earthscan. London.

Taylor R.D. 1988. 'The indigenous resources of the Zambezi Valley: An overview',*The Zimbabwe Science News* **22**: 1–2.

Taylor R.D. 1985. 'The response of buffalo, *Syncerus caffer* (Sparrman), to the Lake Kariba lakeshore grassland (*Panicum repens* L.) in Matusadonha National Park.' *PhD thesis*. University of Zimbabwe. Harare.

Vincent V. & Thomas R. G. 1962. *The Agro-ecological Survey of Southern Rhodesia.* Government Printers. Harare.

Wunder W.B. (1997). *Of Elephant and Men: Crop Destruction, CAMPFIRE and Wildlife Management in Zambezi Valley, Zimbabwe.* A Bell and Howell Company. Michigan, USA.

Kariba dam wall with flood gates discharging. Photo: Zambezi River Authority

8. Defragmenting natural resources management within the Lake Kariba environs

Kefasi NYIKAHADZOI, Lindah MHLANGA, Mafaniso HARA and Tobias HALLER

8.1. Introduction

In this book, the authors have shown that resource management within the Lake Kariba environs is fragmented. Resource sectors such as land, water, fish, other aquatic resources, wildlife, woodlands and grasslands are managed as single units that are not inter-connected with each other. For all these resources, fragmentation is negatively impacting on resource sustainability and the livelihoods of people dependent on the resources.

The pieces of legislation are fragmented at national level where many different ministries have specific mandates of managing specific resources. Typical legislation include the Parks and Wildlife Act, Forestry Act, Water Act, Communal Lands Act, Environmental Management Act, Rural District Council Act and Regional Town and Country Planning Act. Different authorities thus administer protected areas, agricultural land, forestry areas and water resources. The major challenge becomes the proliferation of institutions and the ensuing problems of fragmented administration of the area and lack of co-ordinated planning and management. The emerging paradigm of ecosystem management contrasts with the traditional management efforts that have been focused on specific uses such as agriculture, fishing and tourism, which resulted in separate governance regimes for each use. This book has shown that challenges related to resource sustainability have ensued due to fragmented sector-based management.

This chapter maps the existing cross-sectoral links and resource interactions. It provides a synthesis of all the critical interactions identified in the preceding chapters. It details the nature and impact of inter-sectoral interactions between and among the various resource-specific sectors. The methods of this analysis were discussed in Chapter 1. It is anticipated that this information will give all stakeholders a clear integrated view of interactions within the Lake Kariba ecosystem and prompt them to seek ways of strengthening and protecting the ecosystem to ensure sustainable exploitation of the lake and lakeshore resources. Based on experiences from other sectors (such as agriculture and integrated water resource management), practices from other countries, theory and recent trends in natural resources management, this chapter recommends ways of defragmenting the management of natural resources within Lake Kariba environs so that there is effective and efficient management, which will ultimately result in resource sustainability.

8.2. Characterisation of inter-sectoral interactions

This section discusses how the activities in the resource sectors (in horizontal axis) affect those in the vertical axis in Table 20. The Table shows the results of the inter-sectoral interactions of the six resource sectors. The analysis is based on the following categorisation:

1. Very high (score = 15) – interactions are very critical and can lead to serious and irreversible damage if not attended to.
2. High (score 14) – such interactions need attention and close monitoring so that they are sustained in the long run.
3. Moderate (score 10–13) – these interactions need to be managed so that they are sustained in the long run.
4. Low (score 5–9) – resource interactions in this category are not a cause for concern.

Table 20: Matrix of inter-sectoral interactions within the Lake Kariba environs

Sectors	Sectors					
	Wildlife	**Fish**	**Land**	**Other aquatic organisms**	**Woodlands & grass-lands**	**Water**
Wildlife		5	15	7	15	13
Fish	5		6	14	9	14
Land	14	8		8	14	14
Other aquatic resources	5	5	5		5	12
Woodlands and grass-lands	10	5	5 (Zim) 13 (Zam)	5		8
Water	5	5	8	8	12	

The analysis in this chapter is based on the highest score (score = 15) interactions that might lead to serious and irreversible damage to the natural resources in question if not attended to. Interactions that need attention and close monitoring so that the natural resources in question are sustained even in the long run are also discussed. Such interactions have a score of 14 (see Table 1). As shown in Table 20, resources that are likely to suffer most due to fragmentation are wildlife, fish and land. The table shows that activities based on the exploitation of woodlands and grasslands are impacting negatively on wildlife. Similarly, land-based activities are also negatively affecting the viability of wildlife. This is pointing to the fact that the current rate of exploitation of land-based resources, such as woodlands and grasslands, could lead to the depletion of wildlife within the Lake Kariba environs. The second set of connections that are critical with aggregated scores of 14 are the effects of water-based activities on fish, the effects of wildlife on land-based resources, the effects of water-based activities on land and the effects of woodlands and grasslands utilisation on land-based activities. While the impact of these connections is not yet very serious, they need very close monitoring in order to ensure long-term sustainability.

8.3. Very critical ecosystem interactions

Land-based activities are encroaching into wildlife areas. If the current resource use trends are allowed to persist in the near future, wildlife populations are likely to decline in the short run. We identify the following activities as leading to the expropriation of land designated for wildlife areas:

- Agriculture is taking up land that hitherto had been used by wildlife. This is especially true for areas that are under local authorities (e.g. Binga Rural District Council and Nyaminyami Rural District Council). Other smaller portions of land are also being set aside for other agriculture activities such as banana farming, fish farming in ponds and crocodile farming.
- As the trend of rural to urban migration continues, urban authorities will continue to expropriate wildlife areas for housing and other social amenities.
- As more commercially viable mineral deposits are found in the area, more land that is reserved for wildlife will continue to be taken up by mining companies. For example, the glitter-stone mining activities being carried out on the outskirts of Kariba town have already taken up a considerable piece of the wilderness area that is reserved for wildlife.
- Land-based activities that reduce the size of woodland and grassland areas are impacting negatively on the wildlife. The woodland and grassland areas are important both as a food source and as a habitat for wildlife. Uncontrolled veld fires are also modifying the vegetation structure. Woodlands and grasslands are viewed as prime land for agriculture and residential developments.

The net impact of the land designated for wildlife being converted to other land uses is driven by population growth, as well as the expansion of agriculture and tourism. If current practices (unco-ordinated planning processes), trends (population growth, unemployment levels) and development emphasis (promotion of crop production, tourism, urbanisation and mining) persist, wildlife populations will continue to decline.

8.4. Critical ecosystem interactions

The interactions we have identified are not yet a serious threat, but they need very close monitoring to sustain the resources in question in the long run. The two main ecosystem interactions are the impact of wildlife on land and land-based activities and the impact of woodlands and grasslands exploitation on land-based activities.

The impact of wildlife on land and land-based activities

Wildlife impacts on land and land-based activities in several ways. Animals cause soil erosion if occurring in dense populations, a problem that is accentuated by the fact that soils within the Lake Kariba environs are very fragile and easily erodible. The same wild animals are also destroying vegetation cover, thus leaving soils bare and vulnerable to soil erosion. Finally, they compete with other land uses, such as agriculture and urban development.

The impact of woodlands and grasslands exploitation on land-based activities

The availability of a healthy woodland and grassland cover is very important for the maintenance of compact soil and gully-free landscape. Woodland and grassland cover also provide nutrient enrichment to the soils necessary for healthy flora and fauna.

Activities that are threatening the availability of healthy woodlands and grasslands include an increase in deforestation especially due to land cleared for agriculture and timber/wood harvesting (e.g. for charcoal production). Woodlands are also threatened by large elephant populations, which modify vegetation structure when occurring in large numbers, converting woodland to shrubland and modifying species composition. The woodlands are also threatened by uncontrolled fires, which may kill off the woody component and reduce grass cover and consequently result in desertification. The interaction of elephants and fire is a major threat to woodlands. Woodlands are also opened up for tourism development and for construction of houses.

8.5. Threats to other aquatic organisms and their impact on fish

Other aquatic organisms (such as phytoplankton and zooplankton) provide food sources for fish and hence their availability is crucial for enhancing fish productivity. Enrichment is favouring the dominance of cyanobacteria which is less palatable to fish and can produce algal toxins which have ecological implications on other biota. Activities and processes that are threatening other aquatic organisms include:

- outbreaks of invasive plant species (especially aquatic plant species) with detrimental effects on the aquatic ecosystem;
- nutrient loading from sources outside the aquatic environment such as agriculture in the catchment;
- mining activities that pollute the water through both the introduction of chemicals as well as through increased suspended solids loading;
- water pollution from commercial agriculture mainly through the introduction of pesticides;
- organic pollution from sewage effluent from houseboats (a localised problem, mainly through increased nutrient loading and faecal coliforms);
- pollution from sewage effluent and industrial effluent in urban centres; and
- aquaculture: the main type of aquaculture that causes water pollution is cage culture, while there may be some pollution from land-based aquaculture fish ponds as well.

8.6. Fragmentation of national legislation on natural resources management

Table 21 shows fragmented resource management within the Lake Kariba environs.

Table 21: Fragmentation of national legislation on natural resources management

Common pool resources	**Legislations and statutory instruments for management of selected common pool resources**								
	Land Act	Wildlife Act (Zimbabwe)	Traditional leaders Act	Fisheries (Za)	EMA ZAWA	Water Act	Forestry Act	Local Councils	Navigation Act
Woodlands and grasslands	xx	xx	xxx		xxx	xx	Xxx	xx	
Fisheries		xxx	x	xxx	xxx	xx		xx	
Wildlife		xxx	xx		xxx	xx		xx	
Land	xxx	x	xxx		xxx	xxx	Xx	xxx	
Other aquatic organisms		x	x		xxx	x		x	
Water		x	xx		xxx			xx	X

x= *less involved* xx= *moderately involved* xxx= *very involved*

The major critical resources that are impacted negatively by activities happening in other sectors are wildlife, fish and land. With regards to wildlife, Table 21 shows that Ministry of Lands, local authorities (in communal areas), Parks and Wildlife (state land) and environmental management agencies are heavily involved in the management of land. This shows that there is geographical fragmentation. However, local authorities seem to have little interest in setting apart land solely for wildlife as there is a very high demand for agricultural space. Even within the Parks and Wildlife area, it seems national policies and strategies that support mining are failing to safeguard the interests of wildlife.

Effects of wildlife on land, woodlands and grasslands have been difficult to manage. Both Environmental Management Agencies (EMA) and the Parks and Wildlife Authorities that seek to preserve and protect that natural landscape, plants and wildlife, have put more emphasis on managing the impact of human activities on land. The effects of elephants on their own habitats are not adequately dealt with.

8.7. Scale fragmentation

In Zimbabwe, Statutory Instrument 12 of 2007 requires that large commercial agricultural enterprises acquire a licence in order to use herbicides, fungicides, pesticides and any toxic substance. This exonerates the numerous small-scale cotton growers within the catchment area. The recent thrust by governments to increase crop production by smallholder farmers also increased the use of agrochemicals and fertilisers. This has resulted in increased fertiliser-rich runoff from agriculture and has promoted the problems of aquatic plants. Nutrient enrichment leads to the invasion of water hyacinth, making gill netting a challenge, something experienced within the mouths of all rivers in the Sanyati basin in the 1990s.

In Zimbabwe, small-scale mining is viewed as a major source of employment and income. The promotion of small-scale mining and gold panning operations within the catchment areas has increased the production of highly toxic substances such as cyanide, arsenic, cadmium and mercury. These metals accumulate and biomagnify within the aquatic biota, posing a threat to the organisms and to humans who consume, for example, fish.

Tourism, which has been viewed as a major contributor to gross domestic product, also brings with it increased water pollution. The number of boats on Lake Kariba, for example, is very high and oil and fuel pollution is caused by accidental leakages or spillage from engines and/or deliberate waste oil dumping into the lake. Oil is hazardous to animals and people and it also reduces water quality. There is no co-ordinated approach to dealing with water quality for domestic consumption and for sustaining a healthy aquatic ecosystem for fish. Policies and legislation to deal with the habitats of wildlife and fish are fragmented. While the government is promoting the development of certain sectors, the remaining habitats for fish and wildlife continue to be threatened.

Natural resource management within the area is characterised by sector fragmentation with a number of government departments and NGOs managing specific resources. If uncontrolled this fragmentation can lead to localised overexploitation of certain resources. Murombedzi (1991) discusses how overgrazing in Omay communal areas as a results of higher livestock numbers has threatened the herds of buffalo in those areas. Nyikahadzoi (1998) and Malasha (2001) report the isolated cases of overfishing, which gill net fishers attributed to pesticides and herbicides that enter the water body from agricultural areas. Such fragmentation fails to harness synergies between and among various government departments which is necessary for sustainable utilisation of ecosystem goods and services. Without the inclusive participation of all stakeholders involved in managing specific resources within the ecosystem, localised overexploitation and depletion of certain resources is inevitable. It is important therefore to defragment the management of natural resources in order to sustain livelihoods of people dependent on the exploitation of such resources.

8.8. Defragmentation through innovative systems

The major management challenge facing Lake Kariba and its environs is the incompatibility of resource uses and the presence of multiple planning authorities with diverse and incompatible interests. In order to address this, an integrated shoreline management system should be adopted. This would require the active and sustained involvement of all resource users and stakeholders on how the available resources are allocated, managed and how conflicts are mitigated. The diversity of statutory instruments, if properly co-ordinated, can make the management of Lake Kariba, its environs and natural resources very effective. This might entail forging some new innovative institutions that bring together government departments, researchers, NGOs and fishing communities. The new institution's mandate would be to find ways of synthesising key management challenges of the lake and lakeshore resources with respect to resource use conflict and rationalisation of stakeholder interests and management of natural resources using an ecosystem approach. This is in line with the new thrust in managing natural resources and the environment, which encourages moving from the sectoral approach towards the ecosystem-based management approach (IUCN 2008). Table 22 identifies the major shifts that are necessary for shifting from sector-based management to an ecosystem approach in natural resources management.

Table 22: Ecosystem-based management as a paradigm shift

Paradigm shift	
From	**To**
Individual species	Ecosystems
Small spatial scale	Multiple scales
Short-term perspective	Long-term perspective
Humans independent of ecosystems	Humans as an integral part of ecosystems
Management divorced from research	Adaptive management
Managing commodities	Sustained production potential for ecosystem goods and services

Sources: Lubchenco 1994, Sherman & Duda 1999

8.9. Guiding principles for resource management in Lake Kariba and its environs

Governments and regional bodies involved in the management of Lake Kariba, its environs and resources should be guided by four principles. First, the sustainable use of the ecosystem requires that management planning be conducted with the carrying capacity of the ecosystem and different resource sectors in mind, so as to ensure that the ecological and socio-economic functions of the system are maintained for the long-term in a sustainable manner. This calls for the active and collaborative participation of researchers in the process. Second, conservation and sustainable management of the ecosystem should be based on total ecosystem value and not economic value. Some resources within the ecosystem have an important socio-cultural value for local communities. This allows for the needs of all people dependent on the ecosystem goods and services to be taken into account.

Third, ecosystem functions are inextricably linked to their surroundings, particularly aquatic ecosystems. In this regard, ecosystem management should be pursued in the context of an integrated systems approach to environmental management and sustainable development. It is therefore important to have an inclusive multi-stakeholder partnership. Finally, ecosystem management should be based on continuous development and refinement of scientific knowledge and expertise. Management should be based on research that takes the ecosystem dynamics into consideration. Management should also be informed by indigenous knowledge systems where applicable.

8.10. Designing ecosystem management strategies

In order to conserve the ecosystem and promote rural livelihoods and food security, it is important to design regional, national and local structures for managing natural resources using an ecosystem approach.

8.11. Establishing a high-level institution for technical co-operation

It is important to establish an institution for technical co-operation among the riparian countries. The institution must be at ministerial level, which will give it political clout and status accorded to international arrangements in order to justify fiscal allocation by the riparian countries for collaborative activities. The high-level institution could be supported by a protocol that will form the legal basis for the joint institution among the riparian countries. The implementation of this proposal is highly dependent on both strong political will and provision of adequate funding by the riparian states.

8.12. Establishing a Regional Ecosystem Coordination Committee

Resources and their management have implications on communities upstream, downstream and on either side of the main river course. Therefore, it is critical that attention be paid to the specific interests of all users. Thus, the co-ordination of activities is necessary to ensure that the ecosystem provides maximum benefits to all. It is important to establish an international committee comprising of all the riparian states. Its mandate will be to provide technical advice to the riparian governments on ecosystem management and development. The committee should foster an inter-sectoral approach, harmonised policies, integrated management and conflict resolution strategies and the definition of priorities. It should encourage multi-sectoral co-operation taking into consideration not only ecosystem management but socioeconomic polices and programmes. In order to make informed decisions, the committee should encourage the carrying out of collaborative research and collection of necessary data on stocks and production levels of different resources.

Unfortunately, there is no specific policy or protocol that guides the governance and management of the ecosystem and its resources. Nor is there a policy framework that co-ordinates the regional policies and agreements to maintain the ecosystem. Instead, regional protocols, just like the national policies and legislation, are sectoral. They fail to acknowledge and appreciate the fact that the ecosystem is an interlinked system and action in one sector can lead to changes elsewhere in the ecosystem.

8.13. Establishing a National Ecosystem Management and Development Committee

In both countries, there is an agency that promotes environmental management. However, the focus is not on the proper functioning of the ecosystem. Therefore, it is important to establish a National Ecosystem Management and Development Committee, which draws its membership from all government departments with jurisdiction over lake and lakeshore resources and a mandate to manage them on a sustainable basis. It should consist of government departments, NGOs, local authorities, researchers from local universities, donors, and representatives of resource users. This approach is aimed at fostering social interactions and learning whereby knowledge from numerous sources is integrated and effectively used to manage the ecosystem. There is a need for direct and continuous interaction, communication and knowledge sharing with regards to the status of the ecosystem, activities to be monitored and implications of proposed developmental programmes on the ecosystem services.

The new innovative institution requires rationalised and co-ordinated roles and responsibilities of government departments to minimise conflicts, duplication and inefficient use of administrative resources. This approach implies shared ownership of programmes, activities and an overall sense of joint responsibility for the outcome. If properly constituted, the new institutional arrangement can positively affect the ways that institutions co-operate or compete for sustainable utilisation of the ecosystem goods and services.

This unfied approach is based on the notion that, if all stakeholders are aware that they depend on one another for the realisation of their goal or mandate, they are most likely going to co-operate. There is need for a lot of adjustment from the current approach so as to accommodate the multi stakeholder partnership. Firstly, there is need to situate research for development in organisations that need to respond to changes in production conditions, trends, changing policies and the regulatory environment. This calls for a more participatory action research approach, which Habermas (1989) called the 'ideal speech situation', one that is immune to repression and inequality. We need therefore to deconstruct government's belief systems, which rely on law enforcement, and establish a culture of equity. In this scenario, government should not view users as poachers but rather as partners with something valuable to offer that is complementary to their own scientific knowledge.

At bilateral level, the Lakeshore Combination Master Plans developed in both countries to address governance and physical fragmentation can form the basis of integrated natural resources management. On the Zimbabwean side the Combination Master Plan is a legal document that brings together local authorities, the Zimbabwe Parks and Wildlife Management Authority, the Environmental Management Agency, agricultural extension officers, the Forestry Commission and the Department of Physical Planning. The network should also incorporate researchers and local resources users and their traditional leaders. Having researchers in the committee allows for a shift from the developmental mode of the legal tool to research for development approaches. Co-opting resource users as part of the new institutional arrangement will ensure timely integration of new knowledge with practical use. The new institutional reforms should furthermore help overcome the shortcomings of a silo approach to natural resources management.

Responsibilities of the new committee

The responsibilities of the proposed committee should be to:
– create stakeholder awareness of the ecosystem approaches;
– co-ordinate government activities and programmes;
– co-ordinate developmental programmes within the lake environs; and

– promote sustainable livelihoods and food security.

Creating stakeholder awareness

The new technical committee should promote public awareness and understanding of the ecosystem management approaches and actively encourage community and private participation in the management of the lake's ecosystem. It should also inform stakeholders of the status of the ecosystem and its resources on a regular basis. The committee should also ensure that research results are available to all interested stakeholders, including local communities. This can be achieved through the promotion of targeted ecosystem education and outreach material.

Co-ordinating government activities and programmes

In this respect, the technical committee should promote the use of National Parks, safari areas, state forests, land and water (within Kariba environs) secured for conservation purposes and design networks for communicating the functions and values of the ecosystem to government ministries responsible for their management. It should also be the role of the same committee to commit all government departments to the goal of no net loss of ecosystem functions. Where ecosystem losses have been severe in some areas, the committee should design measures to ensure that there is no further loss of any remaining resources. To help supervise government activities and programmes, the committee should develop guidelines to ensure the mitigation of the impacts of developmental activities affecting ecosystem functions and where appropriate, develop compensatory measures. Where possible, the committee should pursue opportunities to expand or enhance national policies, programmes and regulations that have a positive effect on ecosystem conservation, improve those that would result in its conservation and also improve those that would result in degradation of the ecosystem.

In order to facilitate the engagement of local users in the management of the ecosystem, the national technical committees should facilitate training of government agencies on how to make use of local level institutions to manage resources within the Lake Kariba environs. There is a need to also facilitate community level training on ecosystem management, entrepreneurship and business skills.

Coordinating development programmes within the lake environs

The technical committee should identify links between national legislation and policy instruments – including water, fisheries, land, forestry policies that serve to advance ecosystem conservation. This task may involve facilitating the signing of agreements and memoranda of understanding between government departments or agencies, as well as revising certain pieces of legislation so as to redefine respective departmental roles and responsibilities with regard to ecosystem conservation. The committee should also encourage the recognition of ecosystem functions in natural resource conservation and development strategies such as those for forestry, minerals, fisheries, agricultural lands and water.

Promoting sustainable livelihoods and food security

Given the fact that women in sub-Saharan Africa are mostly responsible for household food security, the technical committee should adopt gender-sensitive approaches to ensure that the concerns of women are taken into consideration at the right time and at the point of decision-making. In addition to a wider scientific understanding of the role and significance of the ecosystem, the committee should find ways of complimenting and enhancing indigenous knowledge, thereby significantly increasing the opportunities for the development of sustainable ecosystem management for rural livelihood security.

The research that the national committee promotes should be sensitive to the inter-relationships between variables such as the ecosystem, household socio-economic and natural resource uses, among other variables. Where possible, the committee should institute the 'user pay and polluter pay' principle to discourage pollution and conversions that threaten local communities' livelihood and food security, and to ensure that the money is ploughed into the affected communities. The 'polluter pays' principle is already enshrined in some legislation, such as Zimbabwe's EMA Act.

Creating local-level ecosystem management committees

The creation of a system that can institutionalise common property resource management by creating new systems of group ownership of such resources should also be the responsibility of the committee. The two countries have legislation that provide for the establishment of water management bodies and village development committees to introduce the involvement of local communities in the planning and management of the ecosystem. It is imperative to assist communities in developing their own by-laws to deal with illegal exploitation, and unsustainable use of the ecosystem and its resources.

8.14. Capacity building

Defragmentation implies new ways of doing things (research and disseminating results, law enforcement etc). This calls for capacity development among stakeholders designed to create new links that support interactions and learning, new institutions that fosters new forms and patterns of behaviour, routines, norms and new roles. The creation of new patterns of interaction and learning is a long-term process through incremental change in habits and practices to better achieve a common goal and allow for the adoption of an incremental process of reflection and learning.

Capacity building should be designed to create a new organisational culture whose elements should include openness to partnership, consensus and dialogue, a willingness to respect the views of stakeholders and a willingness to participate in knowledge sharing and exchange of ideas.

References

Hambermas J. 1989. *Theory of Communicative Action*. Volume 1. Heineman. London.

IUCN 2008. The Ecosystem Approach. Learning from Experiences.*Ecosystem management. Series No. 5. IUCN. Gland, Switzerland.*

Lubchenco J. 1994. 'The scientific basis of ecosystem management: framing the context, language and goals.' In: Committee on Environmental and Public Works, United States Senate. Proceedings of a Workshop by the Congressional Research Service.103*rd Congress, 2nd Session, United States Government Printing Office, Washington DC. pp 33-39.*

Malasha I. 2001. 'Fisheries co-management: A comparative analysis of the Zambian and Zimbabwean inshore fishery of Lake Kariba.' *PhD thesis*. Centre for Applied Social Sciences, University of Zimbabwe. Harare.

Murombedzi J. 1991. Wetland Conservation Under Common Property Regimes in Zimbabwe.*CASS Publication, University of Zimbabwe. Harare.*

Nyikahadzoi K. 1998. 'A socio-economic evaluation of management techniques used for controlling fishing effort in the Lake Kariba gill net fishery on Lake Kariba on the Zimbabwean side.' Master's thesis. *University of Zimbabwe. Harare.*

Sherman K. & Duda A.M. 1999. 'An ecosystem approach to global assessment and management of coastal waters', Marine Ecology Progress Series ***190****: 271-287.*

Peter Mvula, Meya Kalindekafe, Paul Kishindo,
Erling Berge, Friday Njaya (Eds.)
Towards Defragmenting the Management System of Lake Chilwa Basin, Malawi
PLAAS
LIT